PINES

Center Point
Large Print

**This Large Print Book carries the
Seal of Approval of N.A.V.H.**

PINES

Blake Crouch

CENTER POINT LARGE PRINT
THORNDIKE, MAINE

ISBN: 978-1-68324-263-5

Library of Congress Cataloging-in-Publication Data

Names: Crouch, Blake, author.
Title: Pines / Blake Crouch.
Description: Center Point Large Print edition. | Thorndike, Maine : Center Point Large Print, 2017.
Identifiers: LCCN 2016049381 | ISBN 9781683242635 (hardcover : alk. paper)
Subjects: LCSH: United States. Federal Bureau of Investigation—Employees—Fiction. | Missing persons—Investigation—Fiction. | Large type books. | GSAFD: Mystery fiction.
Classification: LCC PS3603.R68 P56 2017 | DDC 813/.6—dc23
LC record available at https://lccn.loc.gov/2016049381

Despite evidence that human evolution still functions, biologists concede that it's anyone's guess where it will take us from here.

Time *magazine, February 23, 2009*

Just because you're paranoid doesn't mean they aren't after you.

Joseph Heller

Chapter 1

HE CAME TO lying on his back with sunlight pouring down into his face and the murmur of running water close by. There was a brilliant ache in his optic nerve, and a steady, painless throbbing at the base of his skull—the distant thunder of an approaching migraine. He rolled onto his side and pushed up into a sitting position, tucking his head between his knees. Sensed the instability of the world long before he opened his eyes, like its axis had been cut loose to teeter. His first deep breath felt like someone driving a steel wedge between the ribs high on his left side, but he groaned through the pain and forced his eyes to open. His left eye must have been badly swollen, because it seemed like he was staring through a slit.

The greenest grass he'd ever seen—a forest of long, soft blades—ran down to the bank. The water was clear and swift as it flowed between the boulders that jutted out of the channel. Across the river, a cliff swept up for a thousand feet. Pines grew in clusters along the ledges, and the air was filled with the smell of them and the sweetness of the moving water.

He was dressed in black pants and a black jacket with an oxford shirt underneath, the white cotton speckled with blood. A black tie hung by the flimsiest knot from his collar.

On his first attempt to get up, his knees buckled and he sat down hard enough to send a vibration of searing pain through his rib cage. His second try succeeded, and he found himself wobbly but standing, the ground a pitching deck beneath his feet. He turned slowly, his feet shuffling and spread wide for balance.

With the river behind him, he stood at the edge of an open field. On the far side, the metal surfaces of swing sets and sliding boards glimmered under an intense, midday sun.

Not another soul around.

Beyond the park, he glimpsed Victorian houses, and farther on, the buildings of a main street. The town was at most a mile across, and it sat in the middle of an amphitheater of stone, enclosed by cliff walls rising several thousand feet on every side and composed of red-banded rock. In the highest, shadowed mountain nooks, pockets of snow lingered, but down here in the valley, it was warm, the sky above a deep and cloudless cobalt.

The man checked the pockets of his slacks, and then of his single-breasted coat.

No wallet. No money clip. No ID. No keys. No phone.

Just a small Swiss Army knife in one of the inner pockets.

By the time he'd reached the other side of the park, he was more alert and more confused, and the pulsing in his cervical spine wasn't painless any longer.

He knew six things:

The name of the current president.

What his mother's face looked like, though he couldn't recall her name or even the sound of her voice.

That he could play the piano.

And fly a helicopter.

That he was thirty-seven years old.

And that he needed to get to a hospital.

Outside those facts, the world and his place in it wasn't so much hidden as printed in a foreign nomenclature beyond his comprehension. He could sense the truth hovering on the outskirts of consciousness, but it lay just out of reach.

He walked up a quiet residential street, studying every car he passed. Did one of them belong to him?

The houses that faced each other were pristine —freshly painted with perfect little squares of bright grass framed by picket fences and each household name stenciled in white block letters on the side of a black mailbox.

In almost every backyard, he saw a vibrant garden, bursting not only with flowers but vegetables and fruit.

All the colors so pure and vivid.

Midway through the second block, he winced. The exertion of walking had drawn a deep breath out of him, the pain in his left side stopping him in his tracks. Removing his jacket, he pulled his oxford out of his waistline, unbuttoned the shirt, and opened it. Looked even worse than it felt—all down his left side stretched a dark purple bruise, bull's-eyed with a swath of jaundiced yellow.

Something had hit him. Hard.

He ran his hand lightly over the surface of his skull. The headache was there, becoming more pronounced by the minute, but he didn't feel any signs of severe trauma beyond tenderness on the left side.

He buttoned his shirt back, tucked it into his pants, and continued up the street.

The blaring conclusion was that he'd been involved in some sort of accident.

Maybe a car. Maybe a fall. Maybe he'd been attacked—that could explain why he carried no wallet.

He should go to the police first thing.

Unless . . .

What if he'd done something wrong? Committed a crime?

Was that possible?

Maybe he should wait, see if anything came back to him.

Though nothing about this town struck him as remotely familiar, he realized, as he stumbled up the street, that he was reading the name on every mailbox. A subconscious thing? Because down in the recesses of memory he knew that one of these mailboxes would have *his* name printed across the side? And that seeing it would bring everything back?

The buildings of downtown lifted above the pines several blocks ahead, and he could hear, for the first time, the noise of cars in motion, distant voices, the hum of ventilation systems.

He froze in the middle of the street, involuntarily cocking his head.

He was staring at a mailbox that belonged to a red-and-green two-story Victorian.

Staring at the name on the side of it.

His pulse beginning to accelerate, although he didn't understand why.

MACKENZIE

"Mackenzie."

The name meant nothing to him.

"Mack . . ."

But the first syllable did. Or rather, it prompted some emotional response.

"Mack. Mack."

Was he Mack? Was that his first name?

"My name's Mack. Hi, I'm Mack, nice to meet you."

No.

The way the word rolled off his tongue, it wasn't natural. Didn't feel like anything that belonged to him. If he was honest, he hated the word, because it conjured up . . .

Fear.

How strange. For some reason, the word instilled fear.

Had someone named Mack hurt him?

He walked on.

Three more blocks brought him to the corner of Main and Sixth Street, where he sat down on a shaded bench and took a slow, careful breath. He looked up and down the street, eyes desperate for anything familiar.

Not a chain store in sight.

There was a pharmacy catty-corner from where he sat.

A café next door.

A three-story building next to the café with a sign overhanging the stoop:

WAYWARD PINES HOTEL

The smell of coffee beans pulled him off the bench. He looked up, saw a place called the Steaming Bean halfway up the block that had to be the source.

Hmm.

Wasn't necessarily the most useful piece of

knowledge, all things considered, but it dawned on him that he loved good coffee. Craved it. Another tiny piece of the puzzle that constituted his identity.

He walked to the coffee shop and pulled open the screened door. The shop was small and quaint, and just by the smell of things, he could tell they brewed great product. A bar down the right side faced espresso machines, grinders, blenders, bottles of flavor shots. Three stools were occupied. A few sofas and chairs lined the opposite wall. A bookshelf of faded paperbacks. Two old-timers were at war on a chessboard with mismatched pieces. The walls displayed local artwork—a series of black-and-white self-portraits of some middle-aged woman whose expression never changed from photo to photo. Only the focus of the camera changed.

He approached the cash register.

When the twentysomething barista with blonde dreadlocks finally noticed him, he thought he detected a flicker of horror in her pretty eyes.

Does she know me?

In a mirror behind the register he caught his reflection and immediately understood what had prompted her look of disgust—the left side of his face was blanketed in a massive bruise, and his left eye bulged, nearly swollen shut.

My God. Someone beat the shit out of me.

Aside from his hideous bruise, he wasn't bad

looking. Figured he stood six feet tall, maybe six-one. Short black hair, and a two-day beard coming in like a shadow across the lower half of his face. A solid, muscular build evident in the way his jacket hung on his shoulders and the taut stretch of the oxford across his chest. He thought he looked like some advertising or marketing exec—probably cut a damn striking profile when he was shaved and polished up.

"What can I get for you?" the barista asked.

He might've killed for a cup of coffee, but he didn't have a dime to whatever his name was.

"You brew good coffee here?"

The woman seemed confused by the question.

"Um, yeah."

"The best in town?"

"This is the only coffee shop in town, but yeah, our coffee kicks ass."

The man leaned over the counter. "Do you know me?" he whispered.

"Excuse me?"

"Do you recognize me? Do I ever come in here?"

"You don't know if you've been in here before?"

He shook his head.

She studied him for a moment, as if appraising his candor, trying to determine if this guy with a battered face was crazy or messing with her.

She finally said, "I don't think I've seen you before."

"You're sure about that."

"Well, it's not like this is New York City."

"Fair enough. Have you worked here long?"

"Little over a year."

"And I'm not a regular or anything?"

"You're definitely not a regular."

"Can I ask you something else?"

"Sure."

"Where is this?"

"You don't know where you are?"

He hesitated, a part of him not wanting to admit such complete and total helplessness. When he finally shook his head, the barista furrowed her brow like she couldn't believe the question.

"I'm not messing with you," he said.

"This is Wayward Pines, Idaho. Your face . . . what happened to you?"

"I—I don't really know yet. Is there a hospital in town?" As he asked the question, he felt an ominous current slide through him.

A low-voltage premonition?

Or the fingers of some deep-buried memory drawing a cold finger down his spine?

"Yeah, seven blocks south of here. You should go to the emergency room right now. I could call an ambulance for you."

"That's not necessary." He backed away from the counter. "Thanks . . . what's your name?"

"Miranda."

"Thanks, Miranda."

15

The reemergence into sunlight made his balance falter and cranked his budding headache up a few degrees into the lower range of excruciating. There was no traffic, so he jaywalked to the other side of Main and headed up the block toward Fifth Street, passing a young mother and her little boy who whispered something that sounded like, "Mommy, is that him?"

The woman hushed her son and caught the man's eye with an apologetic frown, said, "I'm sorry about that. He didn't mean to be rude."

He arrived at the corner of Fifth and Main in front of a two-story brownstone with FIRST NATIONAL BANK OF WAYWARD PINES stenciled across the glass double doors. Around the side of the building, he spotted a phone booth standing near the alleyway.

He limped toward it as fast as he could and closed himself inside the booth.

The phonebook was the slimmest he'd ever seen, and he stood there thumbing through it, hoping for some revelatory breakthrough, but it was just eight pages of several hundred names that, like everything else in this town, held no meaning for him.

He dropped the phonebook, let it dangle from its metal cord, his forehead resting against the cool glass.

The keypad caught his eye.

He smiled at the sweet realization.

I know my home phone number.

Before lifting the receiver, he punched in the number several times just to be sure, and it seemed to flow off his fingertips with the ease of rote knowledge and muscle memory.

He'd call collect, hope to God someone was home—assuming he had a someone. Of course, he wouldn't have a name to give them, not a real one at least, but maybe they'd recognize his voice and accept the call.

He picked up the receiver and held it to his ear.

Reached for the zero.

No dial tone.

He tapped the hook several times, but nothing happened.

It surprised him how fast the rage came. He slammed the phone down, an upwelling of fear and anger expanding like a rushed ignition sequence, in search of some out. Cocked his right arm back fully intending to put his fist through the glass, knuckles be damned, but the pain in his busted ribs blazed through everything and doubled him over onto the floor of the phone booth.

Now the throbbing at the base of his skull was surging.

His vision went double, then blurry, then to black . . .

The booth was in shade when he opened his eyes again. He grabbed onto the metal cord attached to the phone book and hoisted himself onto his feet. Through the dirty glass, he saw the upper curve of the sun sliding behind that ridge of cliffs that boxed in the western edge of town.

The moment it vanished, the temperature dropped ten degrees.

He still remembered his phone number, practiced it a few times on the keypad just to be safe, and checked the receiver once more for a dial tone—silence save for the faintest crackling of white noise bleeding through the line that he didn't recall hearing before.

"Hello? Hello?"

He hung up and lifted the phonebook again. The first time, he'd searched the last names, groping for any word that jogged loose a memory or incited an emotion. Now he scanned first names, tracing his finger down the list and trying to ignore that pain at the base of his skull that was already creeping back.

The first page—nothing.

Second page—nothing.

Third—nothing.

Toward the bottom of the sixth page, his finger stopped.

SKOZIE Mack and Jane
403 E 3rd St W Pines 83278
. . . . 559-0196

He skimmed the last two pages—Skozie was the only Mack listed in the Wayward Pines phone directory.

Digging his shoulder into the folding glass door, he stepped out of the booth into the early evening. With the sun now below the ring of cliffs, the light was spilling fast out of the sky, and the temperature had begun to fall.

Where will I sleep tonight?

He staggered down the sidewalk, part of him screaming that he should go straight to the hospital. He was sick. Dehydrated. Hungry. Confused. Penniless. His entire body sore. And it was getting more difficult to breathe with this debilitating pain wracking his ribs every time his lungs inflated against them.

But something in him still resisted the idea of going to the hospital, and as he moved away from the downtown and toward the residence of Mack Skozie, he realized what it was.

Again . . . fear.

He didn't know why. It made no sense. But he didn't want to set foot inside that hospital.

Not in his present condition. Not ever.

It was the strangest sort of fear. Unspecified. Like walking in the woods at night, not knowing exactly what you should be afraid of, and the fear all the more potent precisely because of its mystery.

Two blocks north took him to Third Street, his

chest inexplicably tightening as he turned onto the sidewalk and headed east, away from the downtown.

The first mailbox he passed had 201 printed on the side.

He figured the Skozie residence should only be two blocks away.

Kids were playing in the grass of a yard just ahead, taking turns running through a sprinkler. He tried to walk upright and steady as he reached their picket fence, but he couldn't stop himself from favoring his right side to ease the jarring of his ribs.

The children became still and quiet as he drew near, watching him shuffle past with unrestrained stares—a mix of curiosity and distrust that made him uneasy.

He crossed another road, moving slower still up the next block as he passed under the branches of three enormous pines that overhung the street.

The numbers of the colorful Victorians that populated this block all started with a three.

Skozie's block would be next.

His palms were beginning to sweat and the pulsing in the back of his head sounded like the *thump-thump-thump* of a bass drum buried deep underground.

Two seconds of double vision.

He squeezed his eyes shut tight, and when he opened them again, it had gone away.

At the next intersection, he stopped. His mouth had been dry, but now it turned to cotton. He was struggling to breathe, bile threatening to surge up his throat.

This will all make sense when you see his face.
It has to.

He made a tentative step out into the street.

Evening now, the chill coming off those mountains and settling down into the valley.

Alpenglow had given the rock surrounding Wayward Pines a pinkish tint, the same shade as the darkening sky. He tried to find it beautiful and moving, but the agony prevented this.

An older couple moved away from him, hand in hand, on a quiet stroll.

Otherwise, the street stood empty and silent, and the noise of the downtown had completely faded away.

He moved across the smooth, black asphalt and stepped onto the sidewalk.

The mailbox to 401 was straight ahead.

Number 403 next in line.

He was having to maintain a constant squint now to stave off the double vision and the stabbing throb of his migraine.

Fifteen painful steps, and he stood beside the black mailbox of 403.

SKOZIE

He stabilized his balance, holding fast to the sharp ends of the picket fence.

Reaching over, he unlatched the gate and pushed it with the tip of his scuffed, black shoe.

The hinges creaked as it swung open.

The gate banged softly into the fence.

The sidewalk was a patchwork of ancient brick, and it led to a covered front porch with a couple of rocking chairs separated by a small, wrought-iron table. The house itself was purple with green trim, and through the thin curtains, he could see lights on inside.

Just go. You have to know.

He stumbled toward the house.

Double vision shot through in nauseating flashes that he was fighting harder and harder to stop.

He stepped up onto the porch and reached out just in time to stop from falling, bracing himself against the door frame. His hands shook uncontrollably as he grabbed the knocker and lifted it off its brass plate.

He refused himself even a split second to reconsider.

Pounded the knocker four times into the plate.

It felt like someone was punching him in the back of the head every four seconds, and burning patches of darkness had begun to swarm his vision like miniature black holes.

On the other side of the door, he could hear a hardwood floor groaning under the weight of approaching footsteps.

His knees seemed to liquefy.

He hugged one of the posts that supported the porch's roof for balance.

The wood door swung open, and a man who could've been his father's age stared at him through the screened door. He was tall and thin, with a splash of gray hair on top, a white goatee, and microscopic red veins in his cheeks that suggested a lifetime of heavy drinking.

"Can I help you?" the man asked.

He straightened himself up, blinking hard through the migraine. It took everything in his power to stand without support.

"Are you Mack?" He could hear the fear in his voice, figured this man could too.

Hated himself for it.

The older man leaned in toward the screen to get a better look at the stranger on his porch.

"What can I do for you?"

"Are you Mack?"

"Yes."

He edged closer, the older man coming into sharper focus, the sour sweetness of red wine on his breath.

"Do you know me?" he asked.

"Pardon?"

Now the fear was fermenting into rage.

"Do. You. Know. Me. Did you do this to me?"

The old man said, "I've never seen you before in my life."

"Is that right?" His hands were balling involuntarily into fists. "Is there another Mack in this town?"

"Not that I'm aware of." Mack pushed open the screen door, ventured a step out onto the porch. "Buddy, you don't look so hot."

"I don't feel so hot."

"What happened to you?"

"You tell me, *Mack*."

A woman's voice called out from somewhere in the house, "Honey? Everything OK?"

"Yes, Jane, all's well!" Mack stared at him. "Why don't you let me take you to the hospital? You're injured. You need—"

"I'm not going anywhere with you."

"Then why are you at my house?" A gruff edge had entered Mack's voice. "I just offered to help you. You don't want that, fine, but . . ."

Mack was still talking, but his words had begun to dissolve, drowned out by a noise building in the pit of his stomach like the roar of a freight train barreling toward him. The black holes were multiplying, the world beginning to spin. He simply wasn't going to be able to stay on his feet another five seconds if his head didn't explode first.

He looked up at Mack, the man's mouth still moving, that freight train closing in with a vengeance of noise, its rhythm in lockstep with the brutal pounding in his head, and he couldn't take his eyes off Mack's mouth, the old man's teeth—his synapses sparking, trying to connect, and the noise, God, the noise, and the throbbing—

He didn't feel his knees give out.

Didn't even register the backward stumble.

One second he was on the porch.

The next, the grass.

Flat on his back and his head reeling from a hard slam against the ground.

Mack hovering above him now, staring down at him, bent over with his hands on his knees and his words hopelessly lost to the train that was screaming through his head.

He was going to lose consciousness—he could feel it coming, seconds away—and he wanted it, wanted the pain to stop, but . . .

The answers.

They were right there.

So close.

It made no sense, but there was something about Mack's mouth. His teeth. He couldn't stop looking at them, and he didn't know why, but it was all there.

An explanation.

Answers to everything.

And it occurred to him—stop fighting it.

Stop wanting it so badly.

Quit thinking.

Just let it come.

The teeth theteeth theteeththeteeththeteeth-
teethteethteeth . . .

They aren't teeth.

They're a bright and shiny grille with the letters

MACK

stamped across the front.

Stallings, the man beside him in the front passenger seat doesn't see what's coming.

In the three-hour ride north out of Boise, it's become apparent that Stallings adores the sound of his own voice, and he's doing what he's been doing the entire time—talking. He stopped listening an hour ago, when he discovered he could tune out completely as long as he interjected an "I hadn't thought of it that way" or "Hmm, interesting" every five minutes or so.

He's turned to make just such a token con- tribution to the conversation when he reads the word mack several feet away on the other side of Stallings's window.

Hasn't even begun to react—he's barely read the word—when the window beside Stallings's head bursts in a shower of glass pebbles.

The air bag explodes out of the steering column but it's a millisecond late, just missing his head, which slams into the window with enough force to punch through.

The right side of the Lincoln Town Car implodes in an apocalypse of breaking glass and bending metal, and Stallings's head takes a direct hit from the truck's grille.

He can feel the heat from the truck's engine as it tears into the car.

The sudden reek of gasoline and brake fluid.

Blood is everywhere—running down the inside of the fractured windshield, splattered across the dash, in his eyes, still erupting out of what's left of Stallings.

The Town Car is sliding crosswise through an intersection, being pushed by the truck toward the side of that brownstone with the phone booth near the alley, when he loses consciousness.

Chapter 2

A WOMAN WAS smiling down at him. At least, he thought those were a mouthful of pretty teeth, although his blurred, double vision made it difficult to say for sure. She leaned in a little closer, her two heads merging and her features crystallizing enough for him to see she was beautiful. Her short-sleeved uniform was white with buttons all the way down the front to where the skirt stopped just above her knees.

She kept repeating his name.

"Mr. Burke? Mr. Burke, can you hear me? Mr. Burke?"

The headache was gone.

He took a slow, careful breath until the pain in his ribs cut him off.

He must have winced, because the nurse said, "Are you still experiencing discomfort in your left side?"

"Discomfort." He groaned through a laugh. "Yes, I'm experiencing discomfort. You could certainly call it that."

"I can get something a little stronger for the pain if you'd like."

"I think I can manage."

"All right, but don't you be a martyr, Mr. Burke. Anything I can do to make you more comfortable, just name it. I'm your girl. My name's Pam, by the way."

"Thank you, Pam. I think I remember you from the last time I was here. I'd never forget that classic nurse's uniform. I didn't even know they still made those."

She laughed. "Well, I'm glad to hear your memory's coming back. That's very good. Dr. Miter will be in shortly to see you. Would you mind if I took a blood pressure reading?"

"Sure."

"Wonderful."

Nurse Pam lifted a blood pressure pump from a cart at the foot of the bed and strapped the cuff around his left biceps.

"You gave us a good scare, Mr. Burke," she said as she inflated the cuff. "Walking off like that."

She was quiet while the needle fell.

"Did I pass?" he asked.

"A-plus. Systolic is one twenty-two. Diastolic seventy-five." She un-Velcroed the cuff. "When they brought you in, you were delirious," she said. "You didn't seem to know who you were."

He sat up in bed, the fog in his head beginning to lift. He was in a private hospital room—he thought it looked familiar. There was a window beside the bed. The blinds had been drawn, but the light creeping through seemed timid enough to be either early morning or early evening.

"Where'd you find me?" he asked.

"Mack Skozie's front yard. You'd blacked out. Do you remember what you were doing there? Mack said you seemed pretty agitated and confused."

"I woke up yesterday by the river. I didn't know who I was or where I was."

"You'd left the hospital. Do you remember leaving?"

"No. I went to the Skozie residence because he was the only Mack in the phone book."

"I don't think I understand."

"Mack was the only name that held any meaning for me."

"Why do you think that is?"

"Because Mack is the last word I read before the truck hit us."

"Oh, right . . . it was a Mack truck that T-boned your car."

"Exactly."

"The mind is a weird thing," the nurse said, moving around the end of the bed and walking over to the window. "It works in mysterious ways. Seeks out the strangest connections."

"How long has it been since I was brought back here?"

She raised the blinds.

"Day and a half."

Light streamed in.

It was actually late morning, the sun just clearing the eastern rim of cliffs.

"You had a bad concussion," she said. "You could've died out there."

"I felt like I was dying."

The early light pouring down into the town was stunning.

"How's your memory?" Pam asked.

"Weirdest thing. It all came back when I remembered the accident. Like someone just flipped a switch. How's Agent Stallings?"

"Who?"

"The man who was riding in the front passenger

30

seat of the car when the collision happened."

"Oh."

"He didn't make it, did he?"

Nurse Pam walked back over to the bedside. She reached down, put her hand on his wrist. "I'm afraid not."

He'd assumed as much. Hadn't seen that sort of trauma since the war. Still, to have that suspicion confirmed was a sobering thing.

"Was he a close friend of yours?" the nurse asked.

"No. I'd met him for the first time earlier that day."

"Must've been just awful. I'm so sorry."

"What's *my* damage?"

"Excuse me?"

"My injuries?"

"Dr. Miter will be able to fill you in better than I can, but you suffered a concussion, which is resolved now. A few cracked ribs. Some superficial cuts and bruises. All things considered, it could have been much, much worse for you."

She turned away and headed for the door, stopping as she started to pull it open for a quick glance back over her shoulder.

"So," she said. "We're sure about your memory coming back?"

"Absolutely."

"What's your first name?"

"Ethan," he said.

"Excellent."

"Could you do me a favor?" Ethan asked.

Big, high-wattage smile. "Name it."

"There are people I need to call. My wife. My SAC. Has anyone been in contact with them?"

"I believe someone from the sheriff's office got in touch with your emergency contacts right after the accident. Let them know what happened, your condition."

"I had an iPhone in my jacket at the time of the collision. Would you happen to know where it is?"

"No, but I can certainly put on my Nancy Drew detective hat and check into that for you."

"I'd appreciate it."

"That little red button on the side of the railing? See it?"

Ethan glanced down at it.

"I'm one click away."

Nurse Pam flashed one more brilliant smile and left.

There was no television in the room, and no telephone. The best and only entertainment was the wall clock hanging above the door, and he lay in bed for several hours watching the second hand make its endless orbit as the morning turned to midday and then to afternoon.

He couldn't be sure, but his room appeared to be three, possibly four floors up. Nurse Pam had left the blinds open, and when he tired of clock-watching, he turned carefully over onto his good side and studied the happenings of Wayward Pines.

From his vantage point, he could see straight down Main Street and several blocks back on either side.

He'd known prior to coming here that it was a tiny, sleepy town, but the sheer inactivity still surprised him. An hour elapsed, and he counted a dozen people strolling down the sidewalk past the hospital, and not a single car driving down the town's busiest thoroughfare. The most effective object of distraction was two blocks away—a construction crew framing a house.

He thought about his wife and son back in Seattle, hoping they were already en route to see him. They'd probably caught the first plane out. They would have had to fly into Boise or Missoula. Rent a car for the long trek out to Wayward Pines.

The next time he glanced at the clock, it was a quarter to four.

He'd been lying in this bed all day, and Dr. Miter, or whatever his name was, hadn't even bothered to stop by. Ethan had spent significant time in hospitals, and in his experience, nurses and doctors never left you alone for more than ten seconds—someone always bringing some new medication, always prodding and poking.

Here, they'd practically ignored him.

Nurse Pam had never even shown up with his iPhone and other belongings. How busy could this hospital in the middle of nowhere be?

He reached for the control panel attached to the railing and jammed his thumb into the NURSE CALL button.

Fifteen minutes later, the door to his room swung open and Nurse Pam breezed through.

"Oh my God, I'm so sorry. I didn't see that you rang until ten seconds ago. I think we're having some issues with our intercom." She stopped at the foot of the bed and put her hands on the metal railing. "How can I help you, Ethan?"

"Where's Dr. Miter?"

She grimaced. "He's been tied up in an emergency surgery all afternoon. One of those five-hour nightmares." She laughed. "But I filled him in on your vitals this morning and the fantastic progress you're making with your memory, and he thinks you're doing A-OK."

She gave Ethan a double thumbs-up.

"When can I see him?"

"It's looking like he'll make his rounds after supper now, which should be coming up in the next half hour."

Ethan struggled to mask his growing frustration.

"Any luck finding my phone and the other things I had with me before the accident? This would include my wallet and a black briefcase."

Nurse Pam gave a half salute and marched in place for several steps.

"Working on it, Captain."

"Just bring me a landline right now. I need to make some calls."

"Of course, Marshal."

"Marshal?"

"Aren't you like a US Marshal or something?"

"No, I'm a special agent with the United States Secret Service."

"Really?"

"Really."

"I thought you guys protected the president."

"We handle some other things too."

"So what are you doing out here in our little slice of heaven?"

Ethan gave her a cool, thin smile.

"I can't discuss that."

He could actually, just didn't feel like it.

"Well, now you've got me all intrigued."

"The phone, Pam."

"Excuse me?"

"I really need the phone."

"I'm on it."

It was when supper finally came—servings of green and brown goo compartmentalized on a shiny metal tray—and the phone didn't that Ethan decided to leave.

Sure, he'd slipped out once before, but he'd

been out of his mind at the time, suffering from a severe concussion.

Now, he was thinking clearly.

The headache was gone, he could breathe easier and with less pain, and if the doctor had any real concern regarding his condition, maybe the asshole would've given him the courtesy of stopping by at some point during the last ten hours.

Ethan waited until Nurse Pam had left, her parting shot assuring him that the hospital food "tastes so much better than it looks!"

When the door closed, he tugged the IV needle out of his wrist and climbed over the railing. The linoleum floor was cold against the soles of his bare feet. He felt a few pegs down from completely stable, but still light-years ahead of his condition forty-eight hours ago.

Ethan padded over to the closet, pulled open the door.

His shirt, jacket, and pants were on a hanger, his shoes on the floor underneath.

No socks.

No briefs.

Guess I'll roll commando.

The only pain came when he bent over to pull on his pants—a sharp twinge high on his left side that went away when he straightened back up.

He caught a glimpse of his bare legs, and as always, the nexus of scarring jogged him out of the moment, fighting to pull him eight years back to a brown-walled room whose stench of death would never leave him.

He checked and found the pocketknife still inside his jacket. Good. It was a relic from his early twenties when he'd worked as a helicopter mechanic—more of a talisman now than a functional tool—but it offered some degree of comfort to know it was there.

He stood in front of a mirror in the bathroom, fumbling with his tie. It took him five attempts to get it right. Fingers misfiring and clumsy, like he hadn't tied one in years.

When he'd finally cinched down a mediocre Windsor knot, he took a step back to appraise himself.

The bruises on his face looked marginally better, but his jacket still bore grass and dirt stains and a small tear across the left pocket. The white oxford shirt underneath was also stained—he could see the smattering of blood near the collar.

He'd lost several inches from his waist over the last few days and had to fasten his belt on the last hole. Still his pants felt too loose.

He turned on the tap, wet his hands, and ran his fingers through his hair.

Fixed his part. Tried to assign it some semblance of order.

He swished with lukewarm water several times, but his teeth still felt mossy.

Sniffed his armpits—*stink*.

He also needed a shave. It had been years since he'd looked this rough.

He stepped into his shoes, laced them up, and headed out of the bathroom toward the door.

His first instinct was to leave without being seen, and this puzzled him. He was a federal agent with the full authority of the United States government. This meant people had to do what he said. Even nurses and doctors. They didn't want him to leave? Tough shit. And yet, some part of him was resisting the hassle of an incident. It was stupid, he knew, but he didn't want Nurse Pam catching him.

He turned the doorknob, opened the door an inch from the jamb.

What he could see of the corridor beyond was empty.

He strained to listen.

No distant chatter of nurses.

No footsteps.

Just blaring silence.

He poked his head out.

A quick glance left and right confirmed his suspicion. For the moment, the place was empty, even the nurses' station fifty feet down the corridor.

He stepped out of his room and onto the checkered linoleum floor and closed the door softly behind him.

Out here, the only sound came from the fluorescent lights overhead—a soft, steady hum.

He suddenly realized what he should have done in the first place and bent down through the pain in his ribs to unlace his shoes.

In bare feet, he moved down the corridor.

Every door on this wing was shut, and with no light slipping through the cracks beneath the doors, none of the rooms but his appeared to be occupied.

The nurses' station stood vacant at the intersection of four corridors, three of which led to additional wings of patient rooms.

A shorter hallway behind the station ran down to a pair of double doors with the word SURGICAL emblazoned on a nameplate above them.

Ethan stopped at the elevator right across from the station and punched the down arrow.

He heard pulleys beginning to turn through the doors.

"Come on."

It took years.

Realized he should've just taken the stairs.

He kept looking over his shoulder, listening for approaching footsteps, but he couldn't hear a thing over the noise of the rising elevator car.

The doors finally separated with a screech that made his teeth ache, and he stepped to the side in the event someone had ridden up.

No one exited the car.

He hurried inside and pressed G.

Studying the illuminated numbers over the doors, he watched as the car began its slow descent from 4, and a full minute had passed—enough time for him to put his shoes back on—before the G illuminated and the doors began to creak open.

He squeezed through, stepped out into another intersection of hallways.

Voices murmured, not far away.

The noise of a stretcher rolling along on a squeaky wheel.

He went the opposite way, tracking through three long corridors, and had begun to suspect he was lost when he spotted an EXIT sign.

He hurried down a half flight of stairs, punched through the door at the bottom, and stumbled outside.

It was early evening, the sky clear and fading, and the mountains taking on the after light of the sun in tones of pink and orange. He stood on a short walkway extending out from the hospital—a four-story, redbrick building that reminded him more of a school, or a mental asylum.

He took as deep a shot of oxygen as he could without bringing the pain, and it felt amazing to inhale this cool, pine-scented air after breathing the hospital's antiseptic stench.

He reached the sidewalk and started down Main Street toward the buildings of downtown.

There were more people out than in the afternoon.

He passed a restaurant situated in a small house with a patio off to the side. People dined outside under aspen trees strung with tiny white lights.

The smell of the food made his stomach growl.

At the corner of Main and Fifth, he crossed the street and returned to the phone booth where he'd lost consciousness two days before.

Stepping inside, he thumbed through the directory until he found the street address of the Wayward Pines Sheriff's Office.

He felt better than he had in days walking toward the east side of town as the light began to fail and the temperature dropped.

He strolled past a barbecue in progress.

The smell of charcoal on the breeze.

The good, sour aroma of beer wafting out of plastic cups.

The sound of children's laughter echoing through the valley.

The cicada-like clicking of a water sprinkler nearby.

Everywhere he looked, it was a painting.

Like the Platonic ideal of a town. There couldn't have been more than four or five hundred people living here, and he found himself wondering what had brought them. How many had discovered Wayward Pines by accident, fell in love, stayed? How many had been born here and never left?

Much as he'd always been a big-city guy, he could understand not leaving a place like this. Why abandon what appeared to be complete and total perfection? Quintessential Americana surrounded by some of the most striking natural beauty he'd ever laid eyes on. He'd seen pictures of Wayward Pines the night before he left Seattle, but none of them had even come close to doing this little valley justice.

And still, *he* was here.

And by virtue of that fact, or rather *because* of it, this place wasn't perfect.

His experience, there was darkness everywhere human beings gathered.

The way of the world.

Perfection was a surface thing. The epidermis. Cut a few layers deep, you begin to see some darker shades.

Cut to the bone—pitch black.

He couldn't take his eyes off the mountains as he walked. The eastern wall must have gone up three or four thousand feet. Toward the top, all rock and ice.

The final strands of horizontal sunlight were striking the cliffs at his back, and he turned around and took a moment to stop and watch the glow fade away.

When the light was gone, the rock turned instantly to the color of blued steel.

And the nature of it changed.

It was still beautiful.

But more remote.

Indifferent.

The placard above the glass double doors:

OFFICE OF THE SHERIFF OF WAYWARD PINES

Moving toward the front entrance down a walkway lined with baby pines, he felt a new impulse of frustration course through him.

Through the glass, he could see that the lobby was dark and empty.

Still, he grabbed the doors and gave them a rough tug.

Locked.

It was after hours, sure, but *Goddammit.*

Ethan backed away from the entrance, glanced down the length of the single-story building. On the far end, it looked like a bit of light was slipping through the blinds behind a window.

He moved forward again, rapped his knuckles against one of the glass doors.

Nothing.

He banged with even more force, pounding the glass so hard the doors rattled in their frames.

Five minutes passed, but no one ever came.

Two stars and a planet had appeared by the time he reached Main Street, and the chill that had been pleasant fifteen minutes ago had become uncomfortable, cutting through his thin oxford shirt, his sockless feet beginning to tingle with numbness.

Worse, the first sign of real hunger was manifesting itself as a hollow ache in the pit of his stomach and a dizziness behind his eyes.

He walked several blocks down to the Wayward Pines Hotel and climbed the stone steps to the entrance.

Through the panes of glass in the door, he saw lights on inside, and a young woman sitting behind the front desk.

Ethan entered the lobby into a welcome blast of warmth.

A grand piano occupied a corner across from the massive hearth, which presently housed a roaring fire.

He stopped for a moment and held his hands out to the heat. The boiling pine resin gave off the sweet smell of a candle. He could've stretched out on the couch and napped for days.

After a moment, he dragged himself away and walked over to the front desk.

The woman smiled at Ethan as he approached.

She struck him as midtwenties. Cute, though a little on the heavy side, her black hair pulled into a short ponytail. She wore a white dress shirt under a black vest, and her name tag identified her as LISA.

Ethan sidled up to the desk and rested his forearms on the high counter to steady his balance.

"Good evening," Lisa said. "Welcome to the Wayward Pines Hotel. How may I help you tonight?"

Her greeting seemed off. Not the words, but the delivery. Like she was struggling through something she rarely had to say.

"Do you have any vacancies tonight?"

"We sure do."

Lisa typed on a keyboard.

"Just tonight?" she asked.

"Yes. For now at least."

Ethan glanced at the computer monitor—an ancient monstrosity. Like something from the late eighties. He couldn't remember the last time he'd seen such a dinosaur.

"I have a nonsmoking, nonpet room on the second floor with a king bed."

"That'll be fine."

She finished typing. "And would you like to put this on a credit card?"

Ethan smiled. "That's an interesting question."

"Really? How so?"

"I was involved in a car accident several days ago. A truck slammed into the side of my car. Just

45

up the block from here actually. Maybe you saw it?"

"No, I sure didn't."

"Well, I was just released from the hospital, and the thing is . . . I haven't been able to locate my wallet. None of my personal belongings, in fact."

"Oh, I'm so sorry to hear that."

He thought he saw Lisa's smile lose just a touch of its initial enthusiasm.

"So how exactly will you be paying then, Mr. . . . ?"

"Burke. Ethan Burke. See, that's what I'm trying to tell you. I won't be able to pay for the room until I get my wallet back tomorrow. I'm informed the sheriff is in possession of my things. Not sure why, but . . ." He shrugged. "Is what it is."

"Hmm. See, I'm not really allowed to open a reservation without a cash advance or at least a credit card number. It's hotel policy. In case —and of course I'm not saying that this would necessarily happen—but in case there was any damage to the room or charges incurred that—"

"I understand that. I'm well aware of the purpose of deposits. What I'm telling you is that I will be able to pay you tomorrow morning."

"You don't even have a driver's license?"

"Everything's in my wallet."

Lisa bit her bottom lip, and he could see what was coming—a nice girl working herself up to be the bad guy.

"Sir—Mr. Burke—I'm afraid that without a credit card or cash or identification, I'm just not going to be able to give you a room tonight. I would love to. Really. But this is just hotel policy and . . ."

She stopped talking when Ethan leaned over the counter.

"Lisa, do you know why I'm wearing a black suit?"

"No."

"I'm a special agent with the United States Secret Service."

"You mean those guys who guard the president?"

"That's only one of our duties. Our primary mission is to protect the integrity of our nation's financial infrastructure."

"And so you're, like, on an investigation in Wayward Pines?"

"I am. I had just arrived in town when the accident happened."

"What kind of investigation?"

"I can't discuss any details."

"You're not pulling my leg, are you?"

"If I was, I'd be committing a federal crime."

"You're really a special agent?"

"Yes. And I'm tired and I'm asking you to give

me a break. I need a room for the night. I promise you—I'm good for it."

"And you'll pay tomorrow? First thing?"

"First thing."

Key in hand, he trudged up the steps to the second floor and emerged into a long, quiet corridor. Faux lanterns had been mounted to the walls every twenty feet, and they shed a weak, yellow light on the Persian carpeting.

His room was at the far end, number 226.

He unlocked the door, stepped inside, hit the light.

The decor ran to the folksy side of the spectrum.

Two badly done iconic Western scenes.

A cowboy on a bucking bronco.

Group of ranch hands huddled around a campfire.

The room was stuffy, and there was no television.

Just an old-school black rotary phone sitting on one of the bedside tables.

The bed itself looked soft and enormous. Ethan eased down onto the mattress and unlaced his shoes. Walking around without socks had already started several blisters on the backs of his feet. He took off his jacket, his tie, and undid the first three buttons of his oxford shirt.

There was a phone directory in the bedside

table drawer, and he took it out, set it on the bed, and lifted the antique phone.

Dial tone.

Thank God.

Strangely, his home phone number didn't immediately spring to mind. He had to spend a minute visualizing it, trying to picture how the number appeared when he smart-dialed on his iPhone. He'd had it just the other day, but . . . "Two . . . zero . . . six." He knew it started with those three numbers—the Seattle area code—and five times, he spun them out on the rotary phone, but five times he blanked after the six.

He dialed 411.

After two rings, an operator answered with, "What city and listing?"

"Seattle, Washington. Ethan Burke. B-U-R-K-E."

"One moment please." Over the line, he could hear the woman typing. There was a long pause. Then: "B-U-R-K-E?"

"That's right."

"Sir, I'm not showing a listing under that name."

"You're sure?"

"Yes."

It was certainly odd, but considering the nature of his job, his number was probably unlisted. Come to think of it, he was almost sure it was. Almost.

"OK, thank you."

He shelved the phone and opened the phonebook, located the number to the sheriff's office.

It rang five times and then went to voice mail.

After the beep, Ethan said, "This is Special Agent Ethan Burke with the United States Secret Service, Seattle field office. As you know, I was involved in the vehicular accident on Main Street several days ago. I need to speak with you at your earliest convenience. The hospital informed me that you're in possession of my personal belongings, including my wallet, phone, briefcase, and firearm. I'll be coming by first thing in the morning to pick them up. If anyone gets this message before then, please call me at the Wayward Pines Hotel. I'm staying in room two twenty-six."

It was full-on night as Ethan walked down the steps from the hotel entrance, his feet killing him, hungry as hell.

The café adjacent to the hotel was closed, so he headed north under a sky filled with stars, past a rare bookstore, a couple of gift shops, and a law office.

It wasn't that late, but with everything closed for the night, the sidewalks of Main had emptied out. He'd begun to come to terms with the horror of not having dinner on top of everything else when he spotted light spilling onto the pavement on the next block down. His pace involuntarily quickened as he caught the first whiff of hot food exhausting out of a vent in the building up ahead.

When he reached the entrance, he stared through the storefront glass into a dimly lighted pub called the Biergarten.

His heart swelled—still open.

He walked inside.

Three tables occupied, but otherwise, the place was dead.

He took a corner stool at the bar.

Through a pair of swinging doors drifted the sizzle of meat cooking on an open grill.

Sitting in this pub, his arms resting on the well-worn bar, he felt at peace for the first time in days. The memory of Stallings and the accident was near, threatening to muscle its way in, but he refused to let it dominate his mind. Simply breathed in and out and tried to stay as firmly planted as possible in the moment.

After five minutes, a tall woman with a pile of brown hair propped up with chopsticks pushed through the swinging doors and opened a hinged section of the bar.

She came around to Ethan, all smiles, and tossed a drink coaster down in front of him.

"Whatcha drinking?"

She wore a black T-shirt with the pub's name screen-printed across the front.

"A beer would be great."

The barkeep grabbed a pint glass and moved over to the taps. "Something light? Dark?"

"You have Guinness?"

"I got something like that."

She'd already pulled the tap when he remembered he didn't have any money.

She set the glass in front of him, cream foam spilling down the sides, said, "You just drinking, or you wanna see a menu?"

"Food for sure," he said, "but you're gonna kill me."

The woman smiled. "Not yet. I hardly know you."

"I don't have any money."

Her smile died. "OK, maybe you're onto something."

"I can explain. You see the car wreck that happened on Main a few days ago?"

"No."

"You hear about it?"

"No."

"Well, there was one, just a few blocks south of here, and I was involved in it. Just got out of the hospital, in fact."

"So that's where you got those pretty bruises?"

"Right."

"I'm still trying to figure out what this has to do with you not paying me."

"I'm a federal agent."

"Same question."

"Apparently, the sheriff has my wallet and phone. Everything actually. It's been a huge headache."

"So what are you, like, FBI or something?"

"Secret Service."

The woman smiled, leaned toward him across the bar. It had been hard to tell in the low light, but in proximity she was damn good looking— a few years younger than Ethan, with model cheekbones, short-torsoed and long-legged. Had probably been a stone-cold knockout in her twenties, although thirty-four or thirty-five— whatever she was now—didn't seem to be treating her too badly.

"I don't know if you're a confidence man, and this is just a part of your game coming in here with your black suit and this crazy—"

"I'm not lying—"

She touched a finger to his lips. "The way I figure, you're either exactly who you say you are, or you're a spectacular liar. I mean, this is a good story, and I love good stories. Either way, of course I'll let you have dinner on credit."

"It's not a lie . . . What's your name?"

"Beverly."

"I'm Ethan."

She shook his hand. "Pleased to meet you, Ethan."

"Beverly, as soon as I get my wallet and things tomorrow morning, I'm gonna come in here—"

"Lemme guess . . . and lay a big tip on me."

Ethan shook his head. "Now you're mocking me."

"I'm sorry."

"If you don't believe me, I'll—"

"I just met you," she said. "By the time you're finished with dinner, I'll know whether or not I'll ever see you again."

"Too early to say, huh?" He smiled, feeling like he might be winning her over.

She brought him a menu, and he ordered potato wedges and a cheeseburger as rare as the health department would allow.

When Beverly had disappeared into the kitchen with his order, he sipped his beer.

Hmm. Something was off. It was flat, and aside from the faintest suggestion of bitterness in the finish, almost completely devoid of taste.

He set the pint glass on the bar as Beverly returned.

"I'm getting a free meal, so I'm hesitant to complain," he said, "but something's wrong with this beer."

"Really?" She gestured to the glass. "You mind?"

"Go ahead."

She lifted the glass and took a sip, licked the foam off her upper lip as she set it back down.

"Tastes fine to me."

"Really?"

"Yeah."

"No, it's flat and . . . I don't know . . . it's just . . . it doesn't have any taste."

"Weird. I don't get that at all. You want to try a different beer?"

"No, I probably shouldn't be drinking anyway. I'll just have a water."

She got him a fresh glass, squirted water over the ice.

He lifted a steaming-hot cheeseburger from his plate with both hands.

Beverly was wiping down the other end of the bar when he called her over, the burger poised in front of his mouth.

"What's wrong?" she asked.

"Nothing. Yet. Come here."

She came over, stood facing him.

"My experience," he said, "is that about eighty percent of the time, when I order a hamburger rare like I just did, I get one well done. I don't know why most cooks are incapable of cooking a hamburger the right way, but there it is. And you know what I do when I get one overcooked?"

"You send it back?" She didn't look amused.

"Exactly."

"You're pretty goddamned difficult to please, you know that?"

"I'm aware," he said, and dove in.

He chewed for a good ten seconds.

"Well?" Beverly asked.

Ethan set the burger back on his plate, swallowing as he wiped his hands on the linen napkin.

He pointed at the burger. "That's an amazing piece of work."

Beverly laughed and rolled her eyes.

By the time Ethan had finished the last crumb on his plate, he was the only customer left in the restaurant.

The barkeep took his plate away and then came back to refill his water.

"You gonna be all right tonight, Ethan? Got a place to stay?"

"Yeah, I sweet-talked the desk clerk at the hotel into letting me have a room."

"She bought your bullshit story too, huh?" Beverly smirked.

"Hook, line, and sinker."

"Well, since this is on me, can I offer you dessert? Our death-by-chocolate is out of this world."

"Thanks, but I should probably get going."

"What is it exactly that you're doing here? In your official capacity, I mean. I understand if you can't talk about it—"

"It's a missing person's investigation."

"Who went missing?"

"Two Secret Service agents."

"They disappeared *here?* In Wayward Pines?"

"About a month ago, Agent Bill Evans and Agent Kate Hewson came here on a classified investigation. As of this evening, they haven't been heard from in ten days. A total loss of contact. No e-mail. No phone calls. Even the GPS tracking chip in their company car went dark."

"And they sent you to find them?"

"I used to work with Kate. We were partners when she lived in Seattle."

"Is that all?"

"Excuse me?"

"*Just* partners?"

He could feel a tremor of something—sadness, loss, rage—vibrating through him.

But he hid it well.

"Yeah, we were just partners. Friends too, though. Anyway, I'm here to pick up their trail. Find out what happened. Bring them home."

"You think something bad happened?"

He didn't answer, just stared at her, but it was an answer.

"Well, I hope you find what you're looking for, Ethan." Beverly pulled a check out of the front pocket on her apron and slid it across the bar.

"So this is my damage, huh?"

Ethan glanced down at the check. It wasn't an itemized bill. Beverly had handwritten an address across the columns.

604 1st Ave

"What's this?" Ethan asked.

"That's where I live. If you need anything, if you run into trouble, whatever . . ."

"What? You worried about me now?"

"No, but with no money, no phone, no ID, you're in a vulnerable state."

"So you believe me now?"

Beverly reached across the bar, let her hand rest on top of his for just a second.

"I always believed you."

Outside the pub, he took off his shoes and started down the sidewalk in bare feet, the concrete cold, but at least he could walk without pain.

Instead of going back to the hotel, he followed one of the streets that intersected Main and headed into a neighborhood.

Thinking about Kate.

Victorian houses lined both sides of the block, set off by the glow of their porch lights.

The silence was staggering.

You never got nights like this in Seattle.

There was always the distant moan of some ambulance or car alarm or the patter of rainfall on the streets.

Here, the complete, dead quiet was broken only by the soft slap of his feet against the pavement—

Wait.

No, there was another sound—a solitary cricket chirping in a bush up ahead.

It took him back to his childhood in Tennessee and those mid-October evenings sitting on the screened porch while his father smoked his pipe, staring across the soybean fields when the chorus of crickets had dwindled down to a lonely one.

Hadn't the poet Carl Sandburg written about this very thing? Ethan couldn't recall the verse verbatim, knew only that it had something to do with the voice of the last cricket across the frost.

A splinter of singing.

There it was—that was the phrase he'd loved.

A splinter of singing.

He stopped beside the bush, half-expecting the chirping to abruptly stop, but it kept on at a rhythm so steady it almost seemed mechanical. Crickets rubbed their wings together to make that sound—he'd read that somewhere.

Ethan glanced at the bush.

Some species of juniper.

Strong, fragrant smell.

A nearby streetlight threw a decent splash of illumination down onto the branches, and he leaned in to see if he could catch a glimpse of the cricket.

The chirping went on, unabated.

"Where are you, little guy?"

He cocked his head.

Now he was squinting at something barely poking up between the branches. But it wasn't the cricket. Some sort of box instead, about the size of his iPhone.

He reached through the branches and touched the face of it.

The chirping grew softer.

He took his hand away.

Louder.

What the hell was the point of this?

The chirp of the cricket was emanating from a speaker.

It was nearly ten thirty when he unlocked his hotel room and stepped inside. He dropped his shoes and stripped naked and climbed into bed without even bothering to turn on the lights.

He'd cracked one of the windows before leaving for dinner, and he could feel a thin, cool draft breezing across his chest, driving out the day's stuffy accumulation of heat.

Within a minute, he was cold.

He sat up, turned back the covers and the sheet, and crawled under.

Fighting for his life, losing, the creature on top of him frenzied as it tried to tear his throat out, the only thing keeping Ethan alive the crushing grip he had around the monster's neck—squeezing, squeezing—but the thing had pure, brute strength. He could feel the hard ripples of muscle as his fingers dug into the milky, translucent skin. But he wasn't stopping it, his triceps beginning to cramp and his arms bending back as the face, the teeth, inched closer . . .

Ethan bolted up in bed, dripping with sweat, gasping for breath, his heart racing so fast it was less like beating than a steady shuddering in his chest.

He had no concept of where he was until he saw the painting of the cowboys and the campfire.

The alarm clock on the bedside table changed to 3:17.

He turned on the light, stared at the phone.

Two . . . zero . . . six . . .

Two . . . zero . . . six . . .

How could he not remember his home landline? Or even Theresa's cell? How was that possible?

Swinging his legs over the side of the bed, he stood and walked over to the window.

Split the blinds, looked down at the quiet street below.

Dark buildings.

Empty sidewalks.

Thinking, *Tomorrow will be better.*

He'd get his phone back, his wallet, his gun, his briefcase. Call his wife, his son. Call Seattle and talk with SAC Hassler. Get back to the investigation that had brought him here in the first place.

Chapter 3

HE WOKE TO a headache and sunlight streaming into his room through the gap in the blinds.

Rolled over, stared at the alarm clock.

"Shit."

12:21.

He'd slept past noon.

Ethan crawled out of bed, and as he reached for his pants—balled up on the floor—he heard someone knocking on his door. Revise that—someone had been knocking on his door for quite awhile, and he was just realizing for the first time that the distant pounding wasn't solely confined to his head.

"Mr. Burke! Mr. Burke!"

Lisa, the front desk clerk, shouting through his door.

"Just a sec!" he called out. He pulled his pants on and staggered over to the door. Undid the locks, the chain, tugged it open.

"Yes?" Ethan asked.

"Checkout is at eleven."

"Sorry, I—"

"What happened to 'first thing'?"

"I didn't realize—"

"Have you been able to get your wallet yet?"

"No, I'm just now waking up. Is it really after twelve?"

She wouldn't answer, just glared at him.

"I'm going to the sheriff's office right now," he said, "and as soon as I get—"

"I need your key back, and I need you to evacuate the room."

"To what?"

"Evacuate the room. Get out. I don't appreciate being taken advantage of, Mr. Burke."

"No one's taking advantage of you."

"I'm waiting."

Ethan took a hard look into her face, searching for something—softness, cracks in her resolve—but he didn't find a shred of compassion.

"Just let me get dressed." He started to close the door, but she put her foot across the threshold.

"Oh, you wanna watch me? Really?" He backed away into the room. "Fine. Enjoy the show."

And she did. Stood in the doorway watching him lace up the shoes over his bare feet, button his stained, white oxford, and struggle for two agonizing minutes to knot his tie.

When he'd finally slid his arms into his black jacket, he grabbed the room key off his bedside table and dropped it into her open palm on the way out.

Said, "You're gonna feel terrible about this in two hours," as he walked down the corridor toward the stairs.

At the drugstore on the corner of Main and Sixth, Ethan grabbed a bottle of aspirin off the shelf and carried it up to the register.

"I can't pay for this," he said as he set it down on the counter. "But I promise I will be right back here with my wallet in thirty minutes. It's a long story, but I have a headache from hell, and I've got to take something right now."

The white-jacketed pharmacist had been in the midst of filling a prescription—counting out pills on a plastic tray. He lowered his chin and looked at Ethan over the top of his square, silver-frame glasses.

"What exactly is it that you're asking me?"

The pharmacist was a balding man on the depressing side of forty. Pale. Thin. With large, brown eyes that looked even larger through his thick-as-plate-glass lenses.

"To help me out. I am . . . really hurting here."

"So go to the hospital. I run a pharmacy, not a credit and loan."

A flash of double vision jarred Ethan for a split second, and he could feel that terrible throbbing beginning to crank up again at the base of his neck, each pulse sending a wave of stunning pain down his spine.

He didn't remember leaving the pharmacy.

Next thing he knew, he was stumbling down the sidewalk of Main.

Feeling worse by the minute, wondering if he should go back to the hospital, but that was the last thing he wanted. He just needed some goddamned Advil, something to take the edge off the pain so he could function.

Ethan stopped at the next crosswalk. Tried to reorient himself to the direction he needed to go to reach the sheriff's office when he remembered. Sliding his hand into the inner pocket of his jacket, he pulled out the slip of paper and unfolded it.

604 1st Ave

He was dubious. Knock on this perfect stranger's door and ask for medicine? On the other hand, he didn't want to go to the hospital, and he couldn't show up at the sheriff's office in the throes of this mind-crippling headache. He was planning to chew some ass, and that usually went better when you weren't overcome by the desire to crawl up into a fetal position in a dark room.

What was her name?

That's right—Beverly.

She'd probably closed last night, which meant there was a good chance she was home now. Hell, she'd offered. He could swing by, borrow a few pills, get this headache under control before heading over to the sheriff's.

He crossed the street, stayed on Main until he'd

reached Ninth, and then took a turn around the block and headed east.

Streets intersected Main.

Avenues ran parallel.

Figured he had about seven blocks to walk.

After the third, he could feel his feet rubbing raw, but he didn't stop. It was pain, but a welcome distraction from the pounding in his head.

The school occupied an entire city block between Fifth and Fourth Avenues, and he limped alongside a chain-link fence that enclosed a playing field.

It was recess hour for a class of eight- or nine-year-olds, and they were engaged in an elaborate game of freeze tag, a girl with blonde pigtails chasing everyone in sight as a choir of screams echoed between the brick buildings.

Ethan watched their game, trying not to think about the blood that had begun to collect in his shoes—cold between his toes.

Blonde pigtails suddenly stopped in the middle of a group of kids and stared at Ethan.

For a moment, the other kids continued running and screaming, but gradually, they also stopped, taking notice, first, that their pursuer was no longer chasing them, and then, of what had stolen her attention.

One by one, each child turned and stared at Ethan—blank expressions that he could have sworn contained some element of thinly veiled hostility.

He smiled through the pain, gave a little wave. "Hey, kids."

Not a single one of them waved back or otherwise responded. They just stood frozen in place like a collection of figurines, only their heads turning as they watched him pass out of sight around the corner of the gymnasium.

"Weird little shits," Ethan muttered under his breath as their laughter and screams started up again, the game resuming.

On the other side of Fourth Avenue, he picked up the pace, the pain in his feet getting more intense, but he pushed through it, thinking, *Just get there. Grin and bear it and get there.*

Beyond Third Avenue now, and he was jogging, his ribs beginning to ache again. He passed a series of houses that looked more run-down. The seedy side of Wayward Pines? he wondered. Could such a town have a bad side?

At First Avenue, he stopped.

The road had gone to dirt—the gravel long since worn away and the lumpy grade of it heavily washboarded. There was no sidewalk and there was no road beyond this one. He'd come to the eastern edge of Wayward Pines and behind the houses that lined this street, civilization came to an abrupt end. A steep hillside, wooded with pines, ran up several hundred feet to the base of that cirque that enclosed the town.

Ethan limped down the middle of the empty dirt road.

He could hear birds chirping in the nearby woods, and nothing else. Completely isolated from what little bustle downtown Wayward Pines could muster.

He was passing mailboxes that were already in the five hundreds, feeling the first glimmer of relief, knowing Beverly's place would be on the next block.

The light-headedness was threatening again, waves of it—gentle so far—washing over him.

The next intersection stood completely empty.

Not a soul out.

A warm wind sliding down off the mountain sent little whirlwinds of dust across the street.

There it was—604, the second house on the right. He could tell this from the tiny steel plate that had been screwed into what was left of the mailbox, which was completely covered in rust except for the gaping, jagged holes. A quiet tweeping emitted from within, and for a moment, he thought it might be another speaker, but then he glimpsed the wing of the bird that was nesting inside.

He looked up at the house itself.

It had probably been a lovely two-story Victorian once, with a steeply pitched roof and a porch with a swing and a stone path leading through the front yard to the entrance.

The paint had long ago chipped away. Even standing in the street, Ethan could see that not even a fleck of it lingered. The boards still attached to the listing frame had been bleached almost white by the sun, most in the final stages of disintegration from rot. Not a jag of window glass remained.

He pulled the ticket from last night's dinner out of his pocket and rechecked the address. The handwriting was clear—*604 1st Ave*—but maybe Beverly had transposed the numbers, or written "Ave" when she meant "St."

Ethan pushed his way into the waist-high weeds that had overtaken the front yard, only flashes of the stone pathway visible through the undergrowth.

The two steps leading to the covered porch looked like they'd been run through a wood chipper. He stepped up and over them onto a floorboard, his weight upon it producing a deafening creak.

"Beverly?"

The house seemed to swallow his voice.

He carefully crossed the porch, stepped through the doorless doorway, and called her name again. He could hear the wind pushing against the house, its timber frame groaning. Three steps into the living room, he stopped. Springs lay rusting on the floor amid the crumbling frame of an ancient sofa. A coffee table stood covered in cobwebs, and underneath them, the pages of some magazine, sodden and rotted beyond recognition.

Beverly couldn't have wanted him to come here—not even as a joke. She must have accidentally written down the wrong—

The smell brought his chin up. He took a tentative step forward, dodging a trio of nails sticking up through a floorboard.

Sniffed the air again.

Another blast of it swept by as a gust of wind shook the house, and he instantly buried his nose in the crook of his arm. He moved forward, past half a staircase, into a narrow hallway that ran between the kitchen and the dining room, where a cascade of light streamed down onto the splintered remains of where the ceiling had crushed the dinner table.

He went on, picking his way through a mine-field of bad boards and outright holes that gaped into the crawlspace under the house.

The refrigerator, the sink, the stove—rust covered every metal surface like a fungus, this place reminding him of the old homesteads he and his friends would stumble across on summer explorations into the woods behind their farms. Abandoned barns and cabins, the roofs perforated with holes that the sun blazed through in tubes of light. He'd once found a fifty-year-old newspaper inside an old desk announcing the election of a new president, had wanted to take it home and show his parents, but the thing was so brittle it had flaked apart in his hands.

Ethan hadn't ventured a breath through his nose in over a minute, and still he could tell the stench was getting stronger. Swore he could taste it in the corners of his mouth and the sheer intensity of it—worse than ammonia—was drawing tears from his eyes.

The far end of the hallway grew dark—still protected under a ceiling that dripped from the last good rain, whenever that had been.

The door at the end of the hall was closed.

Ethan blinked the tears out of his eyes and reached down for the doorknob, but there wasn't one.

He nudged the door open with his shoe.

Hinges grinding.

The door banged into the wall and Ethan took a step forward across the threshold.

Just like his memory of those old home-steads, bullets of light shot through holes in the far wall, glinting off the labyrinth of cobwebs, before striking the only piece of furniture in the room.

The metal frame was still standing, and through the soupy ruin of the mattress, he could see the bedsprings like coiled copperheads.

He hadn't heard the flies until now, because they had congregated inside the man's mouth—a metropolis of them, the sound of their collective buzzing like a small outboard motor.

He'd seen worse—in combat—but he'd never smelled worse.

White showed through everywhere—the wrist and ankle bones, which had been handcuffed to the headboard and the iron railing at the base of the bed. Where his right leg was exposed, the flesh looked almost shredded. The internal architecture on the left side of the man's face was exposed, right down to the roots of his teeth. His stomach had bloated too—Ethan could see the swell of it underneath the tattered suit, which was black and single-breasted.

Just like his.

Though the face was a wreck, the hair length and color were right.

The height was a match too.

Ethan staggered back and leaned against the doorframe.

Jesus Fucking Christ.

This was Agent Evans.

Back outside on the front porch of the abandoned house, Ethan bent over, his hands braced against his knees, and took deep, penetrating breaths through his nose to purge the smell. But it wouldn't leave. That death-stink had embedded in his sinus cavity, and as a bitter, putrid bite in the back of his throat.

He took off his jacket and unbuttoned his shirt, fought his way out of the sleeves. The stench was in the fibers of his clothing now.

Shirtless, he moved through the riot of undergrowth that had once been a front yard and finally reached the dirt road.

He could feel the coldness of raw skin on the backs of his feet and the bass throb in his skull, but the pain had lost its edge to pure adrenaline.

He set off at a strong pace down the middle of the street, his mind racing. He'd been tempted to search the pockets of the dead man's coat and pants, see if he could score a wallet, some ID, but the smart play had been to hold off. To not touch anything. Let people with latex gloves and face masks and every conceivable state-of-the-art forensic tool descend on that room.

He still couldn't wrap his head around it.

A federal agent had been murdered in this little slice of heaven.

He was no coroner, but he felt certain Evans's face wasn't just rotting away. Part of his skull had been caved in. Teeth broken out. One of his eyes MIA.

He'd been tortured too.

The six blocks seemed to fly by, and then he was jogging up the sidewalk to the entrance of the sheriff's office.

He left his jacket and shirt outside on a bench and pulled open one of the double doors.

The reception area was a wood-paneled room with brown carpeting and taxidermied animal heads mounted on every available piece of vertical real estate.

At the front desk, a sixty-something woman with long, silver hair was playing solitaire with a physical deck of cards. The freestanding nameplate on her desk read "Belinda Moran."

Ethan arrived at the edge of her desk and watched her lay down four more cards before finally tearing herself away from the game.

"May I help—" Her eyes went wide. She looked him up and down, wrinkling her nose at what he supposed was the god-awful stench of human decay that must be wafting off him. "You're not wearing a shirt," she said.

"United States Secret Service Special Agent Ethan Burke here to see the sheriff. What's his name?"

"Who?"

"The sheriff."

"Oh. Pope. Sheriff Arnold Pope."

"Is he in, Belinda?"

Instead of answering his question, she lifted her rotary phone and dialed a three-digit extension. "Hi, Arnie, there's a man here to see you. Says he's a secret agent or something."

"Special Agent with the—"

She held up a finger. "I don't know, Arnie. He isn't wearing a shirt, and he . . ." She turned away from Ethan in her swivel chair, whispered, ". . . smells bad. Really bad . . . OK. OK, I'll tell him."

She spun back around and hung up the phone. "Sheriff Pope will be with you shortly."

"I need to see him right now."

"I understand that. You can wait over there." She pointed to a grouping of chairs in a nearby corner.

Ethan hesitated for a moment, and then finally turned and headed toward the waiting area. Wise to keep this first encounter civil. In his experience, local law enforcement became defensive and even hostile when feds threw their weight around right out of the gate. In light of what he'd found in that abandoned house, he was going to be working with this guy for the foreseeable future. Better to start off with the glad hand than a middle finger.

Ethan eased down into one of the four upholstered chairs in the sitting area.

He'd worked up a sweat on the jog over, but now that his heart rate had returned to baseline, the layer of sweat on his bare skin had begun to chill him as the central air blew down out of a vent overhead.

There wasn't much in the way of current reading material on the small table in front of his chair—just a few old issues of *National Geographic* and *Popular Science.*

He leaned back in the chair and shut his eyes.

The pain in his head was coming back—the cut of each throb escalating on some molecular level perceptible only over a span of minutes. He could actually hear the pounding of his headache in the total silence of the sheriff's office, where there was no sound other than the flipping of cards.

He heard Belinda say, "Yes!"

Opened his eyes in time to see her place the last card, having won her game. She gathered the cards up and shuffled them and began again.

Another five minutes passed.

Another ten.

Belinda finished the game and she was mixing the deck again when Ethan noted the first impulse of irritation—a twitch in his left eye.

The pain was still growing and he'd now been waiting, at his estimation, for fifteen minutes. In that increment of time, the phone had not rung once, and not another soul had entered the building.

He shut his eyes and counted down from sixty as he massaged his temples. When he opened them again, he was still sitting there shirtless and cold, and Belinda was still turning cards over, and the sheriff had yet to come.

Ethan stood, fought a bout of wooziness for ten

seconds before finally establishing his balance. He walked back over to the reception desk and waited for Belinda to look up.

She laid down five cards before acknowledging him.

"Yes?"

"I'm sorry to be a bother, but I've been waiting about twenty minutes now."

"The sheriff's real busy today."

"I'm sure he is, but I need to speak with him right away. Now you can either get him on the phone again and tell him I'm done waiting, or I'm gonna walk back there myself and—"

Her desk phone rang.

She answered, "Yes? . . . OK, I sure will." She shelved the phone and smiled up at Ethan. "You're welcome to go on back now. Right down that hallway. His office is through the door at the very end."

Ethan knocked beneath the nameplate.

A deep voice hollered from the other side, "Yep!"

He turned the knob, pushed the door open, stepped inside.

The floor of the office was a dark and deeply scuffed hardwood. To his left, the enormous head of an elk had been mounted to the wall opposite a large, rustic desk. Behind the desk stood three antique gun cabinets brimming with rifles, shotguns, handguns, and what he calculated were enough boxes of ammo to execute every resident of this little town three times over.

A man ten years his senior reclined in a leather chair, his cowboy-booted feet propped on the desk. He had wavy blond hair that would probably be white within a decade, and his jaw was frosted with a few days' worth of grizzle.

Dark brown canvas pants.

Long-sleeved button-down—hunter green.

The sheriff's star gleamed under the lights. It looked like solid brass, intricately etched, with the letters WP inset in black in the center.

As he approached the desk, Ethan thought he saw the sheriff let slip a private smirk.

"Ethan Burke, Secret Service."

He extended his hand across the desk, and the sheriff hesitated, as if holding some internal debate over whether he felt like moving. Finally, he slid his boots off the desktop and leaned forward in his chair.

"Arnold Pope." They shook hands. "Have a seat, Ethan."

Ethan eased down into one of the straight-backed wooden chairs.

"How you feeling?" Pope asked.

"I've been better."

"I'll bet. You've probably smelled better too." Pope flashed a quick grin. "Rough accident you had a couple days ago. Tragic."

"Yeah, I was hoping to learn a few more details about that. Who hit us?"

"Eyewitnesses say it was a tow truck."

"Driver in custody? Being charged?"

"Would be if I could find him."

"You saying this was a hit-and-run?"

Pope nodded. "Hauled ass out of town after he T-boned you. Long gone by the time I reached the scene."

"And no one got a license plate or anything?"

Pope shook his head and lifted something off the desk—a snow globe with a gold base. The miniature buildings under the glass dome became caught in a whirlwind of snow as he passed the globe back and forth between his hands.

"What efforts are being made to locate this truck?" Ethan asked.

"We got stuff in the works."

"You do?"

"You bet."

"I'd like to see Agent Stallings."

"His body is being held in the morgue."

"And where's that?"

"In the basement of the hospital."

It suddenly came to Ethan. Out of the blue. Like someone had whispered it into his ear.

"Could I borrow a piece of paper?" Ethan asked.

Pope opened a drawer and peeled a Post-it Note off the top of a packet and handed it to Ethan along with a pen. Ethan scooted his chair forward and set the Post-it on the desktop, scribbled down the number.

"I understand you have my things?" Ethan said as he slipped the Post-it into his pocket.

"What things?"

"My cell, gun, wallet, badge, briefcase . . ."

"Who told you I had those?"

"A nurse at the hospital."

"No clue where she got that idea."

"Wait. So you *don't* have my things?"

"No."

Ethan stared at Pope across the desk. "Is it possible they're still in the car?"

"Which car?"

He struggled to keep the tone of his voice in check. "The one the tow truck hit while I was in it."

"I suppose it's possible, but I'm fairly certain the EMTs took your things."

"Jesus."

"What?"

"Nothing. Would you mind if I made a few phone calls before I leave? I haven't talked to my wife in days."

"I spoke to her."

"When?"

"Day of the accident."

"Is she on her way?"

"I have no idea. I just let her know what had happened."

"I also need to call my SAC—"

"Who's that?"

"Adam Hassler."

"He sent you here?"

"That's right."

"Did he also instruct you not to bother calling me ahead of time to let me know the feds would be rolling up in my world? Or was that all you?"

"You think I had some obligation to—"

"Courtesy, Ethan. Courtesy. Then again, being a fed, maybe you aren't familiar with that concept—"

"I would've contacted you eventually, Mr. Pope. There was no intent to cut you out of the loop."

"Oh. Well, in that case."

Ethan hesitated, wanting to be clear, to communicate the information he wished to impart and not a shred more. But his head was killing him and the double vision threatened to split the sheriff into two assholes.

"I was sent here to find two Secret Service agents."

Pope's eyebrows came up. "They're missing?"

"For eleven days now."

"What were they doing in Wayward Pines?"

"I wasn't provided a detailed briefing on their investigation, although I know it involved David Pilcher."

"Name sounds vaguely familiar. Who is he?"

"He always shows up on lists of the world's richest men. One of these reclusive billionaires. Never talks to the press. Owns a bunch of biopharmaceutical companies."

"And he has a connection to Wayward Pines?"

"Again, I don't know that. But if the Secret Service was here, there was probably some investigation involving a financial crime. That's all I know."

Pope stood suddenly. Ethan could tell he was a large man sitting behind the desk, but standing in his boots, Ethan saw that he was an inch or two shy of six and a half feet.

"You're welcome to use the phone in the conference room, Agent Burke."

Ethan didn't move from his chair.

"I wasn't quite finished, Sheriff."

"Conference room's right this way." Pope came around his desk and started toward the door. "And maybe a shirt next time? Just a suggestion."

The pounding in Ethan's head was becoming laced with anger.

"Would you like to know why I'm not wearing a shirt, Sheriff?"

"Not particularly."

"One of the agents I came looking for is decomposing in a house six blocks from here."

Pope stopped at the door, his back to Ethan.

"I just found him before coming here," Ethan said.

Pope turned and glared down at Ethan.

"Elaborate on 'I just found him.' "

"Last night, a bartender at the Biergarten gave me her address in case I needed anything. I woke up this morning with a terrible headache. No money. Got kicked out of my hotel room. I went to her house to get some medicine for my headache, only the address she gave was wrong or something."

"What's the address?"

"Six-oh-four, First Avenue. It turned out to be an old, abandoned house. In ruins. Agent Evans had been chained to a bed in one of the rooms."

"You're sure it's this man you came here to find?"

"Eighty percent sure. There was a great deal of decay and his face had suffered extensive blunt-force trauma."

The scowl the sheriff had maintained since Ethan had walked into his office disappeared, and his features seemed to soften. He walked toward Ethan and eased down into the empty chair beside him.

"I apologize, Agent Burke. I kept you waiting out in reception. I got angry that you didn't call before coming to town, and well, you're right. There was no obligation. I've got a nasty temper—one of my many failings—and my behavior was unacceptable."

"Apology accepted."

"You've had a rough couple of days."

"I have."

"Go make your phone calls and we'll talk when you're finished."

A long table crowded the conference room, with barely enough space between the chairs and the wall for Ethan to make his way toward the rotary phone down at the end.

He dug the Post-it Note out of his pocket and lifted the phone.

Dial tone.

He spun out the number.

It rang.

Afternoon sun slicing between the blinds and striking the table's polished wood veneer in blades of blinding light.

Three rings in, he said, "Come on, baby, pick up."

After the fifth ring, he got the machine.

Theresa's voice: "Hi, you've reached the Burkes. Sorry we aren't here to take your call . . . unless of course you're a telemarketer . . . then we're thrilled to have missed your call, and, in fact, we're probably dodging it and encourage you to forget this number. Otherwise, leave it at the beep."

"Theresa, it's me. God, I feel like I haven't heard your voice in years. I guess you know that I was in a car accident out here. No one can seem to find my phone, so if you've been trying to call, I'm sorry. I'm staying at the Wayward Pines Hotel, Room Two Twenty-Six. You might try calling the sheriff's office also. I hope you and Ben are OK. I'm all right. Still a little sore, but doing better. Please call me at the hotel tonight. I'll try you again soon. I love you, Theresa. So much."

He hung up the phone, sat there for a moment trying to conjure the number to his wife's cell. Got as far as the first seven digits but the final three remained shrouded in mystery.

The number to the Seattle field office came to him instantly. He dialed, and after three rings, a woman whose voice Ethan didn't recognize answered.

"Secret Service."

"Hi, it's Ethan Burke. I need to speak with Adam Hassler, please."

"He's not available at the moment. Was there something I could help you with?"

"No, I really need to speak with him. Is he out of the office today?"

"He's not available at the moment. Was there something I could help you with?"

"How about I try him on his cell? Could I have that number, please?"

"Oh, I'm afraid I'm not allowed to give out that information."

"Do you understand who I am? *Agent* Ethan Burke?"

"Was there something *I* could help you with?"

"What's your name?"

"Marcy."

"You're new, right?"

"This is my third day."

"Look, I'm up here in Wayward Pines, Idaho, in the middle of a shitstorm. Get Hassler on the phone immediately. I don't care what he's doing. If he's in a meeting . . . if he's taking a shit . . . put him on the goddamned phone."

"Oh, I'm sorry."

"What?"

"I'm not going to be able to continue this conversation with you speaking to me like that."

"Marcy?"

"Yes?"

"I apologize. I'm sorry I raised my voice with you, but I have to speak with Hassler. It is urgent."

"I'd be happy to slip him a message if you'd like."

Ethan closed his eyes.

He was grinding his molars together to keep from screaming through the phone.

"Tell him to call Agent Ethan Burke at the Wayward Pines Sheriff's Office, or at the Wayward Pines Hotel, Room Two Twenty-Six. He has to do this the moment he gets the message. Agent Evans is dead. Do you understand me?"

"I'll give him the message!" Marcy said brightly and hung up the phone.

Ethan pulled the receiver away from his face and slammed it five times into the table.

As he was hanging the phone back up, he noticed Sheriff Pope standing in the doorway to the conference room.

"Everything all right, Ethan?"

"Yeah, it's . . . just having a little trouble getting through to my SAC."

Pope came inside and closed the door. He sat down at the end of the table opposite Ethan.

"You said there were two missing agents?" Pope asked.

"That's right."

"Tell me about the other one."

"Her name's Kate Hewson. She worked out of the Boise field office, and, prior to that, Seattle."

"Did you know her there?"

"We were partners."

"So she got transferred?"

"Yes."

"And Kate came here with Agent . . ."

"Bill Evans."

". . . on this top-secret investigation."

"Right."

"I'd like to help. Would you like my help?"

"Of course, Arnold."

"OK. Let's start with the basics. What does Kate look like?"

Ethan leaned back in his chair.

Kate.

He'd so thoroughly trained himself over the last year *not* to think of her that it took him a moment to retrieve her face, the memory of it like tearing open a wound that had just begun to scar over.

"She's five-two, five-three. Hundred and five pounds."

"Little gal, huh?"

"Best lawman I've ever known. Short brown hair last time I saw her, but it could have grown out. Blue eyes. Uncommonly beautiful."

God, he could still taste her.

"Any distinguishing marks?"

"Yeah, actually. She has a faint birthmark on her cheek. A café au lait about the size of a nickel."

"I'll put the word out to my deputies, maybe even have a sketch of her drawn to show around town."

"That'd be great."

"Why did you say Kate was transferred out of Seattle?"

"I didn't say."

"Well, do you know?"

"Some sort of internal reshuffling was the rumor. I'd like to see the car."

"The car?"

"The black Lincoln Town Car I was driving when the accident happened."

"Oh, of course."

"Where might I find that?"

"There's a salvage yard on the outskirts of

town." The sheriff stood. "What was that address again?"

"Six-oh-four First Avenue. I'll walk you over."

"No need."

"I want to."

"I *don't* want you to."

"Why?"

"Was there anything else you needed?"

"I'd like to know the results of your investigation."

"Come back tomorrow after lunch. We'll see where we're at."

"And you'll take me to the salvage yard to see the car?"

"I think we can swing that. But for now, let's go. I'll walk you out."

Ethan's jacket and shirt smelled marginally better as he slid his arms into the sleeves and started down the street, away from the Wayward Pines Sheriff's Office. He still reeked, but figured the offensive smell of decay would draw less attention than a man walking around town in nothing but dress slacks.

He pushed as strong a pace as he could manage, but the wooziness kept coming in waves, and his head was alive with pain, each step sending new tendrils of agony into the far reaches of his skull.

The Biergarten was open and empty save for

one bored-looking bartender sitting on a stool behind the bar reading a paperback novel—one of F. Paul Wilson's early books.

When Ethan reached the bar, he said, "Is Beverly working tonight?"

The man held up a finger.

Ten seconds passed as he finished reading a passage.

At last, he closed the book, gave Ethan his full attention.

"What can I get you to drink?"

"Nothing. I'm looking for the woman who was tending bar here last night. Her name was Beverly. Pretty brunette. Midthirties. Fairly tall."

The barkeep stepped down off his stool and set the book on the bar. His long, graying hair was the color of murky dishwater, and he pulled it back into a ponytail.

"You were here? In this restaurant? Last night?"

"That's correct," Ethan said.

"And you're telling me that a tall brunette was tending bar?"

"Exactly. Beverly was her name."

The man shook his head, Ethan detecting a whiff of mockery in his smile.

"There's two people on the payroll here who tend bar. Guy named Steve, and me."

"No, this woman waited on me last night. I ate a burger, sat right over there." Ethan pointed to the corner stool.

"Don't take this the wrong way, buddy, but how much did you have to drink?"

"Nothing. And I'm not your buddy. I'm a federal agent. And I know that I was here last night, and I know who served me."

"Sorry, man, I don't know what to tell you. I think you must've been at a different restaurant."

"No, I . . ."

Ethan suddenly lost his focus.

Dug his fingertips into his temples.

He could feel his pulse now in his temporal artery, each heartbeat carrying the punch of those cold headaches he used to get as a kid—that fleeting, excruciating pain that followed too ravenous a bite of popsicle or ice cream.

"Sir? Sir, are you all right?"

Ethan staggered back from the bar, managed to say, "She was here. I know it. I don't know why you're doing . . ."

Then he was standing outside, his hands on his knees, bent over a pool of vomit on the sidewalk that he quickly surmised had come from him, his throat burning from the bile.

Ethan straightened up, wiped his mouth across the sleeve of his jacket.

The sun had already dropped behind the cliffs, the coolness of evening upon the town.

There were things he needed to do—find Beverly, find the EMTs, and recover his personal belongings—but all he wanted was to curl up in bed in a dark room. Sleep off the pain. The confusion. And the base emotion underlying it all that was getting harder and harder to ignore.

Terror.

The strengthening sense that something was very, very wrong.

He stumbled up the stone steps and pushed through the doors into the hotel.

The fireplace warmed the lobby.

A young couple occupied one of the loveseats by the hearth, sipping from glasses of sparkling wine. On a romantic vacation, he figured, enjoying a completely different side of Wayward Pines.

A tuxedoed man sat at the grand piano, playing "Always Look on the Bright Side of Life."

Ethan arrived at the front desk, forcing himself to smile through the pain.

The same clerk who'd evicted him from his room that morning started speaking even before she looked up.

"Welcome to the Wayward Pines Hotel. How may I help . . ."

She stopped when she saw Ethan.

"Hi, Lisa."

"I'm impressed," she said.

"Impressed?"

"You came back to pay. You told me you would, but I honestly didn't think I'd ever see you again. I apologize for—"

"No, listen, I wasn't able to find my wallet today."

"You mean you haven't come back to pay for your room last night? Like you promised me you were going to multiple times?"

Ethan shut his eyes, breathing through the exquisite pain.

"Lisa, you cannot imagine the day I've had. I just need to lie down for a few hours. I don't even need a room for the whole night. Just a place to clear my head and sleep. I'm in so much pain."

"Hold on." She slid off her chair and leaned toward him across the counter. "You still can't pay and now you're asking me for *another* room?"

"I don't have anywhere else to go."

"You lied to me."

"I'm sorry. I really thought I would have it by—"

"Do you understand that I went out on a limb for you? That I could lose my job?"

"I'm sorry, I didn't mean—"

"Go."

"Excuse me?"

"Did you not hear me?"

"I don't have any place to go, Lisa. I don't have a phone. I have no money. I haven't eaten since last night, and—"

"Explain to me again how any of this is my problem."

"I just need to lie down for a few hours. I am begging you."

"Look, I've explained this to you as clearly as I possibly can. It's time for you to leave."

Ethan didn't move. He just stared at her, hoping she might see the agony in his eyes, take pity.

"Now," she said.

He raised his hands in a gesture of surrender, backing away from the counter.

As he reached the doors, Lisa called after him. "I don't want to see you back in here ever again."

Ethan nearly fell descending the steps, his head spinning by the time he reached the sidewalk. The streetlamps and the lights from passing cars began to swirl, Ethan noting the strength flooding out of his legs like someone had pulled a drain plug.

Regardless, he started up the sidewalk, saw that redbrick building looming up the street, eight blocks away. There was still fear of it, but now he needed the hospital. Wanted the bed, the sleep, the meds. Anything to stop this pain.

He was either going to the hospital or he was sleeping outside—in an alley, or a park, exposed to the elements.

But it was eight blocks, so far, each step now requiring a crushing expenditure of energy, and the lights were disintegrating all around him— swirling, long tails getting more intense, more pronounced, skewing his vision as if he could see the world only as a long-exposure shot of a city at night, the car lights stretching into rods of brilliance, the streetlamps burning like blow-torches.

He bumped into someone.

A man pushed him, said, "Do you drive that way?"

At the next intersection, Ethan stopped, doubtful he could make it across.

He stumbled back and sat down hard on the sidewalk against a building.

The street had become crowded—he couldn't see anything distinctly, but he could hear foot-steps moving by on the concrete and snippets of passing conversation.

He lost all sense of time.

He might have dreamed.

Then he was lying on his side on the cold concrete, felt someone's breath, their voice right in his face.

Words came at him, though he couldn't assemble them into any sensible order.

He opened his eyes.

Night had fallen.

He was shivering.

A woman knelt beside him, and he felt her hands gripping his shoulders. She was shaking him, speaking to him.

"Sir, are you all right? Can you hear me? Sir?

Can you look at me and tell me what's wrong?"

"He's drunk." A man's voice.

"No, Harold. He's sick."

Ethan tried to pull her face into focus, but it was dark and blurry, and all he could see were those streetlamps shining like minor suns across the road and the occasional streak of light from a passing car.

"My head hurts," he said in a voice that sounded far too weak and pained and fear-filled to be his. "I need help."

She took his hand and told him not to worry, not to be afraid, that help was already on the way.

And though the hand holding his clearly didn't belong to a young woman—the skin too taut and thin, like old paper—there was something so familiar in the voice that it broke his heart.

Chapter 4

THEY TOOK THE Bainbridge Island ferry out of Seattle and headed north up the peninsula toward Port Angeles, a convoy of four cars carrying fifteen of the Burkes' closest friends.

Theresa had been hoping for a pretty day, but it was cold, gray rain, the Olympics obscured, and nothing visible beyond their narrow corridor of highway.

But none of that mattered.

They were going regardless of the weather, and if no one else wanted to join her, she and Ben would hike up alone.

Her friend Darla drove, Theresa in the back seat holding her seven-year-old son's hand and staring out the rain-beaded glass as the rainforest streaked past in a blur of dark green.

A few miles west of town on Highway 112, they reached the trailhead to Striped Peak.

It was still overcast, but the rain had stopped.

They started out in silence, hiking along the water, no sound but the impact of their footfalls squishing in the mud and the white noise of the breakers.

Theresa glanced down into a cove as the trail passed above it, the water not as blue as she remembered, blaming the cloud cover for muting the color, no failing of her memory.

The group passed the World War II bunkers and climbed through groves of fern and then into forest.

Moss everywhere.

The trees still dripping.

Lushness even in early winter.

They neared the top.

The entire time, no one had spoken.

Theresa could feel a burning in her legs and the tears coming.

It started to rain as they reached the summit

—nothing heavy, just a few wild drops blowing sideways in the wind.

Theresa walked out into the meadow.

She was crying now.

On a clear day, the view would've been for miles, with the sea a thousand feet below.

Today the peak was socked in.

She crumpled down in the wet grass, put her head between her knees, and cried.

There was the pattering of drizzle on the hood of her poncho and nothing else.

Ben sat down beside her and she put her arm around him, said, "You did good hiking, buddy. How you feeling?"

"All right, I guess. Is this it?"

"Yeah, this is it. You could see a lot farther if it wasn't for the fog."

"What do we do now?"

She wiped her eyes, took a deep, trembling breath.

"Now, I'm going to say some things about your dad. Maybe some other people will too."

"Do I have to?"

"Only if you want to."

"I don't want to."

"That's fine."

"It doesn't mean I don't still love him."

"I know that."

"Would he want me to talk about him?"

"Not if it made you feel uncomfortable."

Theresa shut her eyes, took a moment to gather herself.

She struggled onto her feet.

Her friends were milling around in the ferns, blowing into their hands for warmth.

It was raw up on the summit, a strong gale pushing the ferns in green waves and the air cold enough to turn their breath to steam.

She called her friends over and they all stood in a huddle against the rain and the wind.

Theresa told the story of how she and Ethan had taken a trip to the peninsula several months after they'd started dating. They stayed at a B&B in Port Angeles and, late one afternoon, stumbled upon the trailhead to Striped Peak. They reached the summit at sunset on a clear, calm evening, and as she stared across the strait at the long view into southern Canada, Ethan dropped to one knee and proposed.

He'd bought a toy ring from a convenience store vending machine that morning. Said he hadn't been planning anything like this, but that he'd realized on this trip that he wanted to spend the rest of his life with her. Told her he'd never been happier than in this moment, standing on the top of this mountain and the world spread out beneath them.

"I hadn't been planning anything like it either," Theresa said, "but I said yes, and we stayed up there and watched the sun go into the sea. Ethan and I always talked about coming back here for a weekend, but you know what they say about life and making other plans. Anyway, we had our perfect moments . . ." She kissed the top of her son's head. ". . . and our not so perfect ones, but I think Ethan was never happier, never more carefree and hopeful about the future than that sunset on the top of this mountain thirteen years ago. As you know, the circumstances surrounding his disappearance . . ." She pushed back against the storm of emotion that was waiting, always waiting. ". . . well, we don't really have a body or ashes or anything. But . . ." A smile through the tears. "I did bring this." She dug an old plastic ring out of her pocket, the gold paint of the band long since flaked away, the flimsy prongs still holding the emerald-colored prism of glass. Some of the others were crying now too. "He did eventually get me a diamond, but it seemed appropriate, if not more cost-efficient, to bring this." She pulled a garden spade out of her wet backpack. "I want to leave something close to Ethan here, and this feels right. Ben, would you help me?"

Theresa knelt down and swept away the ferns until she saw the ground.

It was saturated from the rain, and the spade speared through easily. She dug out several chunks of earth and then let Ben do the same.

"I love you, Ethan," she whispered, "and I miss you so much."

Then she dropped the ring into the shallow grave and covered it with the upturned earth and leveled it off with the back of the blade.

That night, back at their home in upper Queen Anne, Theresa threw a party.

Packed the house with friends, acquaintances, coworkers, loads of booze.

Their core group of friends—now responsible, tame professionals—had once upon a time been wild and prone to excess, and on the drive home, they'd all vowed to tie one on in Ethan's honor.

They kept their word.

They drank like fish.

They told stories about Ethan.

They laughed and cried.

At ten thirty, Theresa was standing on their deck that overlooked the small backyard, and on rare clear days, the Seattle skyline and the hulking, white mass of Mount Rainier to the south. Tonight, the buildings of downtown were obscured in mist, their presence relegated to radiating the cloud deck with a neon glow.

She leaned against the railing, smoking a cigarette with Darla—something she hadn't done since her sorority days in college—and nursing her fifth G&T of the night. She hadn't had this much to drink in ages, knew she'd pay for it in the morning, but for now, she reveled in this beautiful padding that protected her from the sharp edges of reality—the unanswered questions, the fear that was always with her. That haunted her dreams.

She said to Darla, "What if his life insurance benefit doesn't pay?"

"Why wouldn't it, honey?"

"No proof of death."

"That's ridiculous."

"I'll have to sell this house. I can't swing the mortgage on my paralegal salary."

She felt Darla's arm slide through hers. "Don't think about that right now. Just know that you have friends who love you. Who'd never let anything happen to you or Ben."

Theresa set her empty glass on the railing.

"He wasn't perfect," she said.

"I know."

"Not by a long, long shot. But the mistakes he made, when it came down to it . . . he owned them. I loved him. Always. Even when I first found out, I knew I'd forgive him. He could've done it again, and the truth is, I would've stayed. He *had* me, you know?"

"So you two had reconciled completely before he left?"

"Yeah. I mean, there were still really . . . tough feelings. What he did . . ."

"I know."

"But we'd come through the worst of it. We

were in counseling. We would've made it. And now . . . I'm a single mother, D."

"Let's get you to bed, Theresa. It's been a long day. Don't touch anything. I'll come over in the morning, help you clean up."

"Almost fifteen months he's been gone, and every day I wake up, I still don't believe this is really happening. I keep waiting for my cell to ring. For a text from him. Ben asks me constantly when Daddy's coming home. He knows the answer, but it's the same thing as with me . . . same reason I keep checking my phone."

"Why, honey?"

"Because maybe this time it'll show a missed call from Ethan. Because maybe this time when Ben asks me, I'll have a different answer for him. I'll tell him Daddy will be home from his trip next week."

Someone called Theresa's name.

She turned carefully, unbalanced by the gin.

Parker, one of the young associates at the law firm where she worked, stood in the threshold of the sliding glass door.

"There's someone here to see you, Theresa."

"Who is it?"

"Guy named Hassler."

Theresa felt a quiver in her stomach.

"Who's that?" Darla asked.

"Ethan's boss. Shit, I'm drunk."

"You want me to tell him you can't—"

"No, I want to talk to him."

Theresa followed Parker inside.

Everyone had hit it too hard, and the party had crashed and burned.

Jen, her college roommate from her junior year, had passed out on the couch.

Several of her other girlfriends had gathered in the kitchen around someone's iPhone, very drunk and attempting to call a cab on speakerphone.

Her sister, Margie, a teetotaler and possibly the only sober adult in the house, grabbed her arm as she passed and whispered that Ben was sleeping peacefully upstairs in his room.

Hassler stood waiting in the foyer in a black suit, black tie loosened, bags under his eyes. She wondered if he'd just come from the office.

"Hi, Adam," she said.

They exchanged a quick hug, quick kiss on the cheek.

"I'm sorry I couldn't come earlier," Hassler said. "It's been . . . well, it's been a day. But I just wanted to drop by for a minute."

"It means a lot. Can I get you a drink?"

"Beer would be great."

Theresa stumbled over to the half-empty keg of Fat Tire and filled a plastic cup.

She sat with Adam on the third step of the staircase.

"I apologize," she said. "I'm a little bit drunk.

We wanted to send Ethan off like the good old days."

Hassler sipped his beer. He was a year or two older than Ethan. Smelled faintly of Old Spice and still wore that same crew cut he'd had since she first met him at the company Christmas party all those years ago. A trace of red—just a day's growth—was coming in across his jaw. She could feel the bulge of his firearm off the side of his hip.

"Are you still running into problems with Ethan's life insurance?" Hassler asked.

"Yes. They're dragging their feet paying. I think they're going to make me bring a lawsuit."

"If it's all right with you, I'd like to call first thing next week. See if I can throw some weight, move things along."

"I'd really appreciate that, Adam."

She noticed she was speaking slowly and with extreme care in an effort to keep her words from slurring.

"You'll send me the adjuster's contact information?" he asked.

"Yes."

"I want you to know, Theresa, that it's the first thing on my mind every day, finding out what happened to Ethan. And I will find out."

"Do you think he's dead?"

A question she would never have asked sober.

Hassler was quiet for a while, staring down into the amber-colored beer.

Said finally, "Ethan . . . was a great agent. Maybe my best. I'm not just saying that."

"And you think we'd have heard from him by now, or—"

"Exactly. I'm sorry."

"No, it's . . ." He handed her a handkerchief and she cried into it for a moment before wiping her eyes. "Not knowing . . . it's so hard. I used to pray that he was still alive. Now I just pray for a body. A physical thing to give me answers and let me move on. Can I ask you something, Adam?"

"Of course."

"What do *you* think happened?"

"Maybe now isn't the time—"

"Please."

Hassler finished off the cup of beer.

He went over to the keg, refilled it, returned.

"Let's just take what we know as a starting point, all right? Ethan arrived in Boise on a direct flight out of Seattle at eight thirty a.m. on September twenty-fourth of last year. He went to the field office downtown in the U.S. Bank Building and met up with Agent Stallings and his team. They had a two-and-a-half-hour meeting, and then Ethan and Stallings left Boise at approximately eleven fifteen a.m."

"And they were going to Wayward Pines to look into . . ."

"Among other things, the disappearance of Agent Bill Evans and Kate Hewson."

106

Just the utterance of her name was like a knife sliding between Theresa's ribs.

She suddenly wanted another drink.

Hassler went on. "You last spoke to Ethan on a cell phone call at one twenty p.m. from Lowman, Idaho, where they'd stopped for gas."

"The connection was bad because they were in the mountains."

"At this point, they were an hour outside of Wayward Pines."

"Last thing he said to me was, 'I'll call you tonight from the hotel, sweetheart,' and I tried to tell him good-bye and that I loved him, but the call dropped."

"And yours was the last contact anyone had with your husband. At least anyone who's still alive. Of course . . . you know the rest."

She did, and she didn't need to ever hear it again.

At 3:07 p.m., at an intersection in Wayward Pines, Agent Stallings had pulled out in front of a Mack truck. He'd been killed instantly, and because of the violence of the collision and the devastation to the front passenger side, the car had to be taken to another location to extricate Ethan's body. Except once they'd torn the door off and pried up enough of the roof to get inside, they'd found the compartment empty.

"The other reason I came by, Theresa, was to share a little bit of news. As you know, we weren't satisfied with the internal examination we had performed on Stallings's Lincoln Town Car."

"Right."

"So I called in a favor from the FBI's scientific analysis team, CODIS. They do amazing work, the best work, and they just finished spending a week with the car."

"And . . ."

"I can e-mail you their report tomorrow, but long story short, they didn't find anything."

"What do you mean?"

"I mean they found nothing. No trace of skin cells or blood or hair or even residual sweat. Not even what they call degraded DNA. If Ethan had ridden in that car for three hours on the drive from Boise to Wayward Pines, this team would've at least found some molecular trace of him."

"How is this possible?"

"I don't know yet."

Theresa grabbed the banister and struggled onto her feet.

Made her way over to the makeshift bar on the dry sink.

Didn't even bother with another G&T. Just scooped some ice into a rocks glass and filled it with premium vodka.

She took a long pull, staggered back over to the staircase.

"I don't know how to process this, Adam," she said, and with the next sip, she knew this would be the drink that pushed her firmly over the edge.

"I don't either. You asked me what I thought had happened?"

"Yeah?"

"I don't have any answers for you. Not yet. Strictly between you and me, we're taking another hard look at Agent Stallings. A hard look at everyone who had access to the scene of the accident prior to my arrival. But so far, we've gotten nowhere. And as you know, this happened over a year ago."

"Something isn't right," she said.

Hassler stared at her, his hard eyes troubled.

"No shit," he said.

Theresa walked him out to his car and stood on the wet street getting rained on and watching the taillights grow smaller and smaller before disappearing over the top of the hill.

All up and down the street, she could see the lights of Christmas trees inside their neighbors' houses. She and Ben hadn't put one up yet, and she doubted they'd get around to it this year. The gesture would feel too much like an acceptance of this nightmare, the final acknowledgment that he was never coming home.

Later, after everyone had cabbed home, she lay on the couch downstairs in the aftermath of the party, fighting the spins.

She couldn't sleep, couldn't pass out.

Every time she opened her eyes, she'd focus on the wall clock as the minute hand trudged between two and three a.m.

At two forty-five, unable to stand the nausea and the dizziness for another second, she rolled off the couch, climbed to her feet, and moved unsteadily into the kitchen.

She took one of the few remaining clean glasses out of the cabinet and filled it under the tap.

Drank and refilled two more times before her thirst was quenched.

The kitchen was a disaster.

She dimmed the track lighting and started loading the dishwasher, something satisfying about watching it fill up. She initiated the wash cycle and then walked around the house with a plastic bag, collecting beer cups, paper plates, discarded napkins.

By four a.m., the house was looking better, and she didn't feel nearly as drunk, although a pounding had become noticeable behind her eyes— the first indication of the approaching headache.

She popped three Advil and stood at the kitchen sink in the predawn silence, listening as the rain pattered on the deck outside.

She filled the sink with hot water and squirted in the dish soap, watching bubbles begin to populate the surface.

Thrust her hands underwater.

Left them there until the heat became unbearable.

She'd been standing in this exact spot that last night when Ethan came home late from work.

Hadn't heard the front door close.

Hadn't heard his footsteps.

She'd been scrubbing a skillet when she felt his hands encircle her waist, his breath on the back of her neck.

"Sorry, T."

She keeps scrubbing, says, "Seven o'clock, eight. That's late. It's ten thirty, Ethan. I don't even know what to call this."

"How's our little man?"

"Fell asleep in the living room, waiting to show you his trophy."

She hates how just the presence of his hands on her body can disarm her anger in a millisecond. She's felt a blinding attraction to him from the first time she spotted him across the bar in Tini Bigs. Unfair advantage.

"I have to fly to Boise first thing in the morning," he says into her ear.

"His birthday's Saturday, Ethan. He turns six only once in his life."

"I know. And I hate it. But I have to go."

"You know what it's gonna do to him, you not being here? How many times he's going to ask me why you aren't—"

"I get it, Theresa, all right? You think this hurts you more than it hurts me?"

She pushes his hands off her hips and turns around to face him.

Asks, "Does this new assignment have anything to do with trying to find *her?*"

"I'm not gonna do this right now, Theresa. I have to be up in five hours to catch my flight. I haven't even packed."

He gets halfway out of the kitchen before stopping and turning back around.

For a moment, they just hold each other's stare, the breakfast table between them and on it the plate of cold food that will be the last meal Ethan eats under this roof.

"You know," he says, "it's over. We've moved on. But you don't act like anything has—"

"I'm just tired of it, Ethan."

"Of what?"

"You work, and you work, and you work, and what's left for us? The dregs."

He doesn't respond, but she can see the muscles in his jaw quiver.

Even this late at night, after a fifteen-hour day, he looks amazing, standing under the track lighting in that black suit she never gets tired of seeing him wear.

Already, her anger is ebbing.

A part of her needing to go to him, to be with him.

He has such a hold on her.

Some kind of magic in it.

Chapter 5

SHE COMES TO him across the kitchen, and he wraps his arms around her, buries his nose in her hair. He does this often, trying as of late to recapture that first-encounter smell—some mix of perfume and conditioner and core essence that once made his heart trip over itself. But it's either changed now, been lost, or become such an integral part of him that he can no longer detect the scent, which, when he could, always carried him back to those first days. More defining even than her short blonde hair and green eyes. A feeling of newness. A fresh turn. Like a sharp October afternoon and the sky blue and bright and the Cascades and Olympics holding fresh snow and the trees in the city just beginning to turn.

He embraces her.

The sting and the shame of all he's put her through are still raw. He can't say for certain, but he suspects that if she'd done the same to him, he'd already be gone. Marvels at her love for him. Her loyalty. So far beyond anything he deserves, it only intensifies the shame.

"I'm gonna go look in on him," Ethan whispers.

"OK."

"When I come back down, you'll sit with me while I eat?"

"Of course."

He drapes his coat over the banister, slips out of his black shoes, and pads up the stairs, skipping over the squeaky fifth step.

There are no bad floorboards the rest of the way, and soon he's standing in the threshold of the bedroom, easing the door open until a splinter of light has carved through the space between the door and the jamb.

For Ben's fifth birthday, they painted the walls to reflect space: Blackness. Stars. The swirl of distant galaxies. Planets. The occasional deep-space satellite or rocket. An astronaut drifting.

His son sleeps in a tangle of blankets, a small trophy clutched in his hands—a golden, plastic boy kicking a soccer ball.

Ethan moves quietly across the floor, dodging stray LEGO pieces and Hot Wheels.

Crouches down beside the bed.

His eyes have adjusted to the darkness just well enough to draw out the details of Benjamin's face.

Softness.

Serenity.

They're shut, but he has his mother's almond eyes.

Ethan's mouth.

There is a tactile ache, kneeling here in the dark by the bed of his soon-to-be-six-year-old son in the wake of another day he's missed completely.

His boy is the most perfect and beautiful thing he's ever laid eyes on, and he feels, acutely, the inexorable passing of a thousand moments with this little person who will be a man sooner than he can possibly imagine.

He touches Ben's cheek with the back of his hand.

Leans forward, kisses the boy's forehead.

Brushes a wisp of hair back behind his ear.

"I'm so proud of you," he whispers. "You can't even imagine."

Last year, the morning of the day he died in a nursing home, wasted from age and pneumonia, his father asked Ethan in a raspy voice, "You spend time with your son?"

"Much as I can," he'd answered, but his father had caught the lie in his eyes.

"It'll be your loss, Ethan. Day'll come, when he's grown and it's too late, that you'd give a kingdom to go back and spend a single hour with your son as a boy. To hold him. Read a book to him. Throw a ball with a person in whose eyes you can do no wrong. He doesn't see your failings yet. He looks at you with pure love and it won't last, so you revel in it while it's here."

Ethan thinks often of that conversation, mostly when he's lying awake in bed at night and everyone else is asleep, and his life screaming past at the speed of light—the weight of bills and the future and his prior failings and all these moments he's missing—all the lost joy—perched like a boulder on his chest.

"Can you hear me? Ethan?"

Sometimes he feels like he can't breathe.
Sometimes his thoughts come so fast he has to find one perfect memory.
Cling to it.
A life raft.

"Ethan, I want you to grab hold of my voice and let it bring you to the surface of consciousness."

Letting it play over and over until the anxiety recedes and the exhaustion comes and he can finally slip under.

"I know it's hard, but you have to try."

Into the only portion of his days that any-more affords him peace . . .

"Ethan."

Dreams.

His eyes shot open.

A light bored down into his face—a small, focused point of bright and blinding blue.

A penlight.

He blinked, it disappeared, and when he opened his eyes again, a man peered down at him through gold wire-rimmed glasses, less than a foot away from his face.

Small, black eyes.

Head shaven.

A faint silver beard the only indication of age, his skin otherwise smooth and clear.

He smiled—small, perfect white teeth.

"You can hear me now, yes?"

There was formality in the man's tone. Implied politeness.

Ethan nodded.

"Do you know where you are?"

Ethan had to think for a moment—he'd been dreaming of Seattle, of Theresa and Ben.

"Let's start with something else. Do you know your name?" the man asked.

"Ethan Burke."

"Very good. And again, do you know where you are, Ethan?"

He could feel the answer on the cusp of memory, but there was confusion too, several realities in competition.

In one, he was in Seattle.

In another, a hospital.

In another, an idyllic mountain town called . . . There was a hole where its name should be.

"Ethan."

"Yes?"

"If I told you that you were in a hospital in Wayward Pines, would that jog anything loose?"

It didn't just jog something loose—it brought everything back at once like a hard, sudden hit from a linebacker, the memory of his last four days jarred into working order, into a sequence of events he felt confident he could lean on.

"OK," Ethan said. "OK. I do remember."

"Everything?"

"I think so."

"What's your last recollection?"

It took a moment to retrieve, to brush the cobwebs off the synapses, but he found it.

"I had a terrible headache. I was sitting on the sidewalk of Main Street, and I . . ."

"You lost consciousness."

"Exactly."

"Do you still have that headache?"

"No, it's gone."

"My name is Dr. Jenkins."

The man shook Ethan's hand and then took a seat in a chair at Ethan's bedside.

"You're what kind of doctor?" Ethan asked.

"A psychiatrist. Ethan, I need you to answer a few questions for me, if that's all right. You said some interesting things to Dr. Miter and his nurse when they first brought you in. Do you know what I'm referring to?"

"No."

"You were talking about a dead body in one of the houses here in town. And that you hadn't been able to get in touch with your family."

"I don't recall speaking with the nurse or doctor."

"You were delirious at the time. Do you have a history of mental illness, Ethan?"

Ethan had been fully reclined in bed.

Now he struggled to sit up.

Threads of brightness slipped through the drawn blinds.

Day out there.

On some primal level, he felt glad for the fact.

"What kind of question is that?" Ethan asked.

"The kind I get paid to ask. You showed up here last night with no wallet, no ID—"

"I was pulled out of a car accident several days ago, and either the sheriff or the EMTs didn't do their fucking job, and now I'm stranded here without a phone, money, or ID. I didn't lose my wallet."

"Relax, Ethan, nobody's saying you've done anything wrong. Again, I need you to answer my questions. Do you have a history of mental illness?"

"No."

"Is there a history of mental illness in your family?"

"No."

"Do you have a history of post-traumatic stress disorder?"

"No."

"But you did serve in the second Gulf War."

"How'd you know that?"

Jenkins motioned to his neck.

Ethan glanced down at his chest, saw his dog tag hanging from a ball chain. Strange. He always kept it in his bedside table drawer. Couldn't remember the last time he'd worn it. Didn't think he'd brought it along on this trip, and certainly didn't remember packing it or making the decision to wear it.

He scanned over his name, rank, social security number, blood type, and religious preference ("NO RELIGIOUS PREF") engraved in the stainless steel.

Chief Warrant Officer Ethan Burke.

"Ethan?"

"What?"

"You served in the second Gulf War?"

"Yeah, I flew the UH-60."

"What's that?"

"The Black Hawk helicopter."

"You saw combat, I assume?"

"I did."

"Extensive?"

"You could say that."

"Were you injured?"

"I don't understand what this has to do with any—"

"Just answer my questions, please."

"I was shot down in the second battle of Fallujah in the winter of 2004. It was a medevac mission, and we'd just loaded up some wounded marines."

"Was anyone killed?"

Ethan took a deep breath in.

Exhaled.

If he was honest, the question had surprised him, and now he found himself bracing against a slideshow of images he'd spent a lot of therapy sessions trying to come to terms with.

The shockwave as the RPG explodes behind him.

The severed tail section and rotor falling a hundred and fifty feet to the street below.

The sudden g-force as the helicopter spins.

Alarms going mad.

The impossible rigidity of the power stick.

The impact not nearly as bad as he feared.

Consciousness lost only for half a minute.

Seat belt jammed, can't reach his KA-BAR.

"Ethan. Was anyone killed?"

Insurgent fire already tearing into the other side of the wreckage, someone opening up with an AK.

Through the cracked windshield, two medics limping away from the chopper.
Shell-shocked.

"Ethan . . ."

Straight into the four-blade rotor still spinning fast enough . . .
There.
Gone.
Blood sheeting down the windshield.
More gunfire.
The insurgents coming.

"Ethan?"

"Everyone was killed except me," Ethan said.

"You were the sole survivor?"

"Correct. I was captured."

Jenkins jotted something on a leather-bound notepad. He said, "I need to ask you a few more questions, Ethan. The more honest you are, the better chance I have at helping you, which is all I want to do. Have you been hearing any voices?"

Ethan tried to suppress the glare.

"Are you kidding?"

"If you could just answer . . ."

"No."

Jenkins scribbled on his pad.

"Have you had any difficulty talking? For instance, maybe your speech has been garbled or mixed up?"

"No. And I'm not delusional. And I'm not having hallucinations, or—"

"Well, you wouldn't really know if you were having hallucinations, now would you? You'd believe the things you were seeing and hearing were real. I mean, if you were hallucinating me and being in this hospital room and this entire conversation we're having, it wouldn't feel any different, would it?"

Ethan slid his legs over the side of the bed and eased his feet down onto the floor.

"What are you doing?" Jenkins asked.

Ethan started toward the closet.

Weak, unstable on his legs.

"You're in no condition to be leaving, Ethan. They're still evaluating your MRI. You could have a closed-head injury and we don't know the severity. We need to continue our evaluation—"

"I'll get an evaluation. Just not here. Not in this town."

Ethan pulled open the closet door, took his suit down off the hanger.

"You did walk into the sheriff's office without a shirt on. Is that correct?"

Ethan slid his arms into his white button-down, which appeared to have been washed since he wore it last. The stink of human decay replaced with the scent of laundry detergent.

"It reeked," Ethan said. "It smelled like the dead man I had just—"

"You mean the one in the abandoned house that you say you found."

"I didn't *say* I found it. I found it."

"And you did go to the residence of Mack and Jane Skozie, whom you'd never met before, and verbally harassed Mr. Skozie on his front porch. Is that a fair statement?"

Ethan started on the buttons, fingers trembling, struggling to fit them through the holes. Got them out of order, but he didn't care. Get dressed. Get out of here. Clear of this town.

"Walking around with a potential brain injury is not on the list of smart things to do," Jenkins said. He had risen out of his chair.

"There's something wrong here," Ethan said.

"I know, that's what I've been trying to—"

"No. This town. The people in it. You. Something's off, and if you think I'm going to sit here, let you fuck with me for one more second—"

"I am not fucking with you, Ethan. No one here is fucking with you. Do you have any idea how paranoid that statement sounds? I'm merely trying to determine if you're in the throes of a psychotic episode."

"Well, I'm not."

Ethan pulled on his pants, got them buttoned, reached down for his shoes.

"Forgive me if I don't take *your* word on that. 'An abnormal condition of the mind, generally characterized by a loss of contact with reality.'

That's the textbook definition of psychosis, Ethan. It could've been caused by the car accident. By seeing your partner killed. Or some buried trauma from the war resurfacing."

"Get out of my room," Ethan said.

"Ethan, your life could be—"

Ethan looked at Jenkins across the room, and something in his stare, his body language, must have suggested the real threat of violence, because the psychiatrist's eyes went wide, and for the first time, he shut up.

Nurse Pam looked up from her paperwork behind the desk in the nurses' station.

"Mr. Burke, what on earth are you doing up and dressed and out of bed?"

"Leaving."

"Leaving?" She said it like she didn't comprehend the word. "The hospital?"

"Wayward Pines."

"You're in no condition to even be out of—"

"I need my personal belongings right now. The sheriff told me the EMTs may have removed them from the car."

"I thought the sheriff had them."

"No."

"You sure about that?"

"Yes."

"Well, I can put on my Nancy Drew hat and—"

"Stop wasting my time. Do you know where they are?"

"No."

Ethan turned away from her, started walking.

Nurse Pam called after him.

He stopped at the elevator, punched the down arrow button.

She was coming now—he could hear her quick footsteps on the checkered linoleum.

Turned and watched her approach in that lovely throwback of a nurses' uniform.

She stopped a few feet away.

He had four or five inches on her. A few years as well.

"I can't let you leave, Ethan," she said. "Not until we know what's wrong with you."

The elevator doors screeched open.

Ethan backed away from the nurse into the car.

"Thanks for your help, and your concern," he said, pressing G three times until the button illuminated, "but I think I got it figured out."

"What?"

"It's this town that's wrong."

Pam stretched her foot across the threshold, blocked the doors from closing.

"Ethan. Please. You're not thinking clearly."

"Move your foot."

"I'm worried about you. Everyone here is."

He'd been leaning back against the wall. Now

126

he pushed off and came forward, stopping inches away from Pam, staring at her through the four-inch space between the doors.

He looked down, tapped the tip of her white shoe with the tip of his black shoe.

For a long moment, she held her ground, Ethan beginning to wonder if he would have to physically remove her from the elevator car.

Finally, she pulled her foot back.

Standing on the sidewalk, Ethan thought the town seemed quiet for late afternoon. He couldn't hear a single car engine. Nothing, in fact, but the sound of birds cheeping and wind pushing through the crowns of three tall pines that loomed over the hospital's front lawn.

He walked out into the middle of the street.

Stood there watching, listening.

The sun felt good and warm in his face.

The breeze carried a pleasant chill.

He looked up at the sky—dark blue crystal.

No clouds.

Flawless.

This place was beautiful, no question, but for the first time, those mountain walls that boxed this valley inside instilled something in him other than awe. He couldn't explain why, but they filled him with fear. A dread he couldn't quite put his finger on.

He felt . . . strange.

Maybe he'd suffered an injury. But maybe not.

Maybe being detached from the outside world now going on five days was beginning to take its toll.

No iPhone, no Internet, no Facebook.

It seemed impossible as he considered it—to have had no contact with his family, with Hassler, with anyone outside of Wayward Pines.

He started walking toward the sheriff's office.

Better to just leave. Regroup. Reevaluate from the other side of those cliff walls.

From the comfort of a normal town.

Because something here was definitely off-kilter.

"Sheriff Pope in?"

Belinda Moran looked up from her game of solitaire.

"Hello," she said. "How can I help you?"

Ethan asked a touch louder this time. "Is the sheriff in?"

"No, he stepped out for a moment."

"So he'll be back shortly?"

"I don't know when he's due back."

"But you said 'for a moment' so I figured—"

"It's just a figure of speech, young man."

"Do you remember me? Agent Burke from the Secret Service?"

"Yes. You have your shirt on this time. I like this look much better."

"Have there been any calls for me?"

She squinted and cocked her head. "Why would there be?"

"Because I told some people they could reach me here."

Belinda shook her head. "No one's called for you."

"Not my wife, Theresa, or an Agent Adam Hassler?"

"No one's called for you, Mr. Burke, and you shouldn't tell them to call for you here."

"I need to use the telephone in your conference room again."

Belinda frowned. "I don't think that's a good idea."

"Why?"

She didn't have an answer to this, just maintained her scowl.

"Theresa, it's me. Just trying to reach you. I was in the hospital again. I don't know if you called the sheriff's office or the hotel, but I haven't gotten any messages. I'm still in Wayward Pines. I haven't been able to find my phone or wallet, but I'm done with this place. I'm going to borrow a cruiser from the sheriff's office. Call you tonight from Boise. Miss you, love you."

He leaned forward in the chair, got a new dial tone, and then shut his eyes and tried to conjure it.

The number was there.

He spun it out, listened to four rings, and then that same voice from the last time answered. "Secret Service."

"This is Ethan Burke calling again for Adam Hassler."

"He's not available at the moment. Was there something I could help you with?"

"Is this Marcy?"

"Yes."

"Do you recall our phone conversation from yesterday?"

"You know, sir, we get a lot of calls here every day, and I just can't keep up with every—"

"You told me you'd slip Agent Hassler a message."

"What was it regarding?"

Ethan closed his eyes, took a deep breath. If he insulted her now, she'd just end the phone call. If he waited until he was back in Seattle, he could publicly eviscerate her, have her fired on the spot.

"Marcy, it was regarding a dead Secret Service agent in Wayward Pines, Idaho."

"Hmm. Well, if I said I would give him the message, then I'm sure I followed through on that."

"But I haven't heard back from him. Don't you find that strange? That an agent from Hassler's field office—me—located another agent who had been murdered, an agent I was sent here to find, and now twenty-four hours have passed and Hassler hasn't even returned my call?"

A slight pause, and then: "Was there something *I* could help you with?"

"Yes, I'd like to speak with Agent Hassler right now."

"Oh, I'm sorry, he's not available at the moment. Was there something—"

"Where is he?"

"He's not available."

"Where. Is. He."

"He's not available at the moment, but I'm sure he'll call you back at his earliest convenience. He's just been very swamped."

"Who are you, Marcy?"

Ethan felt the phone rip out of his grasp.

Pope slammed it down into the cradle, the sheriff's eyes boring through Ethan like a pair of smoldering coals.

"Who told you you could come in here and use my telephone?"

"No one, I just—"

"That's right. No one. Get up."

"Excuse me?"

"I said get up. You can either walk out of here under your own steam, or I can drag you through the lobby myself."

Ethan stood up slowly, faced the sheriff across the table.

"You're speaking to a federal agent, sir."

"I'm not convinced."

"What the hell does that mean?"

"You show up here, no ID, no phone, nothing—"

"I've explained my situation. Did you take a trip over to six-oh-four First Avenue, see the body of Agent Evans?"

"I did."

"And?"

"Under investigation."

"You've called in crime scene specialists to process the—"

"It's all being handled."

"What does that even mean?"

Pope just stared at him, Ethan thinking, *He's unhinged and you have no support in this town. Just get a car, get out of here. Hammer him when you come back with the cavalry. He'll lose his badge, face prosecution for hamstringing a federal investigation.*

"I have a favor to ask," Ethan said, conciliatory.

"What?"

"I'd like to borrow one of your vehicles."

The sheriff laughed. "Why?"

"Well, obviously, since the accident, I don't have one."

"This ain't Hertz Rent-a-Car."

"I need some transportation, Arnold."

"It's just not possible."

"Is this *your* sheriff's department? You can do whatever you want, right?"

The sheriff blinked. "I don't have one to lend you." Pope started walking down the length of the conference table. "Let's go, Mr. Burke."

Pope stopped at the open door and waited for Ethan.

As Ethan drew within range, Pope grabbed his arm and pulled him in close, his large, powerful hand crushing his biceps.

"I may have questions for you in the not too distant," the sheriff said.

"About what?"

Pope just smiled. "Don't even think about leaving town."

Walking away from the sheriff's department, Ethan glanced over his shoulder, saw Pope watching him through a split in the conference room blinds.

The sun had gone behind the mountains.

The town stood silent.

He put a block between himself and Pope's office and sat down on the curb of a quiet street.

"This isn't right," he whispered, and he kept whispering it.

He felt weak and hungry.

Tried to lay everything out, all that had happened since he'd come to Wayward Pines. Scrambling to assemble a snapshot of the entire picture, thinking if he could see it all at once, he might piece these bizarre encounters together into a problem to be solved. Or at least one that made sense. But the harder he tried, the more he felt like he was thinking inside a cloud.

An epiphany: sitting here wasn't going to change a damn thing.

He came to his feet, started toward Main Street.

Go to the hotel. Maybe there's a message waiting from Theresa or Hassler.

False hope. He knew it. There would be no message. Nothing but enmity.

I am not losing my mind.

I am not losing my mind.

He recited his name. His social security number. His physical address in Seattle. Theresa's maiden name. The date of his son's birth. It all felt real. Like scraps of information that formed his identity.

Comfort in names and numbers.

A clinking on the next block caught his attention.

There was a vacant lot across the street with several picnic tables, a few grills, and a horseshoe pit. Families had gathered for a party—a group of women stood talking by a pair of red coolers. Two men flipped burgers and hotdogs on a grill, smoke rising in blue coils into the still evening air. The smell of cooking meat made Ethan's stomach ache, and he realized that he was even hungrier than he thought.

New goal: eat.

He crossed the street to the chirping of crickets

and lawn sprinklers clicking in the distance.

Wondered: are they real?

Kids chased one another in the grass—shouting, laughing, shrieking.

Tag.

The clinking was coming from a game of horseshoes. Two groups of men stood across from each other in opposing sandpits, cigar smoke clouding around their heads like exploded haloes.

Ethan had almost reached the vacant lot, thinking the best move would be to approach the women. Crank the charm. These seemed like decent people living a perfect moment of the American dream.

He straightened his jacket as he moved from the pavement into the grass, smoothing the wrinkles, fixing his collar.

Five women. One in her early twenties, three between thirty and forty, one silver haired, mid to late fifties.

They were drinking lemonade out of clear, plastic cups and discussing some piece of neighborhood gossip.

No one had noticed him yet.

Ten feet out, while trying to invent some nonintrusive way of breaking into their conversation, a woman his age looked over at him and smiled.

"Hello there," she said.

She wore a skirt that dropped below her knees,

red flats, and a plaid blouse. Her hair was short and vintage, like something from a fifties sitcom.

"Hi," Ethan said.

"You come to crash our little block party?"

"I have to admit, the smell of whatever you've got cooking on that grill pulled me over."

"I'm Nancy." She broke away from her group and extended her hand.

Ethan shook it.

"Ethan."

"You new here?" she asked.

"I just got into town a few days ago."

"And how are you enjoying our little hamlet?"

"You have a lovely town. Very welcoming and warm."

"Aw. Maybe we will feed you after all."

She laughed.

"You live around here?" Ethan asked.

"We all live within a few blocks. The neighborhood tries to get together for a cookout at least once a week."

"How Mayberry of you."

The woman blushed deeply. "So what are you doing in Wayward Pines, Ethan?" she asked.

"Just here as a tourist."

"Must be nice. I can't even remember my last vacation."

"When you live in a place like this," Ethan said, gesturing to the surrounding mountains, "why would you ever leave?"

136

"Would you care for a cup of lemonade?" Nancy asked. "It's homemade and delicious."

"Sure."

She touched his arm. "Be right back. Then I'll introduce you around."

As Nancy went to the coolers, Ethan glanced toward the other women, looking for a window to enter the conversation.

The oldest of the bunch—a woman with pure white hair—was laughing at something, and as it occurred to him that he'd heard this laugh before, she brushed her shoulder-length hair back behind her ears.

The nickel-sized birthmark on her face stopped his heart.

It couldn't be, but . . .

Right height.

Right build.

She was speaking now, the voice almost unquestionably familiar. She drew back from the group of women, pointing at the youngest with a mischievous smirk.

"I'm going to hold you to that, Christine," she said.

Ethan watched her turn and walk to the farthest horseshoe pit, where she laced her fingers through those of a tall, broad-shouldered man with a mane of wavy, silver hair.

"Come on, Harold, we're going to miss our show."

She tried to pull him away.

"One more throw," he protested.

She released him, and Ethan stood speechless as Harold lifted a horseshoe out of the sand, took careful aim, and gave it a toss.

The horseshoe arced over the grass and ringed the metal stake.

Harold's team cheered. He gave several dramatic bows and let the snow-haired woman drag him away from the party.

Their friends called good night after them.

"Ethan, here's your lemonade." Nancy offered him the cup.

"I'm sorry, I have to go."

He turned and walked back out into the street.

Nancy called after him, "Don't you want to stay and eat?"

By the time Ethan turned the corner, the older couple were a block ahead of him.

He quickened his pace.

Followed them for several blocks as they walked slowly ahead at the pace of two people who had not a care in the world, holding hands, their voices and laughter lilting up into the pines.

They turned down a street and vanished.

Ethan jogged to the next intersection.

Quaint Victorian houses lined both sides of the street.

He didn't see them anywhere.

The sound of a door closing echoed down the

block. He spotted the house it had come from—green with white trim. Front porch with a swing. Third one down on the left.

He crossed the street and took the sidewalk until he stood in front of it.

Little patch of perfect green grass. The front porch under the shadow of an old pine tree. On the mailbox, a last name he didn't recognize. He put his hands on the picket fence. It was dusk. Lights just beginning to wink on in the houses all around him. The occasional snippet of conversation sliding through a raised window.

The valley silent and cooling and the highest elevations of the surrounding mountains catching the last bit of daylight.

He unlatched the gate, pushed it open.

Walked up an old stone path to the porch.

The steps creaked under his weight.

Then he stood at the front door.

He could hear voices on the other side.

Footsteps.

A part of him didn't want to knock.

He rapped his knuckles on the glass of the outer door, took a step back.

Waited a full minute, but no one came.

He knocked harder the second time.

Footsteps approached. He heard a lock turn. The wood door swung open.

That broad-shouldered man looked at him through the glass.

"Can I help you?"

Ethan just needed to see her up close, under the porch light. Confirm it wasn't her, that he wasn't going mad. Move on with his myriad other problems in this town.

"I'm looking for Kate."

For a moment, the man just stared at him.

Finally, he pushed open the glass door.

"Who are you?"

"Ethan."

"Who are you?"

"An old friend."

The man stepped back into the house, turned his head, said, "Honey, could you come to the door for a minute?"

She responded with something Ethan couldn't make out, and the man said, "I have no idea."

Then she appeared—a shadow at the end of a hallway leading into the kitchen. Passed briefly through the illumination of an overhead light, and padded in bare feet through the living room up to the door.

The man stepped aside and she took his place.

Ethan stared at her through the glass door.

He shut his eyes and opened them again. He was still standing on this porch and she was still, impossibly, behind the glass.

She said, "Yes?"

Those eyes.

Unmistakable.

"Kate?"

"Yes?"

"Hewson?"

"That was my maiden name."

"Oh my God."

"I'm sorry . . . do I know you?"

Ethan couldn't take his eyes off her.

"It's me," he said. "Ethan. I came here to find you, Kate."

"I think you're confusing me with someone else."

"I'd know you anywhere. At any age."

She glanced over her shoulder, said, "It's fine, Harold. I'll be in in a moment."

Kate opened the door, stepped down onto the welcome mat. She wore cream-colored pants and a faded blue tank top.

A wedding ring.

She smelled like Kate.

But she was old.

"What's happening?" Ethan asked.

She took him by the hand and led him over to the swing at the end of the porch.

They sat.

Her house stood on a small rise with a view of the valley, the town. House lights were everywhere now and three stars had popped.

A cricket, or a recording of a cricket, chirped in one of the bushes.

"Kate . . ."

She put her hand on his leg and squeezed, leaned in close.

"They're watching us."

"Who?"

"Shhh." She motioned toward the ceiling, a slight upward gesture with her finger, whispered, "And listening."

"What's happened to you?" Ethan asked.

"Don't you think I'm still pretty?" That snarky, biting tone was pure Kate. She stared down into her lap for a minute, and when she looked up again, her eyes glistened. "When I stand in front of the mirror and brush my hair at night, I still think about your hands on my body. It's not what it used to be."

"How old are you, Kate?"

"I don't know anymore. It's hard to keep track."

"I came here looking for you four days ago. They lost contact with you and Evans and sent me here to find you. Evans is dead." The statement appeared to have little impact. "What were you and Bill doing here?"

She just shook her head.

"What's going on here, Kate?"

"I don't know."

"But you live here."

"Yes."

"For how long?"

"Years."

"That's impossible." Ethan stood, his thoughts swarming.

"I don't have answers for you, Ethan."

"I need a phone, a car, a gun if you have—"

"I can't, Ethan." She stood. "You should go."

"Kate—"

"Right now."

He held her hands. "That was you when I lost consciousness on the street last night." He stared down into her face—laugh lines, crow's-feet, and still so beautiful. "Do you know what's happening to me?"

"Stop." She tried to pull away.

"I'm in trouble," he said.

"I know."

"Tell me what—"

"Ethan, now you're putting *my* life at risk. And Harold's."

"From who?"

She tore away from him, started toward the door. When she reached it, she looked back, and for a moment, standing out of the light, she could have been thirty-six years old again.

"You could be happy, Ethan."

"What are you talking about?"

"You could have an amazing life here."

"Kate."

She pushed open the door, stepped inside.

"Kate."

"What?"

"Am I crazy?"

"No," she said. "Not at all."

The door closed after her, and then he heard the dead bolt turn. He walked to the door and stared at his reflection in the glass, half-expecting to see a sixty-year-old man, but he was unchanged.

He wasn't hungry anymore.

He wasn't tired.

Moving down the steps, down the stone path, and onto the sidewalk, he only felt this tightness in the center of his chest, a familiar sensation that used to hit him just before a mission—walking out to the chopper as the ground crew loaded the fifty-cal Gatling gun and the Hellfires.

Fear.

Ethan didn't see a car until the next block—a mid-1980s Buick LeSabre, its windshield plastered with dried pine needles and sitting on four tires that could have used some air.

The doors were locked.

Ethan crept up onto the porch of the closest house and lifted a stone cherub from its perch under a window. Through the thin curtains, he saw a young boy inside, seated at an upright piano, playing some gorgeous piece of music, the notes drifting out onto the porch through a four-inch crack where the window had been raised off the sill.

A woman sat beside him, turning pages of sheet music.

Though only a foot tall, the cherub was solid concrete and weighed in excess of thirty pounds.

Ethan hauled it back out into the street.

There was simply no way to do this quietly.

He heaved it at the window behind the driver seat, the angel punching easily through. He unlocked the door, pulled it open, climbed inside over the shattered glass, over the seats, and behind the wheel. The impact had decapitated the angel, and Ethan grabbed its head out of the back seat.

Two blows were sufficient to crack open the plastic sheathing under the steering column and expose the ignition cylinder.

The light inside the car was bad.

He worked solely through feel, fingers tugging out the power and starter wires.

The piano playing inside the house had stopped. He glanced toward the porch, saw two silhouettes now standing behind the curtain.

Ethan fished the pocketknife out of his jacket, opened the largest blade, and cut the pair of white wires he was betting fed power to the car. Then he shaved the plastic sheathing off the ends and twisted them together.

The dashboard lit up.

The front door to the house swung open as he found the darker-colored starter wire.

A boy's voice: "Look at the car window."

Ethan shaved some plastic off the end of the starter wire, exposing the threads of copper.

The woman said, "Wait here, Elliot."

Please, please, please.

Ethan touched the starter wire to the power wire, a blue spark crackling in the darkness.

The engine coughed.

The woman was moving toward him through the yard.

"Come on," Ethan said.

He touched the wires together again, and the engine turned over.

Once.

Twice.

Three times.

On the fourth, it caught and sputtered to life.

He revved the RPMs, shifted into drive, and punched on the headlights as the woman reached the passenger-side door, yelling through the glass.

Ethan sped off down the street.

At the first intersection, he turned left and backed off the gas pedal, reducing his speed into the realm of reason—a pace that wouldn't draw attention, somebody out for a nice evening drive.

The gas gauge showed a quarter of a tank remaining. Reserve light not yet on. Not a problem. There was enough fuel to blow out of Wayward Pines. Once he got over the pass, there was a one-stoplight town about forty miles south.

Lowman, Idaho. Right on the highway. They'd stopped there for gas on the way out. He could still picture Stallings by the pump in his black suit, filling the tank. Ethan had walked out to the edge of the empty highway, stared at the abandoned buildings across the road—a shuttered roadhouse and general store, and one diner, still alive but barely kicking, the smell of grease in the smoke that trickled out of a vent on the roof.

He'd called Theresa from that spot with just a single bar of connectivity.

Barely remembered their conversation. His mind had been elsewhere.

Last time he'd spoken to his wife.

He hoped he'd told her he loved her.

The brakes squealed as he brought the Buick to a full stop, left turn signal clicking. Aside from a handful of people on the sidewalks, the downtown was dead and Main Street empty as far as he could see.

Ethan eased out into the road through a gentle left turn and accelerated slowly, heading south.

He passed the pub, the hotel, the coffee shop.

After seven blocks, the hospital.

There were no outskirts.

The buildings simply ended.

He accelerated.

God, it felt good to be going, finally getting out, a palpable weight lifting off his shoulders with every revolution of the crankshaft. He should've done this two days ago.

There were no signs of habitation here, the road on a straight trajectory through a forest of pines so giant they could've been first-growth.

The air rushing into the car was cold, fragrant.

Mist hovered between the trees, and in places, across the road.

The headlights blazed through it, visibility dropping.

The reserve light came on.

Shit.

The road south out of town was on a steep and winding grade for several thousand feet up to the pass, and any minute now, the climb would begin. It was going to burn through what little gas remained. He should turn around now, head back into town, siphon enough to ensure he reached Lowman.

Ethan hit the brake for a long, sharp curve.

The mist was soup through the heart of the turn, the fog blinding white in the high beams, Ethan slowing down to a crawl with nothing to guide him but the faded double yellow.

The road straightened, shot out of the mist, out of the trees.

In the distance: a billboard.

Still an eighth of a mile back, all he could make out were four painted figures standing arm in arm.

Big, white-teeth smiles.

A boy in shorts and a striped shirt.

Mother and daughter in dresses.

The father suited, wearing a fedora, waving.

In block letters, under the perfect smiling family:

WELCOME TO WAYWARD PINES
WHERE PARADISE IS HOME

Ethan accelerated past the sign, the road moving parallel to a split-rail fence, the headlights grazing over a pasture and a herd of cattle.

Lights in the distance.

The pasture fell away behind him.

Soon, he was passing houses again.

The road widened, lost the double yellow divider.

It had turned into First Avenue.

He was back in town.

Ethan pulled over to the curb, stared through the windshield, trying to keep the panic in check. There was a simple explanation: he'd missed the turnoff to the pass. Had shot right past it in that patch of dense fog.

He whipped the car around and burned back up the road, hitting sixty by the time he reached the pasture.

Back in the mist and the towering pines, he searched for a sign, for some indication of where the road veered off toward the pass, but there was nothing.

In the sharpest section of the curve, he pulled off to the side of the road and shifted into park.

Left the car running, stepped out into the night.

He crossed to the other side and started walking along the shoulder.

After a hundred feet, the fog was thick enough to hide his car completely. He could still hear it idling, but the sound grew softer with each step.

He walked two hundred yards before stopping.

He'd come to the other side of the curve, where the road straightened out again and ran back into town.

The rumble of the car engine had died away completely.

There was no wind and the woods stood tall and silent.

Mist drifted by all around him, seemed to carry an electric charge, but he knew that hum was only some microscopic noise within himself, in *his* head, exposed only in the total absence of sound.

Impossible.

The road should not turn here.

It should barrel on through these pines another half mile and then begin the long series of switchbacks up the side of that mountain to the south.

He stepped carefully down off the shoulder into the trees.

The pine needle floor of the forest like walking on cushions.

The air damp and chill.

These trees . . . he'd never seen pines so tall, and with little in the way of undergrowth to contend with, moving between the massive trunks was easy—a forest with breathing room. You could be lost before you knew it.

He walked out of the mist, and now when he looked up, glimpsed icy points of starlight through the tops of the trees.

Another fifty yards, and he stopped. He should go back now. There were certainly other roads out of town, and he could already feel the disorientation creeping in. He glanced back over his shoulder, thought he saw the general route he'd taken to arrive at this spot, but you couldn't be sure. Everything looked the same.

Out of the woods ahead of him: a scream.

He became very still.

There was the thumping of his heart and nothing else.

The scream could only be compared to human suffering or terror. Like a hyena or a banshee. Coyotes at their maddest. The mythologized Rebel Yell. High and thin. Fragile. Terrible. And on some level, humming under the surface like buried electrical cables, was a dim awareness that this wasn't the first time he'd heard it.

Again, the scream.

Closer.

An alarm going off between his eyes, in the pit of his stomach: Leave this place now. Don't think about it. Just. Go.

Then he was running through the trees, gasping after twenty steps, back into the mist and the cold.

Up ahead, the ground sloped upward, and he climbed on hands and knees until he'd stumbled back out into the road. Despite the cold, he was sweating, eyes stinging with salt water. He jogged along the double yellow line, back through the curve, until he saw two cylinders of light in the distance, cutting through the mist.

Slowed to a walk, and above the noise of his exertion, he heard the idle of the stolen car.

He reached it, opened the driver's-side door. Climbed in behind the wheel, put his foot on the brake, and reached for the gearshift, desperate to leave this place.

He caught movement out of the corner of his left eye—a shadow in the side mirror. His eyes cut to the rearview mirror above the dash, and in the red glow of the brake lights, he saw what he'd missed—the cruiser parked thirty feet behind his rear bumper, just shy of complete invisibility in the mist.

When he looked back through the driver's-side window, a shotgun barrel stared him down, just a few inches away. A flashlight blazed inside, firing the interior of the car with a harsh light that glared off the chrome and glass.

"You must be out of your goddamned mind."

Sheriff Pope.

The irate gravel in his voice came slightly muffled through the glass.

Ethan still had his hand on the gearshift, wondering if he jammed it into drive and floored the gas—would Pope fire on him? At this range with a twelve gauge, you were talking decapitation.

"Very slowly," Pope said, "put both hands on the wheel, and use your right to turn off the car."

Ethan said through the glass, "You know who I am, and you ought to know better than to interfere. I'm leaving this town."

"The hell you are."

"I'm an agent of the United States government, with the full—"

"No, you're a guy with no ID, no badge, who just stole a car, who might have murdered a federal agent."

"What are you talking about?"

"I won't tell you again, partner."

Something needled Ethan to comply, whispered that pushing this man could be dangerous. Even fatal.

"All right," Ethan said. "Just give me a second. The car's hotwired. I have to separate the wires to turn it off."

Ethan flicked on the dome light, got his hands under the steering column, pulled the white wires apart.

The lights died.

The engine shut down.

Nothing but the painful brilliance of Pope's flashlight.

"Out!"

Ethan found the handle, had to dig his shoulder into the door to jar it open. He stepped outside. Mist streamed through the light beam. Pope, an angry shadow behind the flashlight and the shotgun, eyes hidden under the brim of his Stetson.

Ethan smelled the gun oil, figured Pope for a man dedicated to the tender loving care of his armory.

"You remember that part where I told you not to leave town?" Pope growled.

Ethan would have answered, but the light beam struck the ground, Ethan realizing a split second before it hit him that the shadow moving toward his head was the stock of the shotgun.

Ethan's left eye had been closed by the blow—it felt hot and huge and it throbbed with his pulse. Through his right, he saw the interrogation room. Claustrophobic and sterile. White cinder-block walls. Concrete floor. A bare wood table, on the other side of which sat Pope, sans Stetson and jacket, the sleeves of his hunter-green button-down rolled up to expose his forearms—thick and freckled and knotted with muscle.

Ethan wiped away the fresh line of blood sliding down the side of his face, oozing out of the gash above his left eyebrow.

He stared at the floor. "May I have a towel, please?"

"No. You can sit there and bleed and answer my question."

"Later, when this is all over, and you're out of prison, I'm going to invite you over to my house to see your badge. It'll be behind glass, in a frame, hanging over my mantel."

This elicited a radiant smile. "Think so, huh?"

"You assaulted a federal agent. That's a career-ender."

"Tell me again, Ethan, how exactly you came to know about the body in six-oh-four? And none of this vanishing-bartender bullshit."

"What are you talking about?"

"The truth."

"What I told you is the truth."

"Really? You want to keep heading down that path? Because I went to the pub." Pope drummed his fingers on the tabletop. "They don't even have a female bartender on staff, and nobody saw you there four nights ago."

"Somebody's lying."

"So what I'm wondering is . . . why'd you *really* come to Wayward Pines?"

"I told you."

"The"—in air quotes—"investigation?"

Ethan took a deep breath, felt the anger rattling in his chest like sand in a bleached-out skull. His head was killing him again, and he knew it was in part owing to the trauma to his face courtesy of Pope. But it also felt like that old, familiar pounding at the base of his skull that had plagued him ever since he'd woken by the river, not knowing who or where he was. And there was something more—the disconcerting déjà vu surrounding this interrogation.

"There's something wrong with this place," Ethan said, the emotion gathering like black clouds in his chest—accumulation of four days' worth of pain and confusion and isolation. "I saw my old partner this evening."

"Who?"

"Kate Hewson. I told you about her. Only she was older. At least twenty years older than she should've been. How is that possible? Tell me."

"It ain't."

"And how can I not make contact with anyone on the outside? How is there no road out of town? Is this some kind of experiment?"

"Of course there's a road out of town. You got any idea how goddamned crazy you sound?"

"There's something wrong with this place."

"No, there's something wrong with you. I have an idea."

"What?"

"How about I give you a sheet of paper. Let you have some time to write down everything you want to tell me. Perhaps I'll give you one hour to do it."

The offer chilled Ethan.

Pope continued. "Or maybe you'd answer my questions faster if I were wearing a black hood? Or if I hung you up by your wrists and cut you. Do you like being cut, Ethan?" Pope dug his hand into his pocket, tossed Ethan something across the table.

Ethan said, "You had it?" He lifted the wallet, flipped it open—Secret Service credentials in the clear plastic sleeve, but they weren't his.

The badge had been issued to William V. Evans.

"Where's mine?" Ethan asked.

"Yeah. Where. William Evans. Special Agent. Secret Service. Boise field office. How again did you know it was him in the abandoned house?"

"I told you. I was sent here to find him and Kate Hewson."

"Oh, that's right. I keep forgetting. I called your Agent Hassler in Seattle, by the way. He'd never heard of you."

Ethan wiped more blood out of his face and leaned forward in his chair.

"I don't know what you're trying to do, what game—"

"My theory, Agent Evans had been pursuing

157

you, finally caught up with you here in Wayward Pines. So you kill him and kidnap his partner, Agent Stallings, intending to flee town in their car. Only on the way out, a little piece of bad luck catches up with you, and you get into a car accident. Stallings is killed, you take a hard blow to the head. Maybe it jars a screw loose, and when you wake up, you actually start believing *you're* this Secret Service agent."

"I know who I am."

"Really? You don't find it odd that no one can locate your identification?"

"Yeah, because it's deliberately being—"

"Right, we're all involved in some big conspiracy." Pope laughed. "You ever consider that maybe no one can locate the badge of Ethan Burke because it doesn't exist? Because *you* don't exist?"

"You're insane."

"I think you may be projecting, partner. You killed Agent Evans, didn't you—"

"No."

"—you sick, psychopathic nut job. Beat him to death with what?"

"Fuck you."

"Where's the murder weapon, Ethan?"

"Fuck you."

Ethan could feel the ire exploding within him. Pure, flammable rage.

"See," Pope said, "I don't know whether you're

just a damn good liar, or if you actually believe this elaborate lie you've constructed."

Ethan stood.

Unstable on his feet.

A deep blossom of nausea spreading in the pit of his stomach.

Blood poured down his face, dripping off his chin into a tiny pool on the concrete.

"I'm leaving," Ethan said, motioning to the door behind the sheriff. "Open it."

Pope didn't move. Said, "You go on and sit back down now before you get yourself really hurt." Said it with the confidence of a man who had many times done the thing he was threatening, who would gladly do it again.

Ethan stepped around the table, moving past the sheriff to the door.

Tugged on the handle.

Locked.

"Sit your ass back down. We ain't even started yet."

"Open the door."

Pope rose slowly to his feet, turned, and crowded into Ethan's airspace. Close enough now to smell the coffee on his breath. See the stains on his teeth. He had four inches on Ethan and probably forty pounds.

"Do you think I *can't* make you sit down, Ethan? That it's beyond my ability to do such a thing?"

"This is an illegal detainment."

Pope smiled. "You're thinking all wrong, boy. There's no such thing as law or government inside this room. It's just you and me. I am the one and only authority in your little world, whose borders are these walls. I could kill you right now if I wanted to."

Ethan let the tension knots in his shoulders relax, lifting both hands, palms open, in what he hoped Pope would mistake for a sign of deference and defeat.

He drew his head back, dipped his chin, said, "OK, you're right. We should keep talk—"

—and came off the balls of his feet like they'd been spring-loaded, driving the plate of his forehead straight into Pope's nose.

Cartilage crunched, and Ethan felt blood gushing down into his hair as he scooped Pope by his cedar-plank thighs, lifting with his legs, the sheriff struggling to catch Ethan's neck between his biceps and forearm, but too late.

The heels of Pope's boots slipped out from under him, greased with some blood that had slicked the floor, and Ethan felt the man's substantial weight go airborne.

He dug his shoulder into the man's stomach and drove him down hard onto the concrete.

A burst of air exploded out of Pope's lungs, and Ethan sat up, straddling the sheriff as he cocked back his right arm for a palm-heel strike.

Pope torqued his hips and drove Ethan's face into the leg of the wooden table with enough velocity to split open his cheek.

Ethan fought to get up amid the motes of excruciating light that starred his vision, but as he got his legs underneath him and struggled to stand, he saw that he'd righted himself a second too late.

Ethan might've parried the haymaker if his head was clear, his reflexes primed, but in his current state, he reacted at half speed.

The force behind the blow made Ethan's head swivel far enough that he felt his thoracic spine pop.

Found himself dazed and prone on the surface of that wooden table, staring up through his one good eye at the maniacal sheriff descending for another blow, his broken nose mushroomed across his face like something that had detonated.

Ethan raised his arms in an effort to protect his face, but the sheriff's fist ripped easily through his hands and crashed into Ethan's nose.

Tears streamed out of his eyes, blood into Ethan's mouth.

"Who are you?" the sheriff roared.

Ethan couldn't have answered if he'd wanted to, his consciousness slipping, what he could see of the interrogation room beginning to spin, interspersed with snapshots of another . . .

He is back in that brown-walled room with a

dirt floor in the Golan slum, watching a bare lightbulb swinging over his head as Aashif stares at him through a hood of black cloth that reveals only a pair of brown, malevolent eyes and a mouthful of smiling teeth too white and perfect to be a product of any fourth-world, Middle-Eastern shithole.

Ethan dangles by his wrists from a chain bolted into the ceiling, his feet just close enough to the floor to ease the circulation-destroying pressure by rising up on his big toes. But he can manage this for only seconds at a time before his phalanges collapse under his weight. When they finally break, he will have no means by which to stop the loss of blood flow to his hands.

Aashif stands inches from Ethan's face, their noses almost touching.

"Let's try a question you should have no problem answering . . . What part of America are you from, Chief Warrant Officer Ethan Burke?" the man asks in excellent English that is tinged with a UK accent.

"Washington."

"Your capital?"

"No, the state."

"Ah. You have children?"

"No."

"But you are married."

"Yes."

"What is your wife's name?"

Ethan doesn't respond, just braces for another blow.

Aashif smiles. "Relax. No more punches for now. You are familiar with the saying 'a death of a thousand cuts'?" Aashif holds up a single razor blade that gleams under the lightbulb. "It comes from a Chinese execution method, abolished in 1905, called lingchi, translated also as 'slow slicing' or 'the lingering death.'"

Aashif motions to the briefcase sitting open on a nearby table, lined with hard, black foam and upon which rests a terrifying collection of cutlery that Ethan has been trying to ignore for the last two hours.

Pope struck Ethan again, and along with the smell of his own blood, the blow jarred loose the memory of the smell of old, rotted blood on the floor of that torture house in Fallujah . . .

"You will now be taken to a room, given a pen, a piece of paper, and one hour. You know what I want," Aashif says.

"I don't."

Aashif punches Ethan in the gut.

Pope punched Ethan in the face.

"I'm growing tired of beating you. You know what I want. How could you not? I've asked you twenty times now. Tell me you know. Just tell me that."

"Who are you?" Pope yelled.

"I know," Ethan gasps.

"One hour, and if what you write down does not make me happy, you will die by lingchi."

Aashif takes a Polaroid out of his black dishdasha.

Ethan shuts his eyes but opens them again when Aashif says, "Look at this or I'll trim away your eyelids."

It is a photo of a man in this very room, also hanging from the ceiling by his wrists.

American. Probably a soldier, though impossible to know.

Three months of combat, and Ethan has never seen mutilation approaching this.

"Your countryman is alive in this photograph," his torturer says, a hint of pride creeping into his voice.

Ethan tried to open his eyes to see Pope. He felt himself on the brink of losing consciousness, wanting it both for the alleviation of his current pain, but also to block the perfect image his mind had conjured of Aashif, of that torture room.

"The next person who hangs from this ceiling will see a similar Polaroid of you," Aashif says. "Do you understand? I have your name. I also have a website. I will post pictures of what I do to you for the world to see. Maybe your wife will see them too. You write down everything I want to know, which up until now, you have held inside."

"Who are you?" Pope asked.

Ethan let his arms fall to the side.

"Who are you?"

No longer even trying to defend himself, thinking, *There is a part of me that never left that room in Fallujah that smelled like rancid blood.*

Willing the coup de grâce from Pope that would mercifully knock him unconscious, kill the old memories, kill his present agony.

Two seconds later, it came—a blow that connected with his chin and brought a burst of white-hot light like a flashbulb going off.

Chapter 6

THE DISHWASHER WAS loaded and groaning through its wash cycle, and Theresa, well past the point of total exhaustion, stood at the sink drying the last serving dish. She returned it to the cabinet, hung the towel on the fridge door, and hit the light.

Moving through the dark living room toward the staircase, she felt something latch onto her far worse than the emotional fallout of this long, long day.

A swallowing emptiness.

In a few short hours, the sun would rise, and in many ways, it would be the first morning of the rest of her life without him. This past day had been about saying good-bye, about scavenging what little peace she could find in a world without Ethan. Their friends had mourned him, would certainly always miss him, but they would move on—were already moving on—and would inevitably forget.

She couldn't shake the sense that beginning tomorrow, she would be alone.

In her grief.

Her love.

Her loss.

There was something so devastatingly lonely at the thought of it that she had to stop at the foot of the steps, put her hand on the banister, and catch her breath.

The knock startled her, kicked her heart rate up a notch.

Theresa turned and stared at the door, the thought crossing her mind that she'd imagined the sound.

It was 4:50 a.m.

What could anyone possibly want—

Another knock. Harder than the first.

She crossed the foyer in bare feet and stood on her tiptoes to see through the peephole.

Under the illumination of the porch light, she glimpsed a man standing on her stoop under an umbrella.

He was short. Completely bald. Face an expressionless shadow under the dripping canopy. He wore a black suit that made something catch inside her chest—a federal agent with news of Ethan? What other reason could there possibly be for someone to knock on her front door at this hour?

But the tie was all wrong.

Striped blue and yellow—too much style and flash for a fed.

Through the peephole, she watched the man's hand reach out and knock once more.

"Mrs. Burke," he said. "I know I'm not waking you. I saw you at the kitchen sink just a few minutes ago."

"What do you want?" she said through the door.

"I need to speak with you."

"About what?"

"Your husband."

She shut her eyes, opened them again.

The man was still there, and she was wide awake now.

"What about him?" she asked.

"It would be simpler if we could just sit down and talk face-to-face."

"It's the middle of the night and I have no idea who you are. There's no way I'm letting you in my house."

"You will want to hear what I have to say."

"Tell me through the door."

"I can't do that."

"Then come back in the morning. I'll speak with you then."

"If I leave, Mrs. Burke, you will never see me again, and trust me, that would be a tragedy for you and for Ben. I swear to you . . . I intend you no harm."

"Get off my property or I'll call the police."

The man reached into his coat and took out a Polaroid.

As he held it up to the peephole, Theresa felt something break inside her.

It was a photo of Ethan lying on a steel operating table, naked under clinical blue light. The left side of his face looked deeply bruised, and she couldn't tell if he was alive or dead. Before she knew what she was doing, her hand was reaching for the chain and turning back the dead bolt.

Theresa pulled the door open as the man collapsed his umbrella and leaned it against the brick. Behind him, a cold steady rain laid down an undercurrent of white noise on the sleeping city. A dark-colored Mercedes Sprinter was parked a few houses down. Not a fixture on her street. She wondered if the van was his.

"David Pilcher," the man said, extending his hand.

"What have you done to him?" Theresa asked, not taking it. "Is he dead?"

"May I come in?"

She moved back as Pilcher stepped over the threshold, his black wingtips glistening with beads of rainwater.

"I can take these off," he said, gesturing to his shoes.

"Don't worry about it."

She led him into the living room and they sat down across from one another, Theresa on the couch, Pilcher on a wooden, straight-backed chair she'd dragged over from the dining room table.

"You hosted a party here tonight?" he asked.

"A celebration of my husband's life."

"Sounds lovely."

She suddenly felt very tired, the lightbulb over her head almost too much for her retinas to bear.

"Why do you have a picture of my husband, Mr. Pilcher?"

"That doesn't matter."

"It does to me."

"What if I were to tell you that your husband is alive?"

For ten seconds, Theresa didn't breathe.

There was the noise of the dishwasher, of rain falling on the roof, of her throbbing heart, and nothing else.

"Who are you?" she asked.

"It doesn't matter."

"Then how can I trust—"

He held up a hand, his black eyes crinkling. "Better to listen right now."

"Are you with the government?"

"No, but again, who I am isn't important. It's what I have to offer you."

"Ethan is alive?"

"Yes."

Her throat tightened, but she held herself together.

"Where is he?" She could only whisper.

Pilcher shook his head. "I could sit here and tell you everything, but you wouldn't believe me."

"How do you know?"

"Experience."

"You won't tell me where my husband is?"

"No, and if you ask me again, I'll get up, walk out that door, and you'll never see me again, which means you'll never see Ethan again."

"Is he hurt?" She could feel a compacted mass of emotion beginning to loosen behind her sternum.

"He's fine."

"Do you want money? I can—"

"Ethan isn't being ransomed. This has nothing to do with money, Theresa." Pilcher scooted forward, now sitting on the edge of the chair and staring at her through those piercing black eyes whose intensity suggested a massive intellect behind them. "I am extending to you and your son a one-time offer."

Pilcher reached into the inner pocket of his coat, carefully removed a pair of half-inch glass vials containing a clear liquid, and set them on the coffee table. They'd been plugged with tiny corks.

"What's that?" Theresa asked.

"A reunion."

"A reunion?"

"With your husband."

"This is a joke—"

"No, it's not."

"Who are you?"

"My name is all I can give you."

"Well, it doesn't mean anything to me. And you expect me to—what?—drink that down, just see what happens?"

"You're welcome to refuse, Theresa."

"What's in the vials?"

"A short-acting, powerful sedative."

"And when I wake up, I'm magically back with Ethan?"

"It's a little more complicated than that, but generally speaking, yes."

Pilcher turned his head, glanced toward the front windows, and then refocused his gaze on Theresa.

"It will be light soon," he said. "I need your answer."

She took off her glasses, rubbed her eyes.

"I'm in no condition to be making a decision like this."

"But you must."

Theresa pushed against her legs and came slowly to her feet.

"That could be poison," she said, pointing at the table.

"Why do you think I'd want to hurt you?"

"I have no idea. Maybe Ethan got mixed up in something."

"If I wanted to kill you, Theresa . . ." He stopped himself. "You strike me as a person adept at reading others. What does your gut tell you? That I'm lying?"

She walked over to the mantel, stood there studying the family portrait they had made last year—Ethan and Ben in white Polo shirts, Theresa in a white summer dress, everyone's skin Photoshopped to perfection and features sharp under the studio lighting. At the time, they'd laughed at how cheesy and staged it had all turned out, but now, standing here in the predawn stillness of her living room, being offered a chance to see him again, the photo of the three of them brought out a lump in the back of her throat.

"What you're doing," she said, her eyes still fixed on her husband, "if it's fake . . . is as cruel as it gets. Offering a grieving widow a chance to see her husband again."

She looked at Pilcher.

"Is this real?" she asked.

"Yes."

"I want to believe you," she said.

"I know."

"I want to so badly."

"I understand it's a leap of faith," he said.

"You come tonight," she said, "of all nights. When I'm tired and drunk and filled to bursting with thoughts of him. I would guess that's not by accident."

Pilcher reached out and lifted one of the vials.

Held it up.

She watched him.

She took a breath in and let it out.

Then she started walking across the living room toward the staircase.

"Where are you going?" Pilcher asked.

"To get my son."

"You'll do it then? You'll come with me?"

She stopped at the base of the stairs and looked back at Pilcher across the living room. "If I do this," she said, "will we have our old life back?"

Pilcher said, "What do you mean by 'old life'? This house? This city? Your friends?"

Theresa nodded.

"If you and Ben choose to come with me, nothing will ever be the same. You will not see this house again. So in that sense, no."

"But I'll be with Ethan. Our family will be together."

"Yes."

She started up the stairs to wake her son. Maybe it was the exhaustion, maybe the emotion, but it felt so surreal. The air electric. There was a part of her screaming in the back of her mind what a fool she was. That no sane person would even consider such a proposition. But as she reached the second floor and moved down the hall toward Ben's room, she acknowledged that she wasn't sane, wasn't operating on the basis of logic or reason. She was broken and lonely, and beyond everything else, she missed her husband so much that even the uncertain possibility of a life with him—with their family reunited—might be worth signing everything else away.

Theresa sat down on Ben's bed and shook his shoulder.

The boy stirred.

"Ben," she said. "Wake up."

He yawned and rubbed his eyes. She helped him to sit up.

"It's still dark," he said.

"I know. I have a surprise for you."

"Really?"

"There's a man downstairs. His name is Mr. Pilcher. He's going to take us to Daddy."

She could see Ben's face glowing in the soft illumination of the nightlight beside his bed.

Her words had hit him like a blast of sunlight, the fog of sleep fast dissolving away, an alertness crystallizing in his eyes.

"Daddy's alive?" he asked.

She didn't even know if she fully believed.

What had Pilcher called it?

A leap of faith.

"Yes. Daddy's alive. Come on. We need to get you dressed."

Theresa and Ben sat down across from Pilcher.

The man smiled at the young boy, extended his hand, and said, "My name is David. And you are?"

"Ben."

They shook hands.

"How old are you, Ben?"

"Seven."

"Oh, very good. Your mother explained to you why I'm here?"

"She said you were going to take us to my daddy."

"That's right." Pilcher picked up the tiny glass vials and handed them to Theresa. "It's time," he said. "Go ahead and pull out the stoppers. You have nothing to fear, either of you. It will take

175

forty-five seconds once you've swallowed it. The effect will be sudden but not unpleasant. Give Ben the vial containing the smaller dose and then take yours."

She pinched the cork between her fingernails and uncapped the vials.

A potent waft of some foreign chemical escaped into the air.

Smelling it somehow made it real, jarred her out of the fugue state that had controlled her for the last several hours.

"Wait," she said.

"What's wrong?" Pilcher asked.

What the hell was she thinking? Ethan would kill her. If it was only her, maybe, but how could she risk her son?

"What's wrong, Mama?"

"We're not doing this," she said, putting the caps back in the vials and setting them on the coffee table.

Pilcher stared at her across the table. "You're absolutely sure about this?"

"Yes. I . . . I just can't."

"I understand." Pilcher gathered up the vials.

As he stood, Theresa looked at Ben, tears shimmering in the boy's eyes. "You go on up to bed."

"But I want to see Daddy."

"We'll talk about this later. Go on." Theresa turned back to Pilcher. "I'm sorry—"

The word stuck in her throat.

Pilcher held a clear oxygen mask to his face with a thin supply tube snaking down into his jacket. In his other hand, he held a small aerosol canister.

She said, "No, please—"

A blast of fine mist exploded out of the nozzle.

Theresa tried not to breathe, but already she could taste it on the tip of her tongue—liquid metal tinged with sweetness. The mist clung to her skin. She felt her pores ingesting it. It was in her mouth, far colder than room temperature, like a line of liquid nitrogen trailing down her throat.

She wrapped her arms around Ben and tried to stand, but she had no legs.

The dishwasher had stopped and the house stood absolutely silent save for the rain drumming on the roof.

Pilcher said, "You're going to serve a more valuable purpose than you could ever conceive of."

Theresa tried to ask him what he meant, but her mouth seemed to freeze.

All the color drained from the room—everything disintegrating into varying shades of gray—and she could feel an unstoppable heaviness tugging her eyelids down.

Already, Ben's little body had gone slack, his torso fallen across her lap, and she stared up at Pilcher, who was now smiling down at her through the oxygen mask and fading toward darkness along with everything else.

Pilcher took a walkie-talkie out of his coat and spoke into the receiver.

"Arnold, Pam, I'm ready for you."

Chapter 7

"ETHAN, I NEED you to relax. Do you hear me? Stop struggling."

Through the fog, Ethan recognized the voice—the psychiatrist.

He fought to open his eyes, but the effort produced only slits of light.

Jenkins peered down at him through those wire-rimmed glasses, and Ethan tried to move his arms again, but they were either broken or locked down.

"Your wrists have been handcuffed to the railing on your bed," Jenkins said. "Sheriff's orders. Don't be alarmed, but you're having a severe dissociative episode."

Ethan opened his mouth, instantly felt the dryness of his tongue and lips like they'd been scorched by a desert heat.

"What does that mean?" Ethan asked.

"It means you're having a breakdown in memory, awareness, even identity. The real concern here is that the car accident triggered it and that you're having these symptoms because your brain is bleeding. They're getting ready to roll you into surgery. Do you understand what I'm telling you?"

"I don't consent," Ethan said.

"Excuse me?"

"I don't consent to surgery. I want to be transported to a hospital in Boise."

"It's too risky. You could die before you got there."

"I want out of this town right now."

Jenkins vanished.

A blinding light bore down on Ethan's face from overhead.

He heard Jenkins's voice. "Nurse, calm him down, please."

"This?"

"No, that one."

"I'm not crazy," Ethan said.

He felt Jenkins pat his hand.

"No one's saying you are. It's just that your mind is broken, and we need to fix it."

Nurse Pam leaned over into Ethan's field of vision.

Beautiful, smiling, something comforting about her presence, and maybe it was just rote familiarity, but Ethan clung to it nonetheless.

"My goodness, Mr. Burke, you look simply awful. Let's see if we can't make you just a pinch more comfortable, OK?"

The needle was goliath, the biggest Ethan had ever seen, its end dripping silver beads of whatever drug the syringe contained.

"What's in there?" Ethan asked.

"Just a little something to steady those jangled nerves."

"I don't want it."

"Hold still now."

She tapped the antecubital vein on the underside of his right arm, Ethan straining so hard against the steel bracelets he could feel his fingers turning numb.

"I *don't* want it."

Nurse Pam looked up, and then leaned in so close to Ethan's face he could feel her eyelashes splay across his when she blinked. He smelled her lipstick and, at close range, could see the pure emerald clarity of her eyes.

"You hold still, Mr. Burke"—she smiled—"or I'll jam this motherfucker straight to the bone."

The words chilled him, Ethan squirming even harder, the handcuff chains rattling against the railing.

"Don't you touch me," he seethed.

"Oh, so you want to play it this way?" the nurse asked. "OK." Her smile never fading, she altered her grip on the syringe, now holding it like a knife, and before Ethan realized her intention, she stabbed the needle into the sidewall of his gluteus maximus, the needle buried to the syringe.

The spearing pain lingered as the nurse strolled back across the room to the psychiatrist.

"You didn't hit a vein?" Jenkins asked.

"He was moving too much."

"So how long before he's under?"

"Fifteen tops. Are they ready for him in the OR?"

"Yeah, roll him out." Jenkins directed his last comment to Ethan as he backpedaled toward the door: "I'll be by to look in on you after they finish the cutting and pasting. Good luck, Ethan. We're gonna get you all fixed up."

"I don't consent," Ethan said with as much force as he could muster, but Jenkins was already out of the room.

Through his swollen eyes, Ethan tracked Nurse Pam's movement around to the head of his gurney. She grasped the railing, and the gurney began to move, one of the front wheels squeaking as it wobbled across the linoleum.

"Why aren't you respecting my wishes?" Ethan asked, struggling to control his voice, trying for a softer approach.

She made no response, just continued to roll him out of the room and into the corridor, which stood as empty and quiet as ever.

Ethan lifted his head, saw the nurses' station approaching.

Every door they passed was closed, not a shred of light filtering out from under any of them.

"There's no one else on this floor, is there?" Ethan asked.

The nurse whistled a tune to the rhythm of the squeaky wheel.

"Why are you doing this to me?" he asked, and there was a note of desperation in his voice that wasn't staged, which sourced straight from the wellspring of terror that was mounting steadily, moment by moment, in the pit of his stomach.

He stared up at her—a strange angle from his supine position on the gurney that showed the underside of her chin, her lips, her nose, the ceiling panels, and long fluorescent lightbulbs scrolling past.

"Pam," he said. "Please. Talk to me. Tell me what's happening."

She wouldn't even look down at him.

On the other side of the nurses' station, she released the gurney, let it roll itself to a stop, and walked on toward a pair of double doors at the terminus of the corridor.

Ethan glanced at the signage above them.

SURGICAL

One of the doors swung open, and a man emerged wearing blue scrubs, his hands already covered in latex gloves.

A face mask hid everything but a pair of calm, intense eyes that matched the color of his scrubs almost perfectly.

He said to the nurse in a soft, quiet voice, "Why is he still awake?"

"He was struggling too much. I couldn't hit a vein."

The surgeon cut a glance toward Ethan.

"All right, keep him here until he's under. How much longer do you think?"

"Ten minutes."

He gave a curt nod and then headed back toward the operating room, shouldering forcefully through the doors, his body language aggressive, angry.

"Hey!" Ethan called after him. "I want to talk to you!"

In the several seconds the doors were open, Ethan took in an eyeful of the OR . . .

An operating table in the center of the room flanked by large, bright lights.

Beside it, a metal cart on wheels bearing an array of surgical implements.

Everything laid out clean and shiny on sterilized cloth.

Scalpels of every size.

Bone saws.

Forceps.

Instruments Ethan couldn't name but which resembled power tools.

A second before the doors swung back together, Ethan watched the surgeon stop beside the cart and unsheathe a drill from its holster.

He looked at Ethan as he squeezed the trigger several times, the high-pitched squeal of the motor filling the OR.

Ethan's chest heaved under his hospital gown and he could feel the bass drum thump of his accelerating pulse rate. He glanced back toward the nurses' station, caught a glimpse of Pam disappearing around the corner.

For a moment, he was alone on the corridor.

No sound but the clink of scalpels and surgical equipment on the other side of those double doors. The patter of the nurse's fading footsteps. The hum of a fluorescent bulb directly above him.

A mad thought—what if he *was* crazy? What if the surgeon in that OR opened him up and actually fixed him? Would all of this disappear? Would he lose this identity? Become another man in a world where his wife and son did not exist?

He managed to sit up.

His head woozy, unwieldy, but that could've been from the beating administered by Sheriff Pope.

Ethan stared down at his wrists, both of them cuffed to the metal railing of the gurney.

He tugged against the bracelets, the chains going taut, his hands turning purple.

Excruciating.

He eased the tension and then jerked back hard enough for the steel edges of the bracelets to dig into his wrists. On his left, it broke skin, blood sprinkling on the sheet.

His legs were free.

He threw his right one over the side of the railing, stretching and straining to reach the wall, but he was three inches short.

Ethan lay back on the gurney, taking a cold, hard look for the first time at how well and truly fucked he was—drugged, chained up, and on the verge of being wheeled into an operating room where they were going to do God knows what to him.

He had to admit that the last time he'd woken in the hospital and spoken to Dr. Jenkins he'd run through a patch of self-doubt, wondering, fearing that maybe he had suffered some injury that had impacted him neurologically.

Skewed his perception of people and space and time.

Because nothing in Wayward Pines made sense.

But these past few moments—Nurse Pam's sociopathic behavior, their refusal to heed his objections to surgery—had confirmed it: there was nothing wrong with him beyond the fact that people in this town meant him harm.

He'd already experienced plenty of fear, homesickness, and hopelessness since arriving in Wayward Pines, but now he bottomed out into complete despair.

For all he knew, death waited for him on the other side of those doors.

Never see Theresa again. Never see his son.

Just the possibility of it was enough to bring tears to his eyes, because he'd failed them. Failed them both in so many ways.

His physical absence. His emotional absence.

He'd brushed up against this level of horror and regret only one other time in his life—Aashif and the Golan slum.

Lingchi.

Now the fear was beginning to fully consume him, dull his ability to process information and properly react.

Or maybe it was the drug finally breaking past the blood/brain barrier and taking control.

Thinking, *God, don't crack up now. Must stay in control.*

He heard the grating screech of the elevator doors opening ten feet behind him, followed by the approach of soft, quick footsteps.

Ethan tried to crane his neck to see who was coming, but by the time he did the gurney was already in motion, someone rolling him back toward the elevator.

He stared up into a beautiful, familiar face, the prominent cheekbones igniting his recognition. In his current state, it took him five seconds to place her as the missing bartender from the pub.

She pushed him into the elevator car, working to fit the gurney inside.

She punched one of the buttons.

Her face was drawn and pale, and she wore a navy poncho that dripped water onto the floor.

"Come on, come on." She kept driving her finger into the lighted B.

"I know you," Ethan said, but he still couldn't recall her name.

"Beverly." She smiled but it was riddled with nerves. "Never got that big tip you promised. Jesus, you look terrible."

The doors started to close—another long, groaning screech worse than nails on a chalkboard.

"What's happening to me?" he asked as the pulleys strained to lower the car.

"They're trying to break your mind."

"Why?"

She lifted the poncho and pulled a handcuff key from the back pocket of her jeans.

Her fingers trembling.

It took her three attempts to finally get the key into the lock.

"Why?" Ethan asked again.

"We'll talk when we're safe."

The bracelet popped open.

Ethan sat up, grabbed the key out of her hand, and started on the other one.

The elevator descended at a crawl between the fourth and third floor.

"If it stops and someone gets on, we fight. You understand?" she asked.

Ethan nodded.

"No matter what happens, you cannot let them take you back into that operating room."

The second bracelet sprung open and Ethan climbed down off the gurney.

Felt reasonably stable on his feet, no sign of the drug's effect.

"Are you gonna be OK to run?"

"They just drugged me. I won't be able to cover much ground."

"Shit."

A bell above the elevator doors dinged.

Third floor.

It kept descending.

"When?" Beverly asked.

"Five minutes ago. But it was a muscular injection, not intravenous."

"What was the drug?"

"I don't know, but I heard them say I'd be unconscious within ten minutes. Well . . . more like eight or nine now."

The car reached the lobby, still dropping.

Beverly said, "When the doors open, we're heading left, all the way down the corridor. There's a door at the end that will put us out on the street."

The elevator shuddered to a stop.

For a long moment, the doors didn't move.

Ethan shifted his weight onto the balls of his feet, ready to explode out into the corridor if there were people waiting for them, adrenaline flooding his system with that electrified alertness he always got just before a mission as the rotors spun up.

The doors creaked open an inch, froze for ten seconds, and then slowly screeched open the rest of the way.

"Wait," Beverly whispered. She stepped over the threshold and peeked out. "Clear."

Ethan followed her out into a long, empty corridor.

Checkered linoleum tile ran for at least a hundred and fifty feet to some doors at the far end, everything spotless and quietly gleaming under the harsh fluorescent light.

A door slam in the distance stopped them in their tracks.

Footsteps became audible, though it was impossible to determine how many people were coming.

"They're heading down the stairwell," Beverly whispered. "Come on."

She turned and ran in the opposite direction, Ethan following, trying to dampen the slap of his bare feet on the linoleum and grunting against the jarring agony of what he could only assume were bruised ribs.

They came to a vacant nurses' station as a door

behind them toward the far end of the corridor banged open.

Beverly accelerated, turning and sprinting down one of the intersecting corridors, Ethan fighting to keep up, venturing a quick glance over his shoulder as he ran, but he was around the corner too soon to see anything.

This wing was empty and shorter by half.

Midway down, Beverly stopped and opened a door on the left-hand side.

Tried to usher Ethan through, but he shook his head, leaned in, and whispered into Beverly's ear instead.

She nodded and rushed into the room, pulling the door closed after her.

Ethan walked to the door on the opposite side of the hall.

The handle turned. He slipped inside.

It was empty, draped in darkness, and, by what little light streamed in from the corridor, appeared to have the same layout as the room they'd kept him in up on the fourth floor.

He shut the door as quietly as he could manage and turned into the bathroom.

Groped in the dark until his finger found the switch.

Flicked the light.

There was a hand towel hanging from a rack beside the shower. He grabbed it, wrapped it around his hand, and faced the mirror.

Cocked his arm back.

You have thirty seconds, maybe less.

But his reflection derailed him.

Oh God. He'd known it was bad, but Pope had beaten the shit out of him—his upper lip twice the size, his nose giant and bruised like a rotted strawberry, a gash across his right cheek closed with what must have been twenty stitches, and his eyes . . .

A miracle that he could see at all. They were black and purple and encased in folds of swollen skin like he was in the throes of a near-fatal allergic reaction.

No time to dwell on it.

He punched the lower right corner of the mirror and held his towel-wrapped fist against the broken glass so it didn't all fall out at once.

He'd struck a perfect blow—minimal damage, large fractures. He quickly picked the pieces away with his free hand, laid them out on the sink, and chose the largest of the bunch.

Then he unwrapped his right hand, hit the lights, and felt his way back out into the bedroom.

There was nothing to see but a razor-thin line of light beneath the door.

Edging forward, he pressed his ear against it.

The sound was faint, but he could hear the distant noise of doors opening and closing.

They were checking every room, and the slams sounded far enough away that he thought they were probably still in the main corridor.

Hoped he wasn't wrong about that.

He wondered if the elevator doors were still open. If they saw the car down here, no doubt they'd surmise he'd fled to the basement. He and Beverly should have sent the elevator back to four, but there was no way to fix their oversight now.

Reaching down, he found the doorknob and grasped it.

As he turned it slowly, he tried to steady his breathing, to drive his BPMs back down into a range that didn't make him feel on the verge of fainting.

When the latch had cleared its housing, Ethan gave the gentlest tug.

The door swung in two inches, the hinges mercifully silent.

A long triangle of light fell across the checkered linoleum under his bare feet.

The sounds of the door slams were louder.

He held the mirror shard and slid it between the open door and the jamb, inching it farther and farther, millimeter by millimeter, until it showed a reflection of the corridor behind him.

Empty.

Another door swung closed.

Between the slams, there was the impact of rubber-soled shoes on the floor and nothing else. One of the fluorescent bulbs nearby was malfunctioning, flickering intermittently and throwing the corridor into alternating bursts of darkness and light.

The shadow preceded the person—a faint darkening across the floor in the vicinity of the nurses' station—and then Nurse Pam strolled into view.

She stopped at the intersection of the four corridors and stood absolutely still, holding something in her right hand that Ethan couldn't identify from this distance, although one end of it cast off shimmers of reflected light.

Thirty seconds elapsed, and then she turned and started down Ethan's corridor, walking carefully, purposefully, in short, controlled strides and with a smile that seemed too wide to fit across her face.

After several steps, she stopped, brought her knees together, and knelt down to inspect something on the linoleum. With her free hand, she wiped a finger across the floor and held it up, Ethan realizing with a jolt of anxiety what it was, how the nurse had known which corridor to take.

Water from Beverly's raincoat.

And it was going to lead her straight to the door across the hall. To Beverly.

Nurse Pam stood up.

Slowly, she began to walk, studying the linoleum as she crossed the tiles.

Ethan saw that the object in her hand was a syringe and needle.

"Mr. Burke?"

He hadn't expected her to speak, and the sound of her bright, malignant voice echoing down the empty corridors of the hospital put a sliver of ice in the small of his back.

"I know you're near. I know you can hear me."

She was getting too close for comfort, Ethan fearing that any second now, she'd spot the mirror in his hand.

Ethan drew the shard of glass back into the room and eased the door closed with even greater care and precision.

"Since you're my new favorite patient," the nurse continued, "I'm going to make you a special deal."

Ethan noted something at the base of his skull —a warmth beginning to stretch down the length of his spine, through the bones of his arms and legs, points of heat radiating into the tips of his fingers and toes.

He could also feel it behind his eyes.

The drug was starting to take effect.

"Be a good sport, come out right now, and I'll give you a present."

He couldn't hear her footsteps, but her voice was getting progressively louder as she moved deeper into the corridor.

"The present, Mr. Burke, is anesthesia for your

surgery. I hope you understand that if it hasn't hit you already, the drug I gave you ten minutes ago will be rendering you unconscious any moment now. And if I have to spend an hour searching every room to find you, that's going to make me very, very angry. And you don't want to see me very, very angry, because do you know what will happen? When we finally find you, we won't roll you into surgery right away. We'll let the current drug that's in your system wear off. You'll wake up on the operating table. No straps, no handcuffs, but you won't be able to move. This is because I'll have injected you with a monster dose of Suxamethonium, which is a paralytic drug. Have you ever wondered what surgery feels like? Well, Mr. Burke, you'll get your own private show."

The way her voice carried, Ethan knew she was standing in the middle of the corridor now, less than four feet away from him on the other side of the door.

"The only movement you'll be capable of performing is blinking. You won't even be able to scream as you feel the cutting and sawing and drilling. Our fingers inside you. The surgery will take hours, and you will be alive, awake, and fully alert for every agonizing second of it. It's the stuff of horror fiction."

Ethan put his hand on the doorknob, the flush of the drug lifting now, enveloping his brain, flooding into the tips of his ears. He wondered how much more of this he could stand before his legs gave out.

Turn it slowly, Ethan. Turn it so, so slowly.

Tightening his grip on the doorknob, he waited for Nurse Pam to speak again, and when she finally did, he began to turn.

"I know you can hear my voice, Mr. Burke. I'm standing just outside the room where you're hiding. Are you in the shower? Under the bed? Perhaps standing behind the door, hoping I'll walk blindly past?"

She laughed.

The latch cleared.

He fully believed she was standing with her back to him, facing Beverly's room, but if she wasn't?

"You have ten seconds to come out, and then my generous offer of anesthesia will expire. Ten . . ."

He edged the door back.

"Nine . . ."

Three inches.

"Eight . . ."

Six inches.

He could see into the corridor again, and the first thing he spotted was the splash of auburn hair down Nurse Pam's back.

She stood straight ahead of him.

"Seven . . ."

Facing Beverly's door.

"Six . . ."

The needle gripped like a knife in her right hand.

"Five . . ."

He kept tugging the door back, letting it glide silently on the hinges.

"Four . . ."

Stopped it before it banged into the wall, now standing in the threshold.

"Three . . ."

He studied the floor to make sure he wasn't throwing a shadow, but even if he had been, that flickering fluorescent bulb would have masked it.

"Two, and one, and now I'm angry. Very, very angry." The nurse lifted something out of her pocket, said, "I'm down in the basement, west wing, pretty sure he's here. I'll wait until you arrive, over."

A walkie-talkie belched static and a male voice answered, "Copy that, on our way."

The drug was hitting Ethan hard now, his knees softening, his sight beginning to come off the rails in bursts of blurriness and double vision.

More people would be here momentarily.

He needed to do this now.

Telling himself *go, go, go,* but he wasn't sure if he even had the strength or presence of mind.

He backed several steps into the room to lengthen his runway, took a long, deep breath, and went for it.

Seven paces covered in two seconds.

Collided into the nurse's back at full speed, driving her across the corridor and slamming her face-first into the concrete wall.

It was a hard, devastating hit that had taken her completely off guard, and so the speed and accuracy of her reaction surprised him, her right arm swinging back, the needle stabbing him through the side.

Deep, penetrating, blinding pain.

He stumbled back, listing, unsteady on his feet.

The nurse spun around, blood sheeting down the right side of her face where it had met with the concrete, the needle cocked back, and charged him.

He could have defended himself if he'd been able to see worth a damn, but his eyesight was lagging, drawing images out across his field of vision like an ecstasy trip.

She lunged and he tried to parry back but misjudged the distance, the needle spearing him through the left shoulder.

The pain when she jerked it back out nearly brought him to his knees.

The nurse caught him with a perfectly placed front kick to the solar plexus, and the sheer force behind it punched him back into the wall and drove the breath out of his lungs. He'd never hit a woman in his life, but as Pam moved in for more, he couldn't shake the thought that it would feel so satisfying to connect his right elbow with this bitch's jaw.

His eyes locked on the needle in her hand, thinking, *No more of that, please God.*

Brought his arms up to defend his face, but they felt like boulders.

Sluggish and cumbersome.

The nurse said, "Bet you're wishing you'd just come out when I asked nicely, huh?"

He lashed out at half speed with a wide-arcing hook that she easily ducked, firing back with a lightning-fast jab that rebroke his nose.

"You want the needle again?" she asked, and he would've charged, tried to get her on the floor, pin her underneath his weight, but proximity, considering the needle and his diminished senses, seemed like a bad idea.

Pam laughed, said, "I can tell you're fading. You know, this is actually kind of fun."

Ethan struggled to slide away against the wall, shuffling his feet to get out of range, but she tracked his movement, staying in front of him and aligned for another strike.

"Let's play a little game," she said. "I poke you with the needle, and you try to stop me."

She lunged, but there was no pain.

Just a feint—she was toying with him.

"Now the next one, Mr. Burke, is going to—"

Something smashed into the side of her head with a hard *thunk.*

Pam hit the ground and didn't move, Beverly standing over her, the frantic light blinking against her face. She still held the metal chair she'd dropped Nurse Pam with by its legs, looking more than a little shocked at what she'd done.

"More people are coming," Ethan said.

"Can you walk?"

"We'll see."

Beverly tossed the chair aside and came over to Ethan as it clattered against the linoleum floor.

"Hold onto me in case your balance goes."

"It's already gone."

He clung to Beverly's arm as she pulled him along back down the corridor. By the time they'd reached the nurses' station, Ethan was struggling just to put one foot in front of the other.

He glanced back as they rounded the corner, saw Nurse Pam struggling to sit up.

"Faster," Beverly said.

The main corridor was still empty, and they were jogging now.

Twice, Ethan tripped, but Beverly caught him, kept him upright.

His eyes were growing heavy, the sedation descending on him like a warm, wet blanket, and all he wanted to do was find some quiet alcove where he could curl up and sleep this off.

"You still with me?" Beverly asked.

"By a thread."

The door at the corridor's end loomed fifty feet ahead.

Beverly quickened the pace. "Come on," she said. "I can hear them coming down the stairwell."

Ethan heard it too—a jumble of voices and numerous footsteps behind a door they passed leading to a set of stairs.

At the end of the corridor, Beverly jerked the door open and dragged Ethan across the threshold into a cramped stairwell whose six steps climbed to another door at the top, over which glowed a red EXIT sign.

Beverly paused once they were through, let it close softly behind them.

Ethan could hear voices on the other side filling the corridor, sounded like the footfalls were moving away from them, but he couldn't be sure.

"Did they see us?" he asked.

"I don't know."

It took all of Ethan's focus to climb those final steps to the exit, where they crashed through the door and stumbled outside into darkness, Ethan's feet on wet pavement and the patter of cold rain on his shoulders already beginning to seep through the paper-thin fabric of his gown.

He could barely stand and already Beverly was pulling him toward the sidewalk.

"Where are we going?" Ethan asked.

"To the only place I know they can't find you."

He followed her into the dark street.

No cars out, just a smattering of streetlights and houselights, everything dim and obscured by the rain.

They took the sidewalk down a quiet street, and after the second block, Ethan stopped and tried to sit down in the grass, but Beverly wouldn't let him quit.

"Not yet," she said.

"I can't go any farther. I can barely feel my legs."

"One more block, OK? You can make it. You have to make it if you want to live. I promise you in five minutes you'll be able to lie down and ride this out."

Ethan straightened up and staggered on, followed Beverly for one more block, beyond which the houses and streetlights ended.

They entered a cemetery filled with crumbling headstones interspersed with scrub oaks and pines. It hadn't been maintained in ages, grass and weeds rising to Ethan's waist.

"Where are you taking me?" His words slurred, felt heavy and awkward falling out of his mouth.

"Straight ahead."

They wove through headstones and monuments, most eroded so badly Ethan couldn't make out the engraving.

He was cold, his gown soaked through, his feet muddy.

"There it is." Beverly pointed to a small, stone

mausoleum standing in a grove of aspen. Ethan struggled through the last twenty feet and then collapsed at the entrance between a pair of stone planters that had disintegrated into rubble.

It took Beverly three digs with her shoulder to force open the iron door, its hinges grinding loudly enough to wake the dead.

"I need you inside," she said. "Come on, you're almost there. Four more feet."

Ethan opened his eyes and crawled up the steps through the narrow doorway, out of the rain. Beverly pulled the door closed after them, and for a moment, the darkness inside the crypt was total.

A flashlight clicked on, the beam skirting across the interior and igniting the color of a stained-glass window inset in the back wall.

The image—rays of sunlight piercing through clouds and lighting a single, flowering tree.

Ethan slumped down onto the freezing stone as Beverly unzipped a duffel bag that had been stowed in the corner.

She pulled out a blanket, unfolded it, spread it over Ethan.

"I have some clothes for you as well," she said, "but you can dress when you wake up again."

He shivered violently, fighting the undertow of unconsciousness, because there were things he had to ask, had to know. Didn't want to risk Beverly not being here when he woke up again.

"What is Wayward Pines?" he asked.

Beverly sat down beside him, said, "When you wake, I'll—"

"No, tell me now. In the last two days, I've seen things that were impossible. Things that make me doubt my sanity."

"You aren't crazy. They're just trying to make you think you are."

"Why?"

"That, I don't know."

He wondered if he could believe her, figured that, all things considered, it was probably wise to err on the side of skepticism.

"You saved my life," he said, "and thank you for that. But I have to ask . . . why, Beverly? Why are you my only friend in Wayward Pines?"

She smiled. "Because we both want the same thing."

"What's that?"

"To get out."

"There's no road out of this town, is there?"

"No."

"I drove here several days ago. So how is that even possible?"

"Ethan, just let the drug take you, and when you wake up, I'll tell you everything I know and how I think we can get out. Close your eyes."

He didn't want to, but he couldn't stop it from happening.

"I'm not crazy," he said.

"I know that."

His shivering had begun to abate, his body heat creating a pocket of warmth under the blanket.

"Tell me one thing," he said. "How did you wind up in Wayward Pines?"

"I was a rep for IBM. Came here on a sales call trying to outfit the local school's computer lab with our PCjrs. But as I drove into town, I got into a car accident. Truck came out of nowhere, slammed into my car." Her voice was becoming softer, more distant, harder to follow. "They told me I suffered a head injury and some memory loss, which is why my first recollection of this town is waking up one afternoon beside the river."

Ethan wanted to tell her that the same thing had happened to him, but he couldn't open his mouth to speak, the drug plowing through his system like a rogue wave, engulfing him.

He'd be gone inside a minute.

"When?" he rasped.

She didn't hear him, had to lean in close, put her ear to his mouth, and it took everything in his power to get the question out.

"When . . . did . . . you . . . come . . . here?" he whispered, clinging to her words now like a life preserver that could keep him afloat, keep him awake, but still he was slipping under, seconds of consciousness remaining.

She said, "I'll never forget the day I arrived,

because in some ways, it's like the day I died. Since then, nothing's been the same. It was a beautiful autumn morning. Sky a deep blue. The aspen turning. That was October third, 1985. In fact, next week is my anniversary. I'll have been in Wayward Pines a whole year."

Chapter 8

SHE DIDN'T DARE open the door, glanced instead through one of the missing panes in the stained-glass window. Found nothing to see through the midnight rainfall and nothing to hear above the sound of it on the weeds and the trees and the mausoleum roof.

Ethan was gone, lost to the drug, and in some ways, she envied him.

In sleep, the dreams came to her.

Of her Life Before.

Of a man whom in all likelihood she would have married.

Of her home with him in Boise.

All the plans they'd made together.

The children they had one day hoped to bring into the world—sometimes, she even dreamed about their faces.

Waking was Wayward Pines.

This beautiful hell.

When she'd first arrived, the surrounding cliffs

had filled her with awe and wonder. Now, she hated them for what they were, what they'd become—prison bars surrounding this lovely town where no one could leave, and those few who tried . . .

She still had nightmares about those nights.

The sound of five hundred telephones ringing at once.

The screaming.

Not tonight . . . that is not going to happen tonight.

Beverly pulled off her poncho and went to him, curled up under the blanket against the wall. When the pattern of his breathing finally slowed into long respirations, she crawled over to the duffel bag and fished the knife out of an exterior pocket.

It was a folder, rusted and dull, but it was all she'd been able to find.

She tugged the blanket away and pulled up Ethan's hospital gown and ran her hand along his left leg until she felt the bump on the back of his thigh.

Let her hand linger there a shade longer than she should have, hating herself for it, but God it'd been so long since she'd even touched or been touched by a man.

She'd considered telling Ethan ahead of time, but his impaired state had prevented this, and maybe that was for the best. Regardless, he was lucky. She hadn't had the benefit of anesthesia when she'd done this to herself.

Beverly set the flashlight on the stone floor so it illuminated the backside of his left thigh.

It was covered in scars.

You couldn't see the bump, only feel it—and just barely—if you knew exactly where to touch.

She pried open the blade, which she'd sterilized two hours ago with cotton balls and alcohol, her stomach lurching at the thought of what she had to do, praying the pain wouldn't break his sedation.

Chapter 9

ETHAN DREAMED HE'D been tied down and that something was eating his leg, taking small, probing bites that occasionally went deep enough for him to cry out in his sleep.

He slammed awake.

Groaning.

Darkness everywhere, and his left leg, high on the back of his thigh, burning with a pain he knew all too well—someone was cutting him.

For a terrible moment, he was back in that torture room with black-hooded Aashif, hanging from the ceiling by his wrists, his ankles chained to the floor, and his body taut so he couldn't struggle, so he couldn't even move, no matter how awful the pain.

Hands shook his shoulders.

A woman's voice said his name.

"Ethan, you're all right. It's over."

"Please stop, oh God, please stop."

"You're safe. I got it out."

He registered a splash of light, blinked several times until it sharpened into focus.

A flashlight beam shone on the floor.

In the indirect light, he glimpsed stone walls, two crypts, a stained-glass window, and then it all came roaring back.

"You know where you are?" Beverly asked.

His leg hurt so much he thought he was going to throw up.

"My leg . . . something's wrong—"

"I know. I had to cut something out of it."

His head was clearing, the hospital, the sheriff, his attempt to leave town all coming back, the memories trying to reassemble themselves into a sequence that made sense. He thought he'd seen Kate as well, but wasn't sure. That piece felt too much like a dream, or a nightmare.

With newfound clarity, the pain in his leg was making it difficult to concentrate on anything else.

"What are you talking about?" he asked.

Beverly lifted the flashlight and let it shine on her right hand, where between her thumb and first finger, she held something that resembled a microchip, specks of drying blood still caught up in the semiconductor.

"What is that?" he asked.

"How they monitor and track you."

"That was in my leg?"

"They're embedded in everyone's."

"Give it to me."

"Why?"

"So I can stomp it into pieces."

"No, no, no. You don't want to do that. Then they'll know you removed it." She handed it to him. "Just ditch it in the cemetery when we leave."

"Won't they find us in here?"

"I've hidden here with the chip before. These thick stone walls disrupt the signal. But we can't stay here long. They can track the chip to within a hundred yards of where the signal drops."

Ethan struggled to sit up. He folded back the blanket to uncover a small pool of blood glistening on stone under the flashlight beam. More red eddies trickled out of an incision site on the back of his leg. He wondered how deep she'd had to dig. Felt light-headed, his skin achy and clammy with fever.

"You have something in the bag to close this wound?" he asked.

She shook her head. "Just duct tape."

"Get it. Better than nothing."

Beverly pulled the duffel bag over and thrust her hand inside.

Ethan said, "Did I dream you told me you came here in 1985, or did that really happen?"

"That happened." She pulled out a roll of tape. "What do I do?" she asked. "I have no medical training."

"Just wrap it around my leg several times."

She started a piece of tape and then moved in, winding it carefully around Ethan's thigh.

"Is that too tight?"

"No, it's good. You need to stop the bleeding."

She made five revolutions and then ripped the tape and smoothed it down.

"I'm going to tell you something," Ethan said. "Something that you won't believe."

"Try me."

"I came here five days ago . . ."

"You already told me that."

"The date was September twenty-fourth, 2012."

For a moment, she just stared at him.

"Ever heard of an iPhone?" Ethan asked.

She shook her head . . .

"The Internet? Facebook? Twitter?"

. . . and kept shaking it.

Ethan said, "Your president is . . ."

"Ronald Reagan."

"In 2008, America elected its first black president, Barack Obama. You've never heard of the *Challenger* disaster?"

He noticed the flashlight beginning to tremble in her hand.

"No."

"The fall of the Berlin Wall?"

"No, none of it."

"The two Gulf Wars? September eleventh?"

"Are you playing some mind game with me?" Her eyes narrowed—one measure of anger, two of fear. "Oh God. You're with them, aren't you?"

"Of course not. How old are you?"

"Thirty-four."

"And your birthday is . . ."

"November first."

"What year?"

"Nineteen fifty."

"You should be sixty-one years old, Beverly."

"I don't understand what this means," she said.

"Makes two of us."

"The people here . . . they don't talk to each other about anything outside of Wayward Pines," she said. "It's one of the rules."

"What are you talking about?"

"They call it 'live in the moment.' No talk of politics is allowed. No talk of your life before. No discussions of pop culture—movies, books, music. At least nothing that isn't available here in town. Don't know if you've noticed, but there are hardly any brand names. Even the money is weird. I didn't realize it until recently, but all the currency is from the fifties and sixties. Nothing later. And there are no calendars, no newspapers. Only way I know how long I've been here is because I keep a journal."

"Why is it like this?"

"I don't know, but the punishment for slipping up is severe."

Ethan's leg throbbed from the constriction of the duct tape, but at least the bleeding had subsided. He let it ride for now, but he'd have to loosen it soon.

Beverly said, "If I find out you're with them—"

"I am not with them, whoever *they* are."

There were tears building in her eyes. She blinked them away and wiped the glistening trails off the sides of her face.

Ethan leaned back against the wall.

The chills and the aches getting worse.

He could still hear the rain beating down above them, and it was still night beyond that stained-glass window.

Beverly lifted the blanket off the floor and draped it over Ethan's shoulders.

"You're burning up," she said.

"I asked you what this place was, but you never really answered me."

"Because I don't know."

"You know more than me."

"The more you know, the stranger it becomes. The less you know."

"You've been here a year. How have you survived?"

She laughed—sad and resigned. "By doing what everyone else does . . . buying into the lie."

"What lie?"

"That everything's fine. That we all live in a perfect little town."

"Where paradise is home."

"What?"

"Where paradise is home. It's something I saw on a sign on the outskirts of town when I was trying to drive out of here last night."

"When I first woke up here, I was so disoriented and in so much pain from the car accident, I believed them when they told me I lived here. After wandering around in a fog all day, Sheriff Pope found me. He escorted me to the Biergarten, that pub where you and I first met. Told me I was a bartender there, even though I'd never tended bar in my life. Then he took me to a little Victorian house I'd never seen before, told me it was home."

"And you just believed him?"

"I had no competing memories, Ethan. I only knew my name at that point."

"But the memories came back."

"Yes. And I knew something was very wrong. I couldn't make contact with the outside world. I knew this wasn't my life. But there was something, I don't know—sinister—about Pope. On some instinctive level, I knew better than to question him about anything.

"I didn't have a car, so I started taking long walks toward the outskirts of town. But a strange thing happened. Every time I'd get near to where the road looped back, guess who showed up? It dawned on me that Pope wasn't really a sheriff. He was a warden. For everyone who lived here. I realized he must be tracking me somehow, so for two months I kept my head down, went to work, went home, made a few friends—"

"And they'd bought into all this as well?"

"I don't know. On a surface level, they never blinked. Never gave any indication that things were out of the ordinary. After a while, I realized it must be fear that was keeping everyone in line, but of what, I didn't know. And I sure didn't ask."

Ethan thought back to the neighborhood party he'd stumbled upon—God, was it just last night? —and how normal it had seemed. How perfectly ordinary. He thought of all the quaint Victorian houses in Wayward Pines and of all the families who lived inside them. How many residents— inmates—kept up a strong, carefree countenance during the day, but then lay awake at night, sleepless, minds racing, terrified and struggling to comprehend why they'd been locked away in this scenic prison? He imagined more than a few. But human beings were, if nothing else, adaptable. He figured just as many had convinced themselves, convinced their children, that things were exactly as they should be. As they'd always been. How many lived day to day, in the moment, banishing any thought or remembrance of the life they had known before? It was easier to accept what could not be changed than to risk everything and seek out the unknown. What lay beyond. Long-term inmates often committed suicide, or reoffended, when faced with the prospect of life outside the prison walls. Was it so different here?

Beverly continued, "One night at the bar, a few months after my arrival, this guy slipped me a note. It said, 'the back of your left thigh.' That night in the shower, I felt it for the first time—a small bump, something under the skin—although I didn't know what I was supposed to do about it. Next night, he was back at my bar. Scribbled a new message, this time on the ticket—'cut it out, keep it safe, it's how they track you.'

"First three times, I chickened out. The fourth, I manned up and did it. By day, I always kept the chip with me. Carried on like everyone else. And the weird thing is that there were moments when it almost felt normal. I'd be at someone's house having dinner, or a neighborhood block party, and I'd catch this feeling like maybe it had always been this way, and that my prior life was the dream. I started to see how people could grow to accept a life in Wayward Pines.

"At night, after my shift ended at the pub, I'd go home, leave the chip in my bed where I was supposed to be, and head out. Each night, a different direction. I kept running into dead ends. To the north, east, and west were these towering cliff walls, and I could climb them for a hundred feet or so, but the ledges inevitably got thinner, and I would always run out of handholds or come to a point where I didn't have the guts to keep climbing. I came across more than a few skeletons at the base of those cliffs—old, broken bones. Human. People who had tried to climb out and taken a fall.

"Fourth time I ventured out, I went south up the main road, the one I'd driven into Wayward Pines. I found what you found—it just looped back into town, back into itself in an endless circle. But I kept heading south into the woods. Must've gone a half mile before I finally came to the fence."

"A fence?"

The throbbing in Ethan's leg had become unbearable, worse than the pain of Beverly's incision. He loosened the duct tape.

"It was twenty feet high and it ran through the forest in either direction as far as I could see. There was barbed wire across the top, and it hummed like it was electrified. The same sign was attached to the fencing every fifty feet. It said, 'Return to Wayward Pines. Beyond This Point You Will Die.' "

Ethan rewrapped his leg.

The throbbing had faded, and there was still pain, but it seemed to have dulled.

"Did you find a way through?"

"No. It was getting near dawn, and I thought I'd better get back to town. But when I turned to go, there was a man standing in front of me. Scared me to death until I realized who it was."

"Guy who told you about the chip?"

"Exactly. He said he'd been following me. Every night I'd gone out."

"Who was he?" Ethan asked, and he couldn't be sure in the low light, but it looked as though a shadow passed across Beverly's face.

"Bill."

A prickling sensation, like a low-amp current, ripped through Ethan's body.

"What was Bill's last name?" he asked.

"Evans."

"Jesus."

"What?"

"Evans was the dead man in the house. The one you steered me toward."

"Right. I wanted you to understand right off how dangerous this place is."

"Message received. Evans was one of the Secret Service agents I was sent to Wayward Pines to find."

"I didn't know Bill was Secret Service. He wouldn't tell me anything about what we called 'our lives before.' "

"How did he die?"

Beverly lifted the flashlight off the floor, its bulb beginning to weaken in intensity.

She switched it off.

Total darkness.

The whisper of rain and nothing else.

"It happened the night we tried to escape. I still don't understand exactly how they found out, because we left our microchips in our beds like we'd done so many times before. Bill and I met up at our predetermined spot with supplies and provisions . . . but we never had a chance."

Ethan could hear the grief splitting her voice.

"We had to go separate ways," she said. "I made it back to my house, but they caught him. Tore him apart."

"Who tore him apart?"

"Everyone."

"Who's every—"

"The entire town, Ethan. I could . . . hear him screaming from my house, but there was nothing I could do. At last, I understood. I realized what it was that kept everyone here."

For what seemed a long, long time, neither of them spoke.

Finally, Ethan said, "I never made it to the fence, but I did wander a ways into the woods beyond the curve in the road at the south end of town. This was just last night. I could swear I heard something."

"What?"

"It was a scream. Or a cry. Maybe something in between. And the weird thing was this feeling like I'd heard it before. In a dream. Or another life. It filled me with terror on such a base level, like the howl of a wolf. Something deeply ingrained. My only response was to run. So now I hear you telling me about this electrified fence, and I'm wondering, why is it there? Is it to keep us in? Or to keep something out?"

At first, Ethan thought the sound was coming from inside his head—some aftereffects of the drug Nurse Pam had given him, or the trauma of Pope's beating and everything he'd experienced since.

But the noise quickly grew.

Something was ringing.

No.

Many things were ringing.

Hundreds and hundreds of them.

"What is that?" Ethan asked, struggling onto his feet.

Beverly was already at the door, fighting to pull it open, the hinges grinding, and then a blast of colder air swept into the crypt and the noise grew suddenly loud.

Ethan realized what it was.

The sound of five hundred rotary telephones going off at once, filling the valley with a bright, eerie ringing.

"Oh God," Beverly said.

"What's happening?"

"This is how it started the night Bill died."

"I don't understand."

"Every telephone in every house in Wayward Pines is ringing right now. People are being told to find and kill you."

Ethan braced for the impact of that piece of information, but he was only vaguely aware that he should be scared shitless, something he knew but didn't feel, his mind already roping itself off, sliding into that numb, adrenalized state of rote survival he'd tasted those few times in his life when he'd had the misfortune to lock eyes with death. No place for extraneous, wasted thought or emotion. All power diverted and channeled so it could heighten the only thing that could keep him alive—sensory perception.

"I'll go ditch the chip and hide here," he said. "Wait them out."

"There are just over five hundred people living in Wayward Pines, and every one of them will be looking for you. I'm thinking eventually someone's going to come through this door, and you don't want to be here when that happens."

Ethan grabbed the flashlight out of her hand and flicked it on, limped over to the duffel bag.

"What's in here?" he asked, going down on his knees beside the bag.

"Clothes for you. Shoes. I had to guess your size."

"Weapons?"

"Sorry. Couldn't get my hands on any."

Ethan started pulling things out—a long-sleeved black T, black jeans, black shoes, two dozen bottles of water—

"Turn off the light!" Beverly hissed at him.

Ethan killed it.

"You have to go right now," she said. "They're coming."

"Just let me get dressed and—"

"They're already in the cemetery. I can see their flashlights."

Ethan left everything strewn across the floor and staggered over to the iron door. Out in the darkness, he spotted four points of light weaving through the headstones.

They appeared to be a few hundred feet away, although judging distance was a challenge in this weather.

The telephones had gone quiet.

Beverly whispered in Ethan's ear, "You need to find the river at the southwest end of town. That's the route Bill and I had planned to take. It's the only direction I haven't thoroughly explored. Bill went up a little ways and thought it looked promising."

"Where do we meet?"

"Just get to the river and follow it upstream. I'll find you."

Beverly pulled the hood of her poncho over her head, stepped down out of the mausoleum, and sprinted off into the night, Ethan listening as the sound of her footsteps dwindled away and were soon lost to the steady rain.

He lingered in the threshold, alternating his attention between the approaching lights and the pitch darkness of the crypt, wondering if he had two minutes to spend getting dressed and gathering supplies or if he just needed to go.

The beams of light drew closer, all four of them moving in the general direction of the mausoleum and bringing voices along with them.

Decide, dammit.

He was wasting precious seconds.

If they reach you while you're in the crypt, you're dead. There is no escape, and they could be here in less time than it will take you to dress.

He ran.

Wearing nothing but a hospital gown, shoeless, his bare feet swishing through grass and squishing through patches of cold mud.

Rain pelting him.

Achy.

Wracked with chills.

His left hamstring screaming with every flexion.

He shut it all away—the fear, the agony, the cold—and tore through the pines, dodging gravestones.

The four points of light behind him didn't appear to have noticed his exit as they were still on an intersecting trajectory with the mausoleum.

In near total darkness, the disorientation was staggering. He had no idea if he was heading north or south, toward town or away, but he kept running until he reached a stone wall that formed the decrepit border of the cemetery.

Climbing over, he straddled it, taking a moment to catch his breath and glance back the way he'd come.

More lights.

At least a half dozen newbies in addition to the original four, and there were more appearing every second behind those, a veritable army of fireflies emerging in the dark and all moving toward him with a kind of bobbling motion that made him fear the people holding them were running.

Ethan dropped the microchip on the stone wall.

Then he swung his legs over and hopped down on the other side, wincing at the biting pain in his left hamstring. But he ignored it and pushed on into a field of cut grass.

On the far side, playground equipment gleamed and he could see the rain pouring through the illumination of an overhanging streetlamp.

Beyond, in a stand of dark pines—more flashlights, more voices.

Someone shouted back in the cemetery, and though he couldn't tell if this was directed at him, it had the effect of accelerating his pace.

Approaching the swing set and sliding board, it occurred to him where he was, and the burbling of running water above the rainfall and the pounding of his heart confirmed it.

Though he couldn't see it in the dark, on his left lay that grassy riverbank where he'd first come to consciousness in Wayward Pines five days ago.

And the river.

He almost course-corrected to move toward it, but then a light winked on down where he imagined the shore should be.

Ethan streaked past the sliding board, shouldered through a hedge of dripping bushes that nearly ripped the flimsy hospital gown off him, and stumbled out into the street.

The gown hung in tatters around his neck like a shredded cape.

He tore it off, desperately needing oxygen—a full minute of deep inhalations wouldn't be enough—but there was no time to stop and replenish his lungs.

Lights from the cemetery, the river, and the pines on the north end of the park had converged in that open field in a luminescent swarm that moved toward him now as a single entity, accompanied by a jumble of voices drunk with the giddy exuberance of a chase.

A fresh shot of adrenaline spiked Ethan's blood.

His muddy feet hammered the wet pavement as he sprinted naked up the middle of the street, rain sheeting down his face.

Realized that his objective had moved.

Forget reaching the river, he needed to find some place to hide and ride this madness out. Didn't know how many people were chasing him, how many had already seen him, but streaking naked through town was going to get him killed in a hurry.

A deep voice shouted, "There!"

Ethan glanced back, saw three shadows dart out of a large Victorian house, the man in front tearing down the steps, through the front yard, and leaping over the white picket fence with considerable grace while his companions bunched up at the gate, fumbling with the latch.

The hurdler hit the sidewalk midstride and accelerated, dressed all in black, boots pounding the street. He carried a machete whose wet blade glimmered under the glancing beam of his head-lamp, running hard, breathing hard, and a voice in Ethan's head said flatly with the dead calm of a filibustering senator reading a phone book at three in the morning—*That man is fifty yards away, he's armed, and he's going to catch you.*

What are you going to do about it?

Chapter 10

ACCESSED FROM THE attic, it is the highest window in the house.

Teardrop-shaped with an overhanging eave that keeps the glass protected from the rain.

It is late and dark and the hush of rainfall on the tin roof above her head would be a peaceful sound on any other night.

A sound to sleep to.

To dream to.

Her telephone didn't ring with all the others, and for this, she is grateful.

She'd prayed they wouldn't expect her to take part in this, and that confirmation is a small comfort in the midst of this nightmare.

From her vantage point on the third floor, she can see the flashlights appearing across the valley like the lights of a great city coming to life. Hundreds of them. Most distant, nothing more than motes of brilliance in the pouring rain. Others close enough to see individual cones of light sweeping through the mist that is beginning to form in the alleys and depressions.

When he comes into view, her heart stops.

Naked.

Pale.

Running like a ghost up the middle of the street

and pursued by a trio of black-garbed men with machetes.

She's known this was coming, thought she'd prepared herself as much as one can for such a thing, but seeing him in the flesh—his fear, his panic, his despair—she has to bite her lip to stop herself from screaming out to him.

I'm watching his execution.

Ethan passes out of view, moving toward the buildings that line Main Street, and it hits her like a load of double-ought buckshot to the chest—she has seen him for the last time, because she will not go to the house on First Avenue to witness what's left of him, to see the damage inflicted upon her husband, the father of her son.

More people flood up the street en masse, everyone racing toward Main.

Despite the dreary weather, it's a carnival atmosphere, and more and more, she sees costumes, many no doubt prepared in advance.

Though no one ever speaks of the *fête*, she knows there are people who long for the telephones to ring.

For the chance to run amok in the wee hours of the night.

To draw blood.

She and Ben joined the mob last time—as if they'd had a choice—and while they hadn't found their way into the eye of the storm that had actually beaten Bill Evans to death, they'd been caught up on the periphery.

Heard his screams and pleas against the laughter and maniacal taunting of the crowd.

Afterward, the entire town had reveled on Main Street until dawn—liquor flowing, fireworks exploding, dancing, singing, feasting—and while she couldn't help but feel sickened by it all, an undeniable oneness buzzed through the crowd like the air itself had been electrified.

Everyone embracing.

Effervescent.

A night for humanity in all its evil, joy, and madness.

A celebration in hell.

Her five years in Wayward Pines, there'd been only four *fêtes*.

Tonight makes five.

Theresa wipes her face and turns away from the window.

Moves quietly through the empty attic, mindful to keep her footsteps gentle on the creaky hardwood. If she wakes Ben and he sees a *fête* in progress, he'll want to go outside, be a part of it.

She descends the drop-down ladder, folds it up, raises the attic door back into the ceiling.

So strange to be standing on the second floor of this silent house, considering what's happening outside.

She walks down the hallway and stops in the open doorway of Benjamin's room.

He sleeps.

Twelve years old and looking more and more like his father every day.

Watching him, she wonders if, when they finally catch him, Ethan will cry out.

Will she hear him?

And if so, will she be able to stand it?

Sometimes things feel so normal, so *as they always have been,* but then come moments when the buried tension of questions she no longer allows herself to ask threatens to shatter her like ancient crystal.

Soon, there will be music on Main Street, and chances are, it will wake her son.

Ben will want to know what's happening, and there will be no lying to him.

No sugarcoating.

He's too smart for that.

And she respects him far too much.

What will she tell him?

And the harder question . . .

A week from now when she wakes in the middle of the night, alone in her dark bedroom, with no possibility of ever seeing her husband again . . .

What will she tell herself?

Chapter 11

ETHAN RUSHED THROUGH the next intersection, more lights appearing every time he glanced back, but his nearest pursuer—the hurdler—was his immediate concern. The man had broken ahead of his slower compatriots, Ethan thinking he looked familiar—the bald head, the huge, silver-frame glasses—and as the man closed to within thirty feet, Ethan realized who it was: that prick pharmacist he'd tried to buy aspirin from two days prior.

Main Street loomed one block ahead, a disturbing noise bubbling up over the two- and three-story buildings—the ebullient chatter of a gathering crowd.

Under no circumstances could he run naked onto Main Street.

But at his current clip and without altering his trajectory, in another twenty seconds he would do that very thing.

One street stood between Ethan and Main, and it wasn't even a street—just a one-lane alley that slashed behind the row of buildings. It gave him one last boost of rage-infused adrenaline to acknowledge that if he rounded the corner into that alley and came upon anybody, anybody at all, he was done.

Hacked to death by a machete-wielding pharmacist.

Nice way to go.

A one-story garage abutted the street, and he figured the corner of the building, when he turned it, would break the pharmacist's line of sight for about two seconds.

If there wasn't a crowd waiting for him in the alley, it might be enough.

Ethan had been sprinting up the dead center of the street, but now it was time to make his move.

He veered right, cutting across the rain-slicked pavement.

Must not fall.

Crossed a strip of grass, then sidewalk, then grass again, and as he reached the opening of the alley, it occurred to him that he didn't even know what he was going to do.

No time to plan. Just react.

By the proximity of the man's footfalls, he estimated the pharmacist to be six strides back.

Ethan shot into the alley.

Concrete to dirt.

Darker.

Mist tinged with the reek of wet garbage.

He saw no one in the immediate vicinity beyond a pair of flashlights several hundred feet down, meandering his way.

Ethan kicked his feet sideways and parallel, as if skidding to a stop on skis, arresting his forward momentum as he skidded to such an abrupt halt he could feel gravity fighting to flip him end over end.

He righted himself and exploded back the way he'd come, accelerating straight at the corner of the building.

Be there. Be there. Be there.

The collision was tremendous, Ethan's forehead smashing flush into the lower half of the pharmacist's jaw in a bone-fracturing wreck so intense the impact left Ethan out on his feet for half a second.

He snapped back, blood sheeting down his face.

The pharmacist sitting stunned and spitting teeth onto the road.

In the aftermath of the brain-scrambling hit, it took Ethan two seconds to realize that the long, metal object lying on the pavement was the man's machete.

He reached down and lifted it as the man looked up at him, the horror of knowing what was about to happen dragging him back into coherence more effectively than a bucket's worth of smelling salts.

Ethan squeezed his fingers into the indentations in the machete's handle, which had been wrapped in duct tape for improved grip in the rain.

The man raised his arms in a feeble attempt to fend off what could not be fended off.

Ethan feigned a strike and drilled the man in the face with a front kick, his heel thrusting through the wreckage of the man's crushed nose and driving the back of his head into the pavement with a skull-fracturing crunch.

The man groaned and stayed down, but his two friends were closing in—they'd be here in ten seconds—and behind them, a block back, that army of flashlights moved like a herd of cattle up the street, the sound of numerous footfalls on wet pavement getting louder and louder.

Ethan fled back into the alley, relieved to find that those pair of lights he'd seen last time had vanished.

He ran, needing to make the most of this brief window of invisibility.

Twenty steps in, he neared a Dumpster and didn't even hesitate.

Ducked around the side, hit the ground, crawled behind it, wedging himself between the metal and the brick wall of the building it nestled against.

He couldn't hear anything over the thundering of his heart and his doglike panting, sweat and blood pouring down his face into his eyes, freezing, muscles blazing with a lactic acid burn like he'd just hit the wall on a marathon.

Footsteps raced past on the other side of the Dumpster and the sound of them moving away, getting steadily softer, was like music.

The side of Ethan's face rested on the ground, dirt and bits of glass and gravel embedding in his cheek.

Rain drummed on his back and collected all around him in pools that shivered with each new droplet.

He could've lain there all night and long into the following day.

Get your ass up. You can't afford to get stiff.

Ethan placed his palms on the wet gravel and struggled up onto his hands and knees.

He backed out of the space between the Dumpster and the building and crouched for a moment beside the trash bin, listening.

Distant voices.

Distant footsteps.

The commotion on Main.

But nothing sounded dangerously close.

He stood, glanced back toward the opening of the alley, and saw the crowd moving past at a jog, climbing the street toward whatever was happening on Main.

Keeping close to the brick wall, Ethan headed in the opposite direction, into the misty darkness of the alleyway.

Thirty feet down, there was a break in the brick—a wooden door.

He looked back toward the Dumpster, to the street beyond.

Now someone was coming—a beam of light sweeping back and forth across the alley, coupled with the crunch of gravel under footsteps.

Ethan tugged the door open, light from inside

throwing a patch of illumination into the alley that diffused through the mist.

He rushed through and into a bright stairwell, pulled the door closed after him, and turned to flip the dead bolt.

The cylinder had been drilled out like a cavity and filled in with solid metal.

No way to lock it.

Ethan raced up the narrow stairwell, the stress of climbing sending new shoots of pain through the back of his left leg.

As he reached the second-floor landing, the alleyway door burst open.

Ethan glanced back down the stairs at a large man standing in a dripping yellow poncho, flashlight in one hand, a butcher knife Ethan figured he'd liberated from a home cutlery block in the other.

The man's eyes stayed hidden under the shadow of the hood, but his jaw was set and his hands, particularly the one holding the knife, were rock-steady, betraying no evidence of nerves.

Ethan rushed across the landing and up the next set of steps as the stairwell filled with the reverberation of booted footfalls.

On the third-floor landing, Ethan crashed through a doorway.

The corridor stood quiet, empty, dimly lit.

Sconces that resembled lanterns had been mounted to the wall at intervals of twenty feet.

Brass numbers centered on each door.

An apartment building?

Ethan heard the footsteps pounding up the stairwell.

Started down the hallway, trying every doorknob he passed.

Locked.

Locked.

Locked.

Locked.

Knowing any second the stairwell door would break open.

Locked.

Locked.

The seventh door he tried, number nineteen, turned.

He tightened his grip on the machete in the event someone waited on the other side, and nudged the door open with his toes.

A small, dark apartment.

Seemingly empty.

He slipped inside and shut the door at the same moment the stairwell door punched open.

Ethan reached up, hooked the chain into the guard.

Lingering by the entrance, he listened as the door out in the hallway swung closed.

The footsteps slowed considerably.

Knocking against the hardwood floor.

No more rushing.

No frantic pounding.

Ethan could almost picture the man in the yellow poncho moving methodically down the corridor. He had to know that Ethan had slipped into one of the apartments, but he'd have no way of knowing which one.

The footsteps approached—

And now that this one was locked as well . . .

—and stopped on the other side, close enough that when Ethan looked down he could see the light slipping under the door broken in two places.

How the hell had the man known exactly where to stop?

Shit.

Muddy footprints.

One of the foot shadows on the floor disappeared and the hardwood in the corridor creaked from wood pressure.

Ethan staggered back, slipping around the right-hand corner into a kitchenette.

The sound of splintering wood.

The chain snapping.

Light from the corridor poured into the dark apartment.

Yellow Poncho had kicked the door in.

Standing with his back against a humming refrigerator, Ethan could see the silhouette of the man's shadow yawning across the carpeting into the apartment.

The shadow lengthened as the man stepped

over the threshold and moved slowly down the short hallway that opened into a living area.

Several feet back from the kitchen, he stopped.

Ethan could hear his poncho dripping on the carpet, the man's elevated breathing as Ethan tried to suppress his own.

A soft click, and then a beam of light shot into the living area and tracked slowly across the wall where bookshelves surrounded two large windows, presently curtained.

Through them, Ethan could hear the noise down on Main steadily increasing.

The light struck a leather sofa and a coffee table, upon which a mug on a coaster exhaled coils of steam that filled the apartment with the sleepy sweetness of chamomile tea.

The light moved across a framed photograph—an aspen grove in full autumn color, snow-dusted mountains in the backdrop, October sky burning blue above it all—and then swept into the kitchen, passing over the stove, cabinets, coffeemaker, gleaming off the stainless-steel sink on its way toward Ethan.

He ducked, crawled across the linoleum, and crouched in the shadow between the island and the sink.

The man came forward, Ethan watching the light beam strike the refrigerator where he'd been standing five seconds ago.

The footsteps moved on.

In the microwave door above the stove top, Ethan locked on the reflection of the man in the yellow poncho who now stood in the living area, staring toward a doorway in the north wall that opened into a bedroom.

Ethan struggled slowly onto his feet, the noise of the crowd masking the popping of his knees. He stood facing Yellow Poncho's back as the man edged forward with careful purpose toward the bedroom.

Ethan crept around the island and then out of the kitchen.

At the coffee table, he stopped.

Yellow Poncho stood in the threshold of the bedroom, twelve feet away, shining his flashlight into the room.

Ethan tightened his grip on the machete's duct-taped handle and scraped the pad of his thumb over the edge of the long blade.

It could've been sharper. A lot sharper. He'd have to swing hard.

Go. Rush him. Right now while you still have the element of surprise.

He hesitated.

Ethan had caused plenty of suffering and death, but the raw intimacy of violence was diluted from the cockpit of a Black Hawk. Sending laser-guided Hellfires into a target two miles away wasn't in the same wheelhouse as killing a civilian with a machete in close quarters like this.

One was a few steps above a video game. The other—

The man spun around in the doorway and faced Ethan.

Both men started breathing faster.

"Why are you doing this?" Ethan asked.

No response.

He couldn't see anything of the man's face now.

Just his profile, the shadow of the knife in his right hand, and a splash of illumination on his boots, the flashlight aimed at the floor.

Ethan had opened his mouth to repeat the question when the light swung up, blazing straight at his face, into his eyes.

Something clattered to the floor.

Darkness resumed.

Ethan couldn't see anything against the retinal overload, standing blind in a gray darkness without form or detail.

Footsteps were coming, the hardwood floor under the carpet straining with each stride, the man's jeans swishing as he charged.

Ethan staggered back, his vision recovering.

Captured a snapshot of Yellow Poncho three feet away, the butcher knife cocked back and poised for a downward strike.

Ethan swung—a hard, lightning slash.

The blade met no resistance, and the force of the swipe spun him around and off balance, Ethan thinking, *I missed. I'm dead.*

The man moved past him, stumbling awkwardly across the room until he finally caught himself on the bar side of the kitchen island.

Ethan regained his balance, and as he improved his grip on the machete, making certain it was sound, he noticed blood dripping off the end of the blade.

Ethan looked back toward the kitchen.

The man had dropped his knife and was facing Ethan, leaning back against the island, both hands clutching the left side of his neck, which made a hissing sound like compressed air escaping from a tire.

Ethan backpedaled to the bedroom doorway, squatted down, lifted the flashlight off the carpet.

He put the beam on the man in the yellow poncho.

The amount of blood was staggering.

It resembled a red spiderweb on the yellow plastic of the jacket, expanding like a time-lapse of a replicating virus, running off in a dozen separate trickles and pooling on the floor. The blood issued from a six-inch gash across the intersection of the man's shoulder and neck, blood spraying from one end in a fine mist and jetting out from the other in pulses of bright arterial red, the arc of each spurt diminishing as the man's heart rate crashed.

His face was sheet-white, and he stared at Ethan

with no expression at all, just blinking slowly, as if lost in some mesmerizing daydream.

He finally slid off the island and crashed through a bar stool and onto the floor.

In the bedroom closet, Ethan requisitioned a pair of jeans, a long-sleeved T-shirt, and a black hoodie. The shirt and jeans were a few sizes small, but nothing Ethan couldn't manage. The tennis shoes he found were another matter. He could squeeze his feet into them, lace them up, but walking around was agony and guaranteed to produce blisters in no time.

The dead man's boots, while much larger, looked promising.

Ethan tugged them off and kept adding layers of socks until his feet fit snugly inside.

It felt good to be clothed again, even better to be out of the rain in this warm apartment. There was a strong temptation to spend another half hour here, patching up what injuries he could, but he needed to keep moving. If a large group happened to search this floor, there'd be nowhere for him to run.

Ethan grabbed the flashlight, the machete, and went to the sink.

Spent a full minute with his mouth under the faucet, half-crazy with thirst and yet trying not to overload on water.

He opened the fridge.

Strange.

There were glass bottles of milk. Fresh veggies. A carton of eggs. Meat wrapped in butcher paper.

But nothing prepackaged.

He reached in, grabbed a bag of carrots and a small loaf of bread, crammed them down into the side pockets of his jeans.

Noise stopped Ethan as he headed for the door —voices and shouts welling up from Main Street.

He rushed back through the apartment to one of the large windows and moved just enough of the curtain for him to peek outside.

Twenty feet below: bedlam.

The buildings and storefronts glowed and darkened under the ceaseless exchange of firelight and shadow, the source of it all a giant bonfire raging in the middle of the street in spite of the rain, fueled with pine saplings and long strips of siding ripped from houses. Two men carried a wooden bench toward the blaze, Ethan watching as they heaved it onto the pyre to the great delight of the rain-drenched masses who packed the block, the concentration of bodies increasing with proximity to the flames.

The people below looked nothing like the residents he'd encountered prior to this moment.

Most had outfitted themselves in extravagant costumes.

Fake, gaudy jewelry dripped from the wrists and necks of women. Beaded necklaces and pearls and tiaras. Their faces were a-sparkle with glitter and heavily made-up, eyes popping with eyeliner, and all scantily clad despite the cold and the rain, like a throng of reveling prostitutes.

The men looked equally absurd.

One wore a sports coat and no pants.

Another, dark slacks and red suspenders and no shirt with a Santa Claus hat perched atop his head. He pointed a baseball bat to the sky, the weapon stark white and covered with grotesque drawings of monsters that Ethan could barely see from his vantage point.

Standing on a brick planter, head and shoulders above the crowd, an immense figure caught his notice. The monstrous man was dressed in the fur of a brown bear—still pinned with his brass star—and he wore some sort of metal headpiece mounted with antlers, his face streaked with lurid war paint, a shotgun slung over one shoulder, a sheathed sword hanging off the other.

Pope.

The man surveyed the crowd like it was something he owned, the liquid pools of his eyes reflecting the bonfire like a pair of stars.

All he had to do was look up across the street, and in the wealth of firelight, he couldn't fail to miss Ethan peeking down from the third-floor apartment.

He knew he should leave, but Ethan couldn't turn away.

A segment of the crowd beyond Ethan's line of sight erupted in shouts that caught Pope's attention, a big smile expanding across the lawman's face.

From an inner pocket in his bearskin coat, Pope took a clear, unlabeled bottle containing some brown liquid, raised it toward the sky, and said something that ignited the crowd into a frenzy of fist-pumping cheers.

While Pope took a long pull from his bottle, the crowd began to part, a corridor forming down the middle of Main Street, everyone straining to see.

Three figures appeared, moving through the crowd toward the bonfire.

The outer two—men dressed in dark clothes with machetes dangling from shoulder straps—held the person in the middle by her arms.

Beverly.

Ethan felt something dislodge inside him, a molten core of rage metastasizing in the pit of his stomach.

He could see that she didn't have the strength to stand, her feet sliding across the pavement as her captors dragged her along. One of her eyes was closed from what must have been a savage blow, and what he could see of her face was covered in blood.

But she was conscious.

Conscious and terrified, her gaze fixed on

the wet pavement under her feet like she was attempting to shut out everything else.

The two men toted her to within ten yards of the bonfire and then pushed her forward, releasing her.

Pope shouted something as Beverly crumpled to the ground.

The people in her immediate vicinity pressed back, forming a circle of open space around her, twenty feet in diameter.

Through the window, Ethan heard Beverly crying.

She sounded like a wounded animal—something so desperate in her high-pitched keening.

Everywhere, people were elbowing their way through the crowd, trying to reach the outskirts of the circle, the cluster of bodies forming the perimeter becoming tighter and tighter.

Pope tucked the bottle back into his coat and took hold of his shotgun.

He pumped it, aimed it at the sky.

The report echoed between the buildings, rattling the glass in the window frame.

The crowd fell silent.

No one moved.

Ethan could hear the rainfall again.

Beverly struggled to her feet and wiped away a line of blood running down the middle of her face. Even from this third-floor window, Ethan couldn't miss the quaking that had enveloped her, the all-encompassing fear that consumes a person who knows exactly what horrible thing they're about to experience.

Beverly stood teetering in the rain, favoring her left foot.

She turned slowly, hobbling, taking in the surrounding faces, and though Ethan couldn't hear her words, the tone of her voice was unmissable.

Imploring.

Desperation.

Rain and tears and blood streaming down her face.

A full minute elapsed.

Someone shouldered his way through the mass of people and broke out into the circle.

Cheers erupted.

Wild applause.

It was the shirtless man with red suspenders and a Santa hat.

At first, he lingered on the edge as if steeling himself—a boxer in his corner, moments before the bell.

Someone handed him a bottle.

He tilted it back, took a long, reckless swig.

Then he gripped his painted bat and stumbled out into the circle.

Toward Beverly.

He circled her.

She backed away, veering close to the edge of the crowd.

Someone gave her a hard shove out into the middle of the circle, the momentum propelling her straight at the man with the bat.

Ethan didn't see it coming.

Neither did Beverly.

Happened fast, as if the man decided at the last possible second.

A single, fluid motion.

Raised the bat and swung.

The sound of maple striking skull made Ethan instinctively shut his eyes and turn away.

The crowd roared.

When he opened them again, Beverly was on the ground, struggling to crawl.

Ethan felt a surge of bile threatening to surface.

The man in the Santa hat dropped the bat on the pavement and strutted off into the crowd.

The bat rolled across the road toward Beverly.

She reached for it, her fingers inches away.

A woman wearing a black bikini, black heels, a black crown, and black angel wings stepped into the circle.

She preened.

The crowd cheered.

The woman strolled across to where Beverly lay straining for the bat.

She squatted down, flashed Beverly a bright, toothy smile, and lifted the weapon, gripping it in both hands and raising it above her head like the battle-ax of some demon queen.

No, no, no, no, no . . .

She smashed it into the dead center of Beverly's back.

Screams of joy filled the street as Beverly writhed on the ground.

What he'd have given to be hovering in a Black Hawk two hundred feet above Main in control of a GAU-19 Gatling, burning two thousand rounds per minute into the crowd, cutting these mother-fuckers in half.

Ethan turned away from the window, lifted the coffee table with both hands, and slammed it into the wall, wood splintering, glass shattering.

The effort only whetted his rage.

He craved violence, a small voice inside him suggesting he go down there into the crowd with the machete right now and hack away. Yes, they would eventually overpower him, but God there was nothing he wanted more than to go slashing through the masses, a one-man massacre.

But then you'll die.

Never see your family again.

Never know what any of this was all about.

Ethan returned to the window.

Beverly lay unmoving on the street, a lake of blood widening around her head.

The circle was breaking down and closing in.

Then all at once, the mob descended upon her.

It was a betrayal to leave, but he couldn't bear to stand there and watch, and there wasn't a damn thing he could do to stop it—five hundred people versus one.

There's nothing you can do for her. She's gone. Now go while you still can.

As Ethan stormed back toward the door, he heard Beverly cry out, the sound of her pain, her utter hopelessness, bringing tears to his eyes.

Calm down.

There could be people outside this door waiting for you.

Must be vigilant.

Ethan stepped out into the hallway.

Empty.

He shut the apartment door.

The commotion on Main became an indistinct murmur.

He wiped his eyes and headed back the way he'd come, up the hallway and then through the door to the stairwell.

On the third-floor landing, he hesitated, listening, staring down through the railing.

No sound.

No movement.

Eerily still.

He descended.

At the bottom, he cracked open the door just wide enough so he could squeeze through.

A sliver of light escaped into the alley.

Ethan stepped down into a puddle and closed the door.

It rained harder than before.

For thirty seconds, he didn't move, waiting for his eyes to readjust to the darkness.

Then, pulling the hood over his head, he moved south, up the middle of the alley.

In the distance, rain poured through the spherical illumination of a streetlamp, but otherwise, the darkness between the buildings was so complete Ethan couldn't see his feet beneath him.

The crowd exploded with its loudest roar yet.

He thought of Beverly, had to stop himself from imagining what was happening to her, his grip tightening around the machete, molars grinding together.

Footsteps up ahead brought Ethan to a sudden halt.

He stood thirty feet back from where the alley intersected the next street, confident of his invisibility in the shadows.

A man in a dark slicker walked into view, heading west from Main.

He stopped under the streetlamp and stared into the alley.

He held a hatchet and a flashlight.

Ethan could hear the rain pattering on his jacket.

The man crossed the street and came into the alley.

Turned his flashlight on, shined the light at Ethan.

"Who's there?"

Ethan could see his own breath steaming in the cold.

"It's me," Ethan said, starting toward him. "Have you seen him?"

"Me who?"

The light was still in Ethan's face, and he hoped the man could see him smiling, hoped he grasped the madness that was coming his way.

The man's eyes went wide as Ethan drew close enough for him to see bruises and blood streaks and stitches and the general ruin of his face, but his reaction—cocking the hatchet back for a strike—came a half second late.

Ethan swung the blade parallel to the ground with a single-handed grip that generated enough force to split him open across the middle.

The man's legs buckled, his knees hit the ground, and Ethan finished him with three devastating slashes.

He began to run, buzzing with the rush of the kill like he'd done a hit of speed.

Ethan streaked out of the alley and across Seventh.

Right—a half dozen points of light two blocks down moving up the street toward the center of town.

Left—fifty or more people flooding around the corner from Main, flashlights winking on as they encountered the darkness of the side street.

Ethan accelerated, blasting into the next alley, no lights ahead, but over his own panting, he could hear multiple footsteps falling in behind his.

He glanced back—a wall of light thundering down the alley.

People shouting.

Up ahead, Eighth Street fast approaching.

He needed a course change, was already calculating the possibilities, but he couldn't pull the trigger until he saw what lay ahead.

Ethan exploded onto Eighth.

Left—no one.

Right—a single light two blocks away.

Ethan veered right, moving at a dead run as he angled across the street.

Leaped over the curb and hit the opposite sidewalk, nearly tripping over a raised lip of concrete, but he somehow managed to stay afoot.

Twenty yards carried him to the next block west of Main, and he looked back two seconds before he made the turn, saw the first group of lights emerging out of the alley.

If he was lucky, they hadn't seen him.

He ripped around the corner.

Blessed darkness.

Kept to the sidewalk, hauling ass under the pitch-black shade of the pines.

The next street stood empty as well, and a quick glance over his shoulder confirmed only a handful of pursuing lights, still a good twenty seconds back if he had to guess.

Ethan dropped another block west and then barreled south.

The street terminated.

He'd come to the edge of town.

Stopped in the middle of the road, bent over with his hands on his knees, gasping for air.

People were coming, both behind him and now from the west.

Figured he could run two blocks uphill back to Main, but that seemed unwise.

Get moving. You're squandering your cushion of distance.

Straight on, a Victorian mansion backed up against the surrounding forest.

Yes.

His legs burned as he pushed on, crossing the street, bolting alongside the house.

Three strides before he reached the pines, the voice of a child shouted, "He's going into the woods!"

Ethan looked back.

Twenty or thirty people swung around the corner of the mansion, flashlights blazing, running toward him as one, and for a moment, Ethan wondered why their proportions seemed all wrong.

Legs too short, heads too big, lights held much closer to the ground.

Children.

It's because they're all children.

He rushed into the trees, gulping air perfumed with the bittersweet fragrance of wet pine.

It had been hard enough to see in town, but inside the forest, it was impossible.

He had to flick on the flashlight, let its wobbly beam steer him between trees, over rotten logs, saplings and low-hanging branches whipping at his face.

The children entered the wood on his heels, footsteps crushing wet leaves, snapping fallen branches. He had a vague idea of where the river might be, thinking if he kept moving right, he couldn't miss it, but already he felt disoriented, his sense of direction unraveling like a poorly tied knot.

A girl screamed, "I see him!"

Ethan glanced back, just a quick turn of the head, but his timing couldn't have been worse—he crossed through a patch of deadfall, his feet entangling in a mass of twisted branches and roots that slammed him to the ground, stripping the flashlight and machete from his hands.

Footsteps all around him.

Approaching from every side.

Ethan struggling to pick himself up, but a vine had ensnared his right ankle, and it took him five seconds to rip free.

The flashlight had gone dark when he'd fallen,

and he couldn't see it or the machete or anything. He ran his hands across the ground, desperate to find them, but all he grasped were roots and vines.

He clambered to his feet, blindly fighting his way through the deadfall as the lights and the voices closed in.

Without a flashlight, he was hamstrung.

Reduced to jogging with hands outstretched—his only defense against plowing into a tree.

Frantic beams of light crisscrossed in front of him, giving fleeting glimpses of the terrain ahead—a pine forest choking to death on underbrush, long overdue for a cleansing fire.

Children's laughter—carefree, giddy, maniacal—filled the woods.

A nightmare version of some game from his youth.

Ethan stumbled out into what he figured for a field or meadow—not that he could see a damn thing, but the rain now hammered him with greater intensity, as if he were no longer protected under the forest's umbrella.

Up ahead, he thought he heard the rush of the river, but then lost it to the sound of hard breathing coming up behind him.

Something crashed into his back—not a particularly jarring blow, but enough to unbalance him for the next.

And the next . . .

And the next . . .

And the next . . .

And the next and then Ethan hit the ground, face jammed in mud, everything drowned out by the laughter of the children, a full-body assault coming from every side, every angle—superficial punches that didn't stand a chance of hurting him, the sting of shallow cuts, the occasional and far more disconcerting heft of blunt objects striking his head, and all of it, with every passing second, increasing in frequency, like he was being attacked by a school of piranhas.

Something stabbed into his side.

He cried out.

They mocked him.

Another stab—oceanic pain.

His face flushed with rage, and he jerked his left arm out of someone's grasp, and then his right.

Got his palms on the ground.

Pushed himself up.

Something hard—a rock or a log—thudded into the back of his head hard enough to jog his fillings.

His arms gave out.

Face-first back in the mud.

More laughter.

Someone said, "Hit him in the head!"

But he pushed up again, screaming this time, and it must have taken the children by surprise, because for a split second the blows stopped coming.

It was all the time he needed.

Ethan got his feet underneath him and forced himself up, took a swing at the first face he saw— a tall boy of twelve or thirteen—and knocked him out cold.

"Get back," he seethed.

There was enough light that for the first time he could actually see what he was dealing with— two dozen children from seven to fifteen years of age encircled him, most holding flashlights and a variety of makeshift weapons—sticks, rocks, steak knives, one with a broom handle with the mop end broken off leaving a jagged splinter of wood.

They looked as if they'd dressed up for Halloween—a ragtag assembly of homemade costumes pieced together from their parents' wardrobes.

Ethan was almost grateful he'd lost the machete, because he would've hacked these little shits into pieces.

There was an opening off to Ethan's left—a weak link in the circle he might have charged through over two children who stood no taller than his waist.

But then what?

They'd give chase, run him to death in these woods like an injured deer.

Turning slowly, he locked eyes with the most intimidating of the bunch, a post-pubescent, blond-haired boy armed with a tube sock stretched to the max, its pocket weighted with an ominous-looking sphere—perhaps a baseball or a globe of solid glass. The teen wore a suit that must have belonged to his father—several sizes too large, the sleeves hanging down to his fingertips.

Ethan roared, approaching the boy with his right arm cocked back, and he would've hit him but the kid backpedaled, tripped, fell, and then ran off into the woods the moment he regained his feet, shouting in full voice that they'd found him.

Half the children, upon seeing their leader turn tail and flee, followed suit.

Those who didn't, Ethan charged, feeling a bit like an elk trying to scatter a pack of predatory coyotes, but eventually he chased off all but one, the children screaming as they vanished into the pines as if the devil was after them.

The boy who stayed behind watched Ethan through the rain.

He might have been the youngest of the bunch —seven, eight at most.

He'd dressed up like a cowboy—red-and-white hat, boots, string tie, and a Western-style button-down.

He held a flashlight and a rock and stood there with no expression at all.

"Aren't you afraid of me?" Ethan asked.

The boy shook his head, water dripping off the brim of his hat. He looked up at Ethan, and as the flashlight beam illuminated the freckles on his face, Ethan could see that he'd lied. He was afraid, his bottom lip trembling uncontrollably. It was the bravest face the boy could muster, and Ethan couldn't help but admire him, wondering what had prompted him to make this stand.

"You should quit running, Mr. Burke."

"How do you know my name?"

"You could have a beautiful life here, and you don't even see it."

"What is this place?"

"Just a town," the boy said.

Adult voices rang out, a new squadron of flashlights twinkling in the pines like emerging stars.

"Where's your home?" Ethan asked.

The boy tilted his head, puzzled at the question.

"What do you mean?"

"Where'd you live before Wayward Pines?"

"I've always lived here."

"You've never left this town?" Ethan asked.

"You can't leave," the boy said.

"Why?"

"You just can't."

"I don't accept that."

"That's why you're going to die." The boy suddenly screamed, "He's over here! Hurry!"

Lights broke out of the pines into the meadow.

Ethan ran, crashing into the forest on the other side, not even bothering to shield his face or glance back at his pursuers, thrashing through the darkness, losing all sense of time and direction, struggling to keep his head against the chord of absolute panic that threatened to drop him to his knees, curl him up in the fetal position, and finally break his mind.

Because of the fear.

Because of the pain.

Because none of this made a goddamned inkling of sense.

It wasn't the sound of the river that stopped him but the smell.

A sudden sweetness in the air.

The terrain dropped away and he scrambled down a muddy bank into frigid, raging water, the river pouring into his boots like liquid steel.

Despite the freezing shock of it, he refused to falter, just kept staggering in, away from the bank, deeper and deeper into the current.

The water reached his waist, Ethan gasping as it chilled him to the core, the current fierce, desperate to drag him downstream.

He took slow, careful steps, the stones on the bed shifting under his weight and tumbling slowly downriver.

Between each step, he braced himself, leaning into the force of the water.

Midway across, it rose to his chest.

The current swept him off his feet.

Driving Ethan downstream.

In the near darkness, he had no idea what boulders jutted out of the channel, just knew that slamming into one could kill him.

He struggled across the current using a hard, deliberate sidestroke.

His arms worked fine, but with his waterlogged boots he couldn't kick with any efficiency or power.

Their weight pulled him under more than they propelled him.

After a frenzied minute, his muscles on the brink of mutiny, he felt the soles of his boots graze the bottom.

Standing, he leaned into the current, the water level dropping back to his waist.

A dozen more steps brought it down to his knees, and then he jogged the rest of the way out of the river, collapsing on the bank.

Rolled onto his side, breathless, spent, shivering.

He stared back across the channel.

Everywhere, new beams of light appeared.

He could hear people shouting, thought it was possible they were calling his name, but from this distance, the crushing noise of the white-water destroyed any chance of hearing them distinctly.

Ethan wanted to move, knew he had to, but he couldn't make himself scramble back onto his feet. Just needed another minute to lie there and breathe.

There were more lights on the opposite shore now than he could count, the highest concentration thirty yards upriver at his point of entry, but more and more, people seemed to be venturing north and south of where he'd gone in, light beams sweeping out over the current in a dozen places.

He rolled over onto his knees.

Hands shaking with cold like he'd been afflicted with palsy.

He began to crawl, fingers groping through wet sand.

Just that minute of lying motionless had stiffened his joints.

When he came to the next large rock, he reached up, got a handhold, and pulled himself onto his feet.

His boots sloshed with water.

There must have been a hundred people across the river, and still more lights appearing on the bank every second. Most beams reached only the midpoint, but a handful carried the potency to shoot all the way across to Ethan's side, their compact tubes of light clearly visible with the rain falling through them.

Ethan scrambled away from the water, hoping to put more distance between himself and the lights, but after ten feet, he reached a sheer wall of rock.

He moved alongside it as the voices of several hundred people overpowered the crush of white-water.

A light struck the cliff ten feet ahead.

Ethan ducked behind a boulder and peeked around the side as the beam traversed the cliff behind him.

A waterfall of light poured down from the shore into the current. From where Ethan crouched, he saw a few people wading knee-deep in the river, searching, but no one was attempting to swim across.

He'd started to step out from behind the boulder when a voice, amplified through a megaphone, blared across the river.

"Ethan, come back to us, and all will be forgiven."

He'd have known it anywhere—the deep, guttural boom of Sheriff Pope's voice, ricocheting off the cliffs, back into the pine forest behind the crowd.

"You don't know what you're doing."

Actually, I know exactly what I'm doing.

With no lights striking the rock anywhere in his general vicinity, Ethan struggled back onto his feet, stumbling south beside the cliff.

"If you come back, we won't hurt you."

Yeah. Be right over.

"You have my word on that."

Ethan wished he had a bullhorn of his own.

Other voices were shouting his name across the river.

"Ethan, please!"

"You don't understand what you're doing!"

"Come back!"

Pope continued to call out to him as well, but Ethan pushed on into pitch-black rain.

The farther he moved away from the crowd, the more impossible it became to see.

Ethan limping now in slow, shuffling steps, his only directional anchor the noise of the river on his left.

Behind—fading voices, shrinking points of light.

His body had cranked out the last available adrenaline, and he could feel a world-class crash coming on.

Total system shutdown.

But he couldn't stop. Not yet.

The urge to curl up in the sand beside the river and sleep was almost overpowering, but those people might decide to cross.

They had lights and weapons and numbers.

He had nothing.

Too great a risk.

And so, with what little gas he had remaining in his reserve tank, he went on.

Chapter 12

ETHAN HAD NO way of knowing how long he'd been walking alone in darkness.

An hour.

Maybe two.

Maybe less.

His pace was such that he couldn't have covered more than a mile. If nothing else, he felt certain of this. Every few minutes, he made himself stop and glance downstream, searching for oncoming lights, listening for footsteps crackling over rocks.

But each time he looked back, it was always the same—complete darkness—and if someone was following him, the roar of the river effectively masked all other sounds.

The rain slowed to a drizzle and then an intermittent sprinkle and then it stopped altogether.

Ethan still trudged along, traveling solely by feel, his hands grasping invisible boulders, his feet taking the smallest possible steps so that when they inevitably collided with an impediment, Ethan's forward momentum didn't throw him to the ground.

• • •

And then he could see.

One moment, darkness.

The next—a bulging, gibbous moon, its light shining down through a break in the clouds, the surfaces of every wet rock gleaming like they had been lacquered.

Ethan sat down on a flat-topped boulder, his legs trembling, at the end of endurance.

The width of the river had narrowed by almost half, but the current was rougher, blasting down through a rock garden in a furious spray of white-water.

Great pines—seventy or eighty feet tall—towered over the riverbank on the other side.

He suddenly realized how thirsty he was.

Falling to his knees, he crawled to the edge of the river and dipped his face into a small pool.

The water tasted deliciously pure and sweet, but bitterly cold.

Between sips, he glanced downstream.

Aside from the madness of the water, nothing moved on either shore.

Ethan wanted to sleep, could've lain here on the rocks and drifted off in seconds, but he knew that would be foolish.

Must find shelter before I lose the light of the moon.

Before I lose the ability to walk.

Already, clouds had begun to roll back in front of the moon.

He forced himself to stand.

A river crossing here, particularly in his weakened state, would be fatal. He'd have to seek out shelter on this side of the river, but that was going to be a challenge. On the other side, an old pine forest swept up a mountainside for several thousand feet into roiling clouds. In such a forest, he felt confident he'd have been able to find someplace to hole up for the night, even if nothing more than covering himself under a latticework of downed limbs. You lay enough of them on top of you and they'd provide a shelter from the rain, maybe even trap enough body heat to create an oasis of warmth.

But that wasn't going to happen.

On Ethan's side of the river, the bank climbed steeply for forty feet to the base of that same red-rock cliff that encircled Wayward Pines.

And above that—ledges upon ledges ascending into darkness.

He was in no condition for a climb.

Ethan staggered on.

Water sloshing in his stomach.

He could feel his feet—swollen and throbbing in his boots. Knew he should've stopped to empty the water out of them an hour ago, but he'd been concerned that if he sat down, he wouldn't have the strength to relace them and continue on.

The going was getting more difficult on this side, with little in the way of level ground, all of it rocky and steeply sloping.

He passed into a grove of soaring pines.

The rocky ground gave way to soft, moist earth covered in a cushion of dead pine needles, Ethan thinking, *Worse comes to worst, I'll sleep here*. Wasn't ideal—too close to the river, no branches to cover himself with, and anyone tracking him couldn't help but find him. But at least he'd have some protection under the canopies of these ancient pines.

He took one last look around, having already decided that if he saw nothing of interest, this would be home for the night.

Ethan glanced up the slope that led to the base of the cliff.

He thought he saw a patch of blackness up there.

Didn't think, didn't debate, just climbed.

Scrambling on all fours up through the pines and then out of them onto a field of shattered rock.

Steeper and steeper.

He was panting again, sweat pouring down his face, his eyes stinging with it.

Near the cliff, the rock became looser and finer, his feet sliding with every step like he was climbing a sand dune.

He reached the cliff.

The darkness setting back in, all but a cuticle of the moon shrouded in clouds, and the air growing heavy with the smell of returning rain.

There it was—that patch of black he'd spotted from the river was a recess in the cliff. It extended back for five or six feet, the interior smooth and dry, protected from the elements.

Ethan climbed up onto the ledge and crawled inside.

The back wall had a natural slope, and he leaned against it, the darkening world framed by the walls of the little alcove. He couldn't see the river from his vantage point, the sound of it vastly diminished to something like a loud whisper.

As the moonlight died, the pine forest on the other side of the river dimmed steadily away, leaving Ethan once more in absolute darkness.

It began to rain.

He sat up, and with trembling fingers, tried to unlace the boots he'd taken from the man he'd killed in the apartment. Took him several minutes to finally unravel the knot and pull off the boots. Dumped at least a pint of water out of each and then peeled off the layers of socks and wrung them out and laid them on the rock to dry.

His clothes were sopping wet.

He took off the hoodie, the T-shirt, the jeans, even his briefs. Spent ten minutes sitting naked in the alcove, twisting water out of the clothes until they were only damp.

He draped the hoodie over his chest, the long-sleeved T over his legs, and folded the jeans into a pillow. Lying against the back wall of the cave, he turned over onto his side and shut his eyes.

Never in his life had he been so cold.

At first, he feared it would keep him from sleep, his body shivering so violently in a failing effort to warm itself that he had to grasp the sleeves of the hoodie so he didn't shake it off.

But as cold as he was, he was even more exhausted.

Within five minutes, sleep won out.

Chapter 13

ETHAN'S RIGHT ANKLE is shackled and chained to an eyebolt in the floor.

He sits at a ramshackle desk that holds three objects . . .

A blank sheet of A4 paper.

A black ballpoint pen.

And an hourglass whose black grains of sand are cascading from one bulb into another.

Aashif has advised Ethan that when the sand runs out, he will return, and if at that time what Ethan has written on the paper doesn't delight him, Ethan will die by lingchi.

But Ethan knows that even if he had

specific, high-clearance knowledge of a major upcoming offensive, wrote down dates, locations, targets, details of the anticipated ground strike and air support, it wouldn't be enough.

Nothing will ever be enough, because no matter what he writes, he will die and die horribly.

All he knows of Aashif is his voice and those brown, evil eyes in which he senses not a desire to learn information but to inflict pain.

The guise of interrogation is merely foreplay.

Something to get Aashif hard and wet.

He is a sadist. Probably al-Qaida.

Somehow, Ethan didn't allow that full realization to set in as he hung by his wrists in the torture room, but sitting here alone at the desk in the quiet, it hits him full force.

No matter what he writes, in a little under an hour, his life will become infinitely worse.

There is a single window in the room, but it has been boarded over with two-by-sixes.

Through tiny cracks between the panels of wood, brilliant strings of Iraqi sunlight tear through.

The heat is scalding, sweat streaming out of every pore.

The hyperrealness of the moment becomes unbearable, Ethan overwhelmed with sensory input.

—A dog barking outside.

—The distant laughter of children.

—Miles away, the eerie, cicada-like clicking of a gunfight.

—A fly buzzing at his left ear.

—The scent of Masgouf roasting nearby.

—Somewhere in the bowels of this compound, a man screaming.

No one knows I'm here. At least no one who can help me.

His thoughts veer toward Theresa— pregnant back home—but the onslaught of emotion and homesickness is more than he can bear in light of what lies ahead. The temptation to replay their last conversation— a VoIP call at the MWR—is powerful, but it would break him.

Cannot go there. Not yet. In my final moments maybe.

Ethan lifts the pen.

Just need something to occupy my mind. Cannot sit here and dwell on what's coming.

Because that's what he wants.

That's all this is about.

Shot out of dreams of the war.

For a full minute, he had no idea where he was, simultaneously shivering and burning with fever.

Ethan sat up, reaching out in the darkness around him, and as his fingers grazed the rocky walls of the alcove, his internal GPS updated and the horror that had become his life came rushing back.

He'd thrown his clothes off in his sleep, and they lay scattered on the stone beside him, cold and damp. He spread them out so they'd have a better chance at drying, and then scooted forward until he perched on the edge of the alcove.

The rain had stopped.

The night sky hemorrhaging starlight.

He'd never had the slightest interest in astronomy, but he found himself searching for familiar constellations, wondering if the stars he saw shone from their proper stations.

Is this the night sky I've always seen?

Fifty feet below him, the river sang.

He stared downslope toward the water, and when he saw it, his blood froze.

Ethan's first inclination was to scramble back into the recess, but he fought against the urge, fearing any sudden movement would draw attention.

Son of a bitch, they followed me.

Crossed the river after all.

They were down in those giant pines by the river and so well hidden in shadow that he couldn't gauge their number.

At a sloth's pace, inch by inch, Ethan withdrew into the recess, lowering himself until his chest was flattened against the freezing rock, now just peeking out over the lip of the alcove.

They vanished into shadow, and for a moment, aside from the river, the world stood absolutely still, Ethan beginning to wonder if he'd actually seen anything at all. Considering what he'd been through in the last five days, rote hallucinations would've been a welcome return to sanity.

Thirty seconds later, they emerged out of the shadow of the pines, onto the crushed rock at the base of the slope.

What the hell?

There was only one, and though it was the size of a man, it didn't move like a man—traveling across the rock on all fours, hairless and pale under the stars.

A metal taste—by-product of fear—coated Ethan's mouth as it struck him that its proportions were all wrong, arms seemingly twice their normal length.

The thing raised its head, and even from this distance, Ethan could see its oversized nose pointed toward the sky.

Smelling.

Ethan wriggled himself away from the opening and as far back into the alcove as he could get, where he huddled with his arms around his legs, shivering and straining to listen for the sound of approaching footsteps or shifting rocks.

But all he could hear was the purr of the river, and the next time he chanced a look outside, whatever he'd seen—or thought he'd seen—was gone.

In the few hours of darkness remaining, sleep eluded him.

He was too cold.

In too much pain.

Too terrorized by everything he'd experienced to venture back into dreams.

He lay on the rock, overwhelmed with one desire. One need.

Theresa.

Back home, he'd often wake in the middle of the night to feel her arm thrown over him, her body contoured to his. Even on the hardest nights. Nights he'd come home late. Nights they fought. Nights he'd betrayed her. She brought so much more to the table than he ever had. She loved at light-speed. No hesitation. No regrets. No conditions. No reservations. While he hoarded his chips and held a part of himself back, she went all in. Every time.

There were moments when you saw the people you loved for who they really were, separate from the baggage of projection and shared histories. When you saw them with fresh eyes, as a stranger might, and caught the feeling of the first time you loved them. Before the tears and the armor chinks. When there was still the possibility of perfection.

He had never had a clearer picture of his wife, had never loved her more—not even in the beginning—than in this moment, in this cold, dark place, as he imagined her holding him.

He watched the stars go dark as the sun breathed fire into the sky, and when it finally cleared the ridge on the far side of the river, he bathed in the rays of gorgeous warmth streaming into his alcove and toasting the frozen stone.

In the new light, he could finally see the damage he'd sustained fleeing Wayward Pines.

Bruises, bull's-eyed with blackish-yellow hematomas, covered his arms and legs.

Puncture wounds from Nurse Pam's needle stabs specked his left shoulder and right side.

He unwound the duct tape from his left leg, uncovering the place along the back of his thigh where Beverly had dug out the microchip. The pressure of the wrap had effectively stopped the bleeding, but the skin around the incision was inflamed. It would need antibiotics and a good stitch job to stave off infection.

He ran his hands along his face, thinking how it didn't feel like anything that belonged to him. The skin was swollen, split in places, and his nose, broken twice in the last twenty-four hours, felt excruciatingly tender. His cheeks were rippled with shallow cuts from branches whipping his face as he'd sprinted through the forest, and a lump had risen on the back of his head, courtesy of one of those rock-wielding children.

Nothing, however, rivaled the blinding ache of his leg muscles, which he'd pushed far beyond their breaking point.

He wondered if he even had the strength to walk.

By midmorning, with his clothes sufficiently dry, Ethan dressed, laced up his still-damp boots, and lowered himself over the alcove's ledge, down to the base of the cliff.

The descent to the river gave him a brutal taste of what the rest of the day held in store, and by the time he reached the bank, his muscles screamed.

No choice but to rest, closing his eyes and letting the sunlight pour onto his face like warm water. At this elevation, it was wonderfully concentrated.

There was the smell of the dried pine needles baking in the sun.

The sweet cold water.

The bright sound of the river tumbling down through the canyon.

The clatter of stones shifting under the current.

The piercing blue of the sky.

To be warm again lifted his spirits, and to be in the wilderness, despite everything, spoke to something buried deep in the pit of his soul.

Last night, he'd been too tired to do anything but lie motionless on the stone.

Now, his hunger returned.

He fished the carrots and squashed bread loaf out of his pockets.

Back on his feet, he scavenged until he found a pine branch in the nearby grove and broke off one end so that its length suited him for a walking stick. Spent several minutes stretching, trying to work the debilitating soreness out of his muscles, but it was a losing battle.

He finally struck off up the canyon at a pace he thought he could maintain, but after ten minutes, the trauma of yesterday's exertion forced him to slow down.

A half mile felt like five.

With every step, he was relying more and more on his walking stick for support, clinging to it like a lifeline, like his only decent leg.

By early afternoon, the nature of the canyon had begun to change, the river narrowing until it could only be called a stream, pines shrinking, growing fewer and farther between, and those he encountered were stunted and gnarled, dwarfed victims of punishing winters.

He was having to stop frequently, now resting more than he was walking, and constantly out of breath, his lungs burning with oxygen deprivation the higher he climbed.

Near dusk, he lay sprawled across a lichen-covered rock beside what was left of the river—a six-foot-wide, fast-moving current that babbled over a bed of colorful stones.

It had been four or five hours since he'd left the alcove, and already the sun was sliding behind the canyon wall on the other side of the stream.

When it disappeared, the temperature plummeted.

He lay there watching the color drain from the sky, curled up against the coming chill, and the grim realization setting in that he wasn't going to be getting back up.

Turning over onto his side, he tugged the hood over his face.

Shut his eyes.

He was cold, but his clothes were dry, and he was trying to sort through a swarm of thoughts and competing emotions, the exhaustion pushing him toward the edge of delirium, and then suddenly he felt the sun beating down on his hood.

He opened his eyes, sat up.

He was still on that rock beside the stream, only now it was morning, the sun just peeking over the canyon wall at his back.

I slept all night.

He dragged himself over to the stream and drank, the water so cold it made his head ache.

He had a carrot and a few bites of bread, and then struggled onto his feet and took a leak. He felt surprisingly better, the pain in his legs less all-consuming. Almost manageable.

He grabbed his walking stick.

• • •

The canyon walls closed in and the stream dwindled into a trickle before finally disappearing altogether into the spring from which it sourced.

In the absence of running water, the silence was blaring.

Nothing but the clink of rocks under his boots.

The lonely croak of a bird passing overhead.

His own panting.

The walls on either side of him were becoming steeper, and there were no more trees or even shrubs.

Just shattered rock and lichen and sky.

By midday, Ethan had abandoned his walking stick, reduced now to moving on all fours over the steepest terrain yet. As he worked his way around a bend in the canyon, a new sound crept in over the constant noise of shifting rocks. He leaned against a boulder the size of a compact car, trying to hone in on the noise over his own ragged breathing.

There it was.

Man-made.

Steady.

A low-decibel hum.

Curiosity pulled him forward, Ethan climbing quickly until he'd cleared the corner, the hum becoming more prominent with every step, his anticipation spiking.

When he finally saw it, a stab of exhilaration coursed through him.

The canyon continued its steep ascent for another mile or two, the cliff walls topped with jagged spires and serrated ridges, an unforgiving cruelty to the landscape that looked almost alien.

Fifty feet upslope, Ethan stared straight at the source of the hum—a twenty-foot-high fence crowned with coils of razor wire that spanned sixty feet across the breadth of the canyon at its most tapered point. Signage on the fence advised:

HIGH VOLTAGE
RISK OF DEATH

and

RETURN TO WAYWARD PINES
BEYOND THIS POINT YOU WILL DIE

Ethan stopped five feet from the barricade and made a thorough inspection—the fence was constructed of square panels of wire, the side of each square approximately four inches long. In proximity, the hum was even more ominous, giving the fence an authentic, not-to-be-fucked-with vibe.

Ethan caught the scent of rot in the vicinity, and it took him only a moment to spot the origin. A large rodent—probably a marmot—had made the mistake of trying to crawl through one of the squares adjacent to the ground. Looked like it had been microwaved between the wires for eight hours. Charred pitch black. Some poor bird, apparently thinking it had stumbled upon a hassle-free meal, had erred in judgment, attempted to help itself to the critter's remains, and suffered the same fate.

Ethan glanced up at the canyon walls.

They were sheer, but the handholds, particularly on the right side, looked feasible for someone who was both motivated and had the nerves to handle a little exposure.

Ethan trucked over to the wall and began to climb.

It wasn't the best rock, and some of the holds felt rotten in his grip, but they were plentiful and spaced closely enough that he didn't have to put his weight on any one for more than several seconds.

Soon, he was twenty-five feet off the ground, a weightless, tingling sensation in his gut as the electrified razor wire hummed just several feet beneath the soles of his boots.

He traversed a ledge on solid rock, carefully sidestepping as he crossed to the forbidden side of the fence. The height rattled him, but even more, the reality of what he'd just done—this illicit boundary crossing.

A nagging premonition in the back of his mind

whispered he'd just willingly placed himself in terrible danger.

Ethan safely reached the canyon floor and went on, the hum of the electrified fence growing softer as his system kicked into an intensified and disconcerting state of alertness. Same thing had happened to him in Iraq—a heightened level of sensory intake always seemed to hit him in the ramp-up to missions that ultimately went to shit. His palms would start sweating, his pulse rate would accelerate, his sense of hearing, smell, taste, everything ratcheted into overdrive. He'd never told anyone, but when he lost the Black Hawk in Fallujah, he'd known the RPG was coming five seconds before it exploded.

It was lonely country up here beyond the fence, the rock all fractured and lightning-blasted.

Empty sky.

The absence of clouds only underscoring the mood of absolute desolation.

After his time in Wayward Pines, it felt surreal to be this alone again, so far removed from other people. But in the back of his mind, a new worry had begun to eat at him. The canyon appeared to climb another thousand feet to a high, wind-ripped ridge. If his strength held, he might reach it by dusk. Spend another long, cold night trying to sleep on shattered rock. But then what? He would soon be out of food, and though water still bloated his stomach from the last drink he'd taken before the stream vanished, the exertion he was putting his body through would bleed him dry again in no time.

But even more than the looming threat of hunger and thirst, he feared what lay beyond that distant ridge at the top of the drainage.

Miles and miles of wilderness, if he had to guess, and though he still retained a modicum of survival training from his military days, when it came down to it, he was beat to shit and tired as hell. The prospect of walking out of these mountains and back into civilization struck him as beyond daunting.

And yet, what choice did he have?

Return to Wayward Pines?

He'd rather freeze to death alone out here than ever set foot in that place again.

Ethan made his way through a section of the canyon clogged with massive boulders, carefully hopping from one to the next. He could hear water running underneath him again, but the stream was invisible, unreachable, hidden down in the black space beneath the dogpile of boulders.

High on the left-hand wall of the canyon, something threw a sharp glint of sunlight.

Ethan stopped and cupped his hand over his eyes and squinted toward the blinding glimmer. From where he stood in the belly of the canyon, all he could see was a square, metal surface a good ways up the wall, its proportions too perfect, too exact, to be anything but man-made.

He jumped to the next boulder, now moving with greater speed, greater intensity, and constantly glancing up at the wall as he went along, but the nature of that reflective surface remained elusive.

On ahead, the canyon looked more reasonable, the boulders downsized into traversable terrain.

He was considering whether he could make the climb to that piece of metal when the crackle of falling rock disrupted his thoughts.

For a terrifying instant, Ethan imagined a landslide heading his way, a thousand tons of rock raining down off the wall, crushing him to death.

But the sound had originated behind him, not above, Ethan turning, glancing back the way he'd come, figuring it was just a boulder he'd moved across and dislodged several minutes ago, now finally shifting in his wake.

Still, there was something eerie about registering a sound other than his own labored breathing or the movement of rocks in his immediate vicinity. He'd grown so accustomed to the stillness of this isolated drainage.

He could see down-canyon for a long ways, his eyes initially fixing on the electrified fence a quarter mile back, but then on movement much closer, inside a hundred yards. At first he thought it must be one of those marmots, but it was scrambling with a weightless, feline agility, almost too quickly from rock to rock, and as he squinted to bring it into focus, Ethan saw that it didn't have fur at all. It looked albino, covered with pale, milky skin.

Ethan instinctively backpedaled as he realized he'd grossly underestimated its size. It wasn't moving over small rocks. It was moving through that field of giant boulders Ethan had just emerged from, which meant it was actually closer in size to a human being and traveling at an intimidating speed, barely even stopping between leaps.

Ethan tripped over a rock and jumped back onto his feet, his respirations revving.

The thing near enough that he could hear it breathing—panting—its claws clicking on the stone each time it landed on a new boulder, each leap bringing it closer to Ethan, just fifty yards away now and a sick heat beginning to ferment in Ethan's stomach.

This is what he'd seen night before last from that alcove above the river.

This is what he'd dreamt about.

But what the hell was it?

How could such a thing exist?

He started up the canyon as fast as he'd dared to move all day, glancing back every other step.

The thing leaped off the last of the large boulders

and came down with the grace of a ballerina, now scuttling on all fours, low to the ground like a wild boar, the grating noise of its panting getting louder as it closed the distance between them at such an alarming rate Ethan arrived instantly at the conclusion that there was no point in trying to outrun it.

He stopped and turned to face what was coming, torn between trying to process what was happening and simply preparing himself to survive.

Twenty yards away now, and the nearer it got, the less Ethan liked what he saw.

It was short-torsoed.

Long legs and longer arms, each tipped with a row of black talons.

Hundred and ten, maybe a hundred and twenty pounds.

Sinewy.

Wiry.

And above all, humanoid, its skin in the sunlight as translucent as a baby mouse's—mapped with a network of blue veins and purple arteries and even its heart faintly visible as a pinkish throb just right of center mass.

At ten yards, Ethan braced himself, the creature's small head lowering for the charge, snarling as strings of bloody saliva dangled from the corners of its lipless mouth, creamy eyes hard-focused on its target.

Ethan caught a whiff of its stench two seconds before impact—fetid, decayed flesh spiced with rotted blood.

It screamed—a strangely human-sounding cry—as it launched, Ethan trying to sidestep at the last possible instant, but it had anticipated this, throwing one of its four-foot arms and hooking Ethan around the waist, talons easily penetrating the thick fabric of the hoodie and piercing into Ethan's side.

A searing flash of pain, and then the creature's forward momentum jerked Ethan off his feet, slamming him to the rocks with enough force to drive the air out of his lungs.

Ethan gasped for oxygen as it attacked.

Pit-bull ferocity.

Lightning-fast.

Brutal strength.

Slashing wildly as Ethan held up his arms in an effort to protect his face from the five-taloned claws that were as sharp as a bird of prey's, tearing easily through his clothing, through his skin.

It had managed, in a matter of seconds, to straddle Ethan, the claws at the ends of its legs digging into his calves like nails pinning him to the ground.

In all the fury, Ethan glimpsed its face.

Large, craterous nostrils.

Small, opaque eyes.

Skull hairless and the skin stretched so tight and thin over its cranium he could see where the skull plates fit together like puzzle pieces.

Gums lined with double rows of tiny, razor cuspids.

It seemed like he'd been fighting this thing for hours—time slowed into sluggish, terrifying increments—though in reality, only seconds had elapsed, Ethan's combat training struggling to kick-start, his mind beginning to rise above the fear and the confusion, struggling to quash the mad panic that had engulfed him. The more dangerous and chaotic the situation, the more clearly you needed to think to evaluate how you were going to survive, and so far, he'd failed. Allowed this encounter to sap most of his strength, and if he didn't get control of his fear and his energy output, in another sixty seconds, he wouldn't have the ability—mental or physical —to even try to fight back.

The creature landed its deepest strike yet—an excruciating score across Ethan's stomach, slicing through fabric, skin, the shallow layer of fat on top of Ethan's well-defined abs, and finally skimming across the surface of raw muscle.

As it burrowed its head into Ethan's stomach, he could feel its teeth tearing through the hoodie, Ethan coming to the horrific realization of what this monster was actually trying to do—gut him with its built-in knives and have a feast right here in the canyon while Ethan watched and bled out.

Ethan smashed his fist into the side of its head—an awkward blow but a hard one.

The thing looked up from Ethan's stomach and produced an angry, roaring screech.

Then raised its right claw and swung at Ethan's neck.

He blocked the oncoming strike with his left arm as he reached across the ground with his right, fingers desperately searching for a weapon.

The luster of pure rage in the creature's eyes was unmistakable.

It pushed off Ethan's stomach, its hideous face driving toward his neck, teeth bared.

It's going to tear my throat out.

Ethan's hand seized on a rock, fingers struggling for a decent grip.

He swung as hard as he'd ever swung at anything in his life, the stone heavy, the size of a paperweight, and when its blunt end crunched into the side of the monster's head, the thing faltered, coal-black pupils dilating in those milky eyes, its jaw gone slack with a kind of stunned amazement.

Ethan didn't hesitate.

Shot straight up and drove the rock through that mouthful of jagged brown canines, teeth breaking as the thing tumbled back, Ethan following with another strike, this one a catastrophic blow to its gaping nose.

It crashed to the ground, deep red blood pouring out of its nose and mouth as it screamed in livid disbelief, throwing weak talon-slashes that didn't have the force or velocity behind them to even break skin.

Ethan straddled the thing, one hand crushing its windpipe, the other clutching the rock.

Seven skull-fracturing strikes, and it finally quit moving.

Ethan tossed the blood-smeared rock away and fell back onto his side, drawing long, deep breaths, his face spattered with blood and the occasional bone splinter.

He forced himself to sit up and lift his shirt.

Jesus.

Looked like he'd been in a knife fight, bleeding from numerous places across his torso—long, ugly cuts from those talons. The one across his stomach had done the most damage—a six-inch canyon carved through his abdomen. An inch deeper, and this slash would have opened him wide.

He glanced down at what was left of whatever the hell this thing was.

Didn't even know how to begin to process it.

He couldn't make his hands stop shaking, still so much adrenaline chugging through his system.

He stood.

The canyon still again.

He glanced up at the nearest wall, that mysterious

metal object still shining in the sun. Impossible to be sure, but from his perspective, it looked like an eighty- or ninety-foot climb, and though he couldn't quite get a fix on the reason, he felt a strong urge to get off the canyon floor as soon as possible.

Ethan wiped the gore off his face with the sleeves of his sweatshirt and scrambled back from the wall so he could get a better look at it. Took a moment to study all possible routes up the cliff face, finally deciding on one that would take him up a series of dwindling ledges to the base of a wide crack that ran all the way up to the object of his curiosity.

He walked to the wall.

In the afterglow of the fight, his body felt absolutely electric.

Be a good thing to plug this energy into a climb.

Reaching up to the first wide ledge, Ethan found a decent lip on the rock and pulled himself up.

The flexion of his stomach muscles was agonizing, compounded by the fact that they were integral to nearly every movement.

But he pushed through the pain.

Twenty feet up the wall, Ethan found a spot on a ledge where he could easily stand, and leaned back into the rock.

It had been years since he'd done any climbing, and his inefficiency was evident in the sheer physical toll just the first twenty feet had taken. He was climbing with his arms instead of relying on the power of his legs, and already he was drenched in sweat, the salt water running down into every nick, every slice, every cut.

He carefully shuffled back around and placed his hands on the rock. The ledge was shadowed from the sun and the stone as cold as ice. From the ground, this next section had seemed fairly straightforward—a wealth of good footholds and the kind of knobby rock that lent itself to climbing. But now, standing twenty feet above the canyon floor and staring up a near-vertical pitch, the handholds didn't look quite so inviting, and the distance to the next ledge—where he might grab a much-needed minute of rest—was at least thirty feet.

Ethan shut his eyes and took two deep breaths in an effort to bring his pulse back down to baseline.

You can do this. You have *to do this.*

A foot above his head, he gripped his smallest handhold yet, and then stepped up onto a gently sloping surface that contained just enough grit to give the soles of his boots several seconds of purchase.

The fear kicked up several notches as Ethan worked his way above the second ledge, trying to ignore that quiet voice lodged in the back of his mind like a splinter, whispering that he was passing out of broken-leg-and-back territory into the caliber of height where a mistake meant death.

He made increasingly risky grabs on progressively smaller hand- and footholds.

Starting out, he'd hesitated between every move, testing and retesting each hold, but no more. Already, his legs had begun to sporadically tighten—a precursor to cramps. If he was hit with one up here on the wall that might very well be the end.

And so he climbed as fast as he could, taking every decent hold he encountered, trying to find comfort in the growing distance between himself and the floor of the canyon, assuring himself that should he fall, it would be far better to just die right off, because a broken leg or back out in this barren wilderness would only mean a slow and agonizing death.

And yet the higher he climbed, the terror gripped him tighter, Ethan fighting the urge to look down, but he couldn't resist the morbid fascination with how far he was taking himself above the ground.

His right hand finally reached the third ledge.

He strained to haul himself up, digging his left knee into the edge.

By the time he realized there was nothing obvious for his left hand to grasp, he was already committed.

There was an endless second where Ethan hung in midair, one knee perched on the ledge as his center of gravity slowly dragged him back from the wall toward that terrible emptiness beneath him.

He lunged out in total desperation, both hands clawing at the rock, his left just managing to find a crimp at chest level.

For a moment, he didn't know if he had a sufficient grip to reverse gravity's undertow and pull himself back onto the ledge, the surface of his fingertips scraping away, his knuckles blanching from the strain.

His backward momentum stopped, and he tugged himself forward by the tips of his fingers until his forehead grazed the wall.

Took everything in his power to swing his right leg up and make himself stand.

This ledge was half the width of the last one and his feet hung off the edge.

Would've been impossible to sit down or to remain here for any extended length of time.

The crack in the wall that climbed the remaining distance to that piece of metal opened up just above him. Looked wide enough for Ethan to squeeze into if he could get there, but he didn't have the strength to try to pull himself up just yet.

He'd nearly died, and his body, head to toe, was still shaking.

The scream ripped him out of his own fear.

He stared fifty feet down to the canyon floor, baffled.

He'd crushed that thing's skull into pieces.

How the hell—

Wait.

It wasn't moving, and it no longer had a mouth to even produce such a noise.

As the next scream—this one a shade lower in pitch—resounded through the canyon, bouncing back and forth between the walls, Ethan looked back toward the electrified fence.

Oh God.

There were five of them moving up-canyon in a pattern that almost resembled a squadron formation, ascending that field of large boulders in fast, elegant leaps.

Ethan pressed his back against the wall, trying to establish as steady a perch as he could find.

The pack leader came sprinting out of the boulder field at full speed, as fast as a dog, and when it reached what Ethan had killed, it skidded to a stop and lowered its head to the ground, sniffing the smashed skull of its compatriot.

As the others closed in, it raised its face to the sky and cut loose a long, brokenhearted moan that resembled the howl of a wolf.

The other four arrived and within ten seconds they were all howling like a choir in mourning, Ethan growing cold as he stood motionless on the ledge listening, his sweat cooling on his skin and the remnants of blood from that thing drying on his face like tiny scabs.

He tried to comprehend what he was seeing and hearing, but there was no explanation.

It was all utterly beyond his experience, and possibly his imagination.

When the howling ended, the group turned to one another and conversed in the strangest language Ethan had ever heard.

Like dreadful birds—an eerie chirping quality to their fast, sharp squawks.

Ethan tightened his grip on the rock, fighting against a wave of dizziness, the world tilting beneath him.

All five of them were sniffing the ground now in the vicinity of the dead one—haunches high, faces jammed down between the rocks.

Ethan tried not to panic as it hit him, but he realized something standing there above the monsters—after they left, there was no way he could climb back down. Not even off this ledge. The only way off this wall, where he'd so thoroughly bitten off more than he could chew, was up.

One of the creatures suddenly barked a high, piercing shriek.

The others rushed over, gathering around and chirping frantically, and then the largest of the bunch—easily twice the size of the one that had attacked Ethan—broke out ahead of the others, its nose still to the ground.

Only as it reached the base of the cliff did Ethan finally understand.

My trail.

The creature pressed its nose into the rock and then came up on its legs.

It backed slowly away . . .

. . . and looked up, straight at Ethan.

They're following my trail.

The canyon fell silent.

Five sets of milky eyes studying Ethan up on the ledge.

He could hear his heart raging in his chest like someone trying to beat a way out of a padded room.

A single thought scrolling through his mind on an endless loop . . .

Can they climb?

As if in answer, the large one who'd first picked up his trail reared back on its hind legs and sprang off the ground in a five-foot jump from a stationary position.

Stuck to the wall as if covered in Velcro, the points of its talons digging into tiny crevices in the rock that Ethan could never have used.

It gazed up the cliff face at Ethan as the others began leaping onto the wall.

Ethan looked up at the crack above his head, searching until he spotted a workable handhold just out of reach.

He jumped, palming a cluster of sharp, dark crystals as he heard the click of talons on rock ascending toward him.

He scrambled up the wall, got his other hand on a level surface inside the crack, and pulled himself the rest of the way into the opening of the chute.

It was tight, less than three feet across, but he forced his boots into the walls and created just enough opposing pressure to keep himself suspended.

He stared down.

The big one had already reached the second ledge, climbing fast, fearless, with no sign of fatigue.

The others close behind.

Ethan turned his attention to what lay above—a chute enclosed on three sides. Not much in the way of handholds, but he figured he could chimney up.

He began to climb, the enclosure of the rock giving a welcome, if false, sense of security.

Every few feet, he glanced down between his legs, his view now obscured by the rock surrounding him, but he could still see that thing out in front, moving effortlessly between the second and third ledges up a section of the wall where Ethan had struggled.

Twenty feet up the crack, seventy above the canyon floor, his thighs burning.

Couldn't tell how much farther he had to go to reach that piece of metal that had gotten him into the shit to begin with. On the other hand, if he'd been down in the canyon when those things had shown up, they'd be eating him right now. So maybe in retrospect that shimmering metal that prompted this ballsy climb had actually prolonged, if not saved, his life.

The monster reached the third ledge and, without a moment's hesitation to rest or consider its next move, leaped off the narrow shelf of rock.

A single talon at the end of its left arm caught on a square millimeter of surface just inside the opening to the crack, and in a feat of brute strength, it pulled itself up with one arm and squeezed into the chute.

Ethan locked eyes with the monster as it began to climb on foot- and handholds so insignificant Ethan had disregarded them, traveling at least twice as fast as Ethan could manage.

Nothing to do but keep climbing.

He struggled up another five feet.

Ten.

The monster twenty-five feet away and close enough that Ethan could see the pink pounding of its massive heart, obscured through its skin as if tucked behind thick, frosted glass.

Ten more feet and then the crack appeared to lead out onto flat, vertical, horrifying wall.

The handholds near the top looked good, Ethan

realizing that if he kept chimneying that thing was going to reach him before he made it out.

He switched to hand-over-hand climbing, racing up the last ten feet.

Just before the top, one of the holds broke loose and he nearly lost his balance.

Caught himself before he fell.

He could feel the wind streaming across the opening to the chute.

Glimpsed something catching sunlight straight above.

Froze.

Looked down.

He'd almost blown the chance to save himself.

With the monster fifteen feet away and two more trailing close behind it in the chute, Ethan reached down, the loose handhold that had nearly killed him just within reach.

He tore the chunk of rock from its housing, hoisted it over his head.

It was a handful, even bigger than he'd thought —two pounds of quartz-laced granite.

He wedged himself between the rock, took aim, and let it fly.

It struck the creature dead center of its face just as it was reaching for a new handhold.

Its grip failed.

It plunged down the chute.

Talons scraping rock.

Its velocity too great to self-arrest.

It hit the one beneath it at a high enough rate of speed to knock it from its perch, the pair crashing as one into the third, and then all three screaming for two long seconds as they shot out of the bottom of the chute, bounced off the third ledge, and accelerated toward the rocks below where they slammed aground in a tangle of badly bent appendages and broken skulls.

Ethan emerged out of the chute squinting against the flash of brilliance now just a few feet above his head.

He was at least a hundred feet above the canyon floor, and his stomach churned. From his new vantage point, he could now see that the opposite wall climbed another five or six hundred feet to a razor ridge, which in itself looked impassable.

If his wall did the same, he might as well jump off now, because he didn't have it in him to climb another hundred feet, much less five.

The two remaining creatures on the wall snapped him out of the despair. Instead of following the others up the chute, they had climbed around, one on each side—slower going, but they were still alive and now thirty feet below Ethan.

He reached up and grabbed a ledge under the shiny metal, got both elbows onto the widest shelf of rock he'd seen, and hauled himself up, face-to-face with a steel vent protruding several inches out of the rock. It was square, approximately twenty-four inches across, the blades of a fan spinning counterclockwise directly behind it.

Talons clicked on the rock below.

Ethan gripped the sides of the vent, pulled.

It didn't budge—it had been welded to the duct.

He stood up on the ledge and ran his hands over the surface of the wall until he came to what he was after—a large, twenty-pound wedge of granite that looked poised to fall.

He lifted it and smashed it down on top of the vent where it joined the duct.

The alloy disintegrated, the upper left-hand edge of the vent popping loose.

The creatures were ten feet below him now, so close he could smell the decay of their last kill wafting off them like some savage cologne.

He raised the rock again, brought it down in a crushing blow to the right-hand corner.

The vent snapped free and clanged down the cliff, bouncing off the rock and nearly striking one of the creatures on its descent.

All that stood between Ethan and the darkness of a ventilation shaft were the spinning blades of the air intake.

He rammed the rock into them and brought their revolutions to a halt.

Three hard blows completely detached the unit from its mount, Ethan reaching in, grabbing it by the blades, and slinging it over the cliff.

He picked up the rock, held it high, and dropped

it on the closest creature as its talons reached for the ledge.

It fell screeching.

Its partner watched until it hit the ground, and then looked back at Ethan.

Ethan smiled, said, "You're next."

The thing studied him, its head tilting like it could understand or at least wanted to. It clung to the rock just below the ledge, within easy reach, Ethan waiting for it to make its move, but it held position.

Ethan spun around, searching the cliff wall within reach for another loose rock and coming up empty.

When he turned back, the monster was still perched on the wall.

Settling in.

Ethan wondered if he should climb on until he came across another sizeable rock.

Bad idea. You'd have to down-climb to get back to this ledge.

Ethan crouched, unlaced his left boot. Pulled it off, and then did the same with his right.

He held it—not nearly the heft of a rock, but perhaps it could do the job. Grasping it by the heel, he made a dramatic show of cocking back his arm as he stared down into the monster's milky eyes.

"You know what's coming, don't you?"

Ethan feigned a throw.

It didn't flinch and come off the rock as he'd hoped, just pressed in closer to the wall.

The next time wasn't a fake, but Ethan threw so hard the boot sailed over the creature's head and took an uninterrupted fall into the canyon.

He lifted the other boot, took aim, threw.

Direct hit to the face.

The boot bounced off and tumbled away as the creature, still clinging to the wall, looked up at Ethan and hissed.

A visage of murderous intent.

"How long can you hold on, you think?" Ethan asked. "You must be getting tired." He reached down, pretending to offer a hand. "I'll help you the rest of the way. You just have to trust." The way it watched him was unnerving—a definite intelligence all the more frightening because he couldn't know how deep it went.

Ethan sat on the rock.

"I'll be right here," he said. "Until you fall."

He watched its heart beating.

He watched it blinking.

"You are one ugly motherfucker." Ethan chuckled. "Sorry. I couldn't resist. It's from a movie. Seriously, what the hell are you?"

Fifteen minutes crept by.

Late afternoon now.

The sun beginning to drop, the floor of the canyon already in darkness.

It was cold up here on the rock.

A few clouds streaming overhead, but they were inconsequential and swallowed up in all that crystal blue like afterthoughts.

The five talons on the creature's left arm began to quiver, rattling against the microscopic hand-hold, and something in its eyes had changed. Still plenty of rage, but now an added element—fear?

Its head swiveled, surveying all the rock within reach.

Ethan had already made the same inspection and arrived at the same conclusion.

"Yeah, this is it, pal. This ledge. My ledge. Your only option."

A tremor moved through its right leg, and Ethan had opened his mouth to suggest the creature just let go when it leaped from its footholds, elevating three feet and simultaneously swiping its right claw in a wide, flat arc.

It would have torn his face open, but he ducked —talons grazing the top of his head—and then Ethan rose up on both legs, ready to kick this thing off the cliff.

But he didn't need to.

It had never had a chance of reaching the ledge in its weakened state—had merely taken one last shot at bringing Ethan down with it.

The fall apparently came as no surprise, because it didn't make a sound and it didn't flail its arms or legs.

Just stared up at Ethan as it plummeted toward the sunless floor of the canyon, body as motionless as if in the midst of a high dive.

Fully resigned, maybe even at peace, with its fate.

Chapter 14

YESTERDAY, SHE HADN'T left her room.

Hadn't even left her bed.

She had prepared for his death.

Had known it was coming.

But watching the sun rise on a world without Ethan had nearly killed her regardless. Somehow, the light had made it real. The people out on morning walks. Even the chattering magpies in the side-yard birdfeeder. It was the continuance of things that crushed her already broken heart. The gears of the world turning on while she lived with his absence like a black tumor in her chest, the grief so potent she could barely bring herself to breathe.

Today, she had ventured outside, now sitting listless in the soft grass of her backyard in a patch of sunshine. She'd been staring up at the surrounding mountain walls for hours, watching the light move across them and trying not to think about a single thing.

The sound of approaching footsteps broke her reverie.

She looked back.

Pilcher was coming toward her.

During her time in Wayward Pines, she'd seen the man around town on numerous occasions, but they'd never spoken—she'd been warned about that from the beginning. Not a word exchanged since that rainy night five years ago in Seattle, when he'd shown up on her doorstep with the most outlandish proposition.

Pilcher sat down beside her in the grass.

He took off his glasses, set them on his leg, said, "I'm told you missed your harvest day at the co-op."

"I haven't left my house in two days."

"And what's that supposed to accomplish?" he asked.

"I don't know. But I can't take people looking at me. We can't talk about him, of course, but I'd see the pity in their eyes. Or worse, they'd ignore me. Act like nothing happened. Like he never existed. I haven't even told my son that his father's dead. I don't know how to begin."

It would be evening soon.

The sky was free of clouds.

The row of aspen saplings that separated her backyard from her neighbor's had turned to gold overnight, the coin-shaped leaves twittering in the breeze. She could hear the wooden wind chimes clanging on the back porch beside the door. It was moments like this—the visual perfection underscored with a reality she could never know—that she feared would one day drive her to insanity.

"You've done well here," Pilcher said. "The difficulties with Ethan were the last thing I ever wanted. I hope you believe that."

She looked at Pilcher, stared straight into his black eyes.

"I don't know what I believe," she said.

"Your son's inside?"

"Yes, why?"

"I want you to go in and get him. I have a car parked out front."

"Where are you taking us?"

He shook his head.

"Are you going to hurt Benjamin?"

Pilcher struggled onto his feet.

He stared down at her.

"If I wanted to hurt you, Theresa, I would take you and your son in the middle of the night, and no one would ever hear from you again. But you already know this. Now go get him. I'll meet you out front in two minutes."

Chapter 15

ETHAN STARED INTO the air duct.

The fit was going to be tight, maybe impossible with the hoodie.

He pulled out of the sleeves and tugged it off and tossed it over the ledge, gooseflesh rising on his bare arms. Figured his feet would be responsible for most of the propulsion and decided to come out of his socks as well so he wouldn't slide.

He got his head through the opening.

At first, his shoulders wouldn't fit, but after a minute of wriggling, he finally maneuvered himself halfway inside, arms splayed out ahead, feet struggling to push him the rest of the way, the thin metal freezing against his toes.

When he was completely inside the air duct, a wave of panic swept over him. He felt like he couldn't breathe, his shoulders squeezed between the two walls, and the realization dawning on him that moving backward was now impossible. At least not without popping both shoulders out of socket.

His only method of movement was the paltry momentum his toes could stir up, and they had no reverse gears.

He inched forward, literally, sliding along the surface of the duct.

Still bleeding.

Muscles in revolt in the wake of the climb and his nerves frayed.

In the distance—nothing but absolute darkness, the tunnel reverberating with the echo of his shuffling.

Except for when he stopped.

Then a perfect silence set in, interrupted only by random *bangs* that gave his heart a start— the expanding and contracting of the metal in response to temperature fluctuations.

Five minutes in, Ethan tried to glance back toward the opening, something in him craving just one last glimpse of light—that smallest consolation—but he couldn't crane his neck far enough back to see.

He crawled and crawled and crawled.

Closed in on all sides in complete darkness.

At some point, maybe thirty minutes in, maybe five hours, maybe a day . . . he had to stop.

His toes cramped from the strain.

He slumped across the metal.

Shivering.

Insanely thirsty.

Maddeningly hungry and unable to reach the food in his pocket.

He could hear his heart heaving in his chest against the metal and nothing else.

He slept.

Or lost consciousness.

Or died for a minute.

When he woke again, he thrashed violently against the sides of the duct, no idea where he was or even when he was, his eyes open to sheer darkness.

For a terrifying moment, he thought he'd been buried alive, the sound of his own hyperventilation like someone screaming in his ear.

Crawled for what seemed like days.

His eyes conjuring strange displays of light that appeared with greater frequency the longer he stayed in darkness.

Vivid bursts of color.

Imaginary auroras.

Haunting radiance in the black.

And the longer he crawled in that confined darkness, the more aggressively one thought kept eating at him—none of this is real.

Not Wayward Pines, or the canyon, or those creatures, or even you.

So what is this? Where am I?

In a long, dark tunnel. But where do you think you're going?

I don't know.

Who are you?

Ethan Burke.

No, *who* are you?

The father of Ben. Husband of Theresa. I live in a neighborhood in Seattle called Queen Anne. I was a Black Hawk helicopter pilot in the second Gulf War. After that, a Secret Service agent. Seven days ago, I came to Wayward Pines—

Those are just facts. They say nothing about your identity, your nature.

I love my wife, but I was unfaithful to her.

That's good.

I love my son, but I was rarely around. Just a distant star in his sky.

Even better.

I have good intentions, but . . .

But what?

But all the time I fail. I hurt the ones I love.

Why?

I don't know.

Are you losing your mind?

I sometimes think I'm still in that torture room. I never left.

Are you losing your mind?

You tell me.

I can't.

Why?

Because I am you.

• • •

At first, he thought it was just another phantom light show, but there were no erratic blooms of color. No optic fireworks.

Just a sustained speck of blue somewhere far ahead, as faint as a dying star.

When he closed his eyes, it disappeared.

When he opened them, it came back again, like the only vestige of sanity left in his claustrophobic world. It was just a point of light, but he could make it vanish and reappear, and even this scintilla of control was something to cling to.

An anchor. A port of call.

Ethan thinking, *Please. Be real.*

The dim blue star grew larger, and with its expansion came a quiet hum.

Ethan stopped to rest, a soft vibration now moving through the ductwork, moving through him.

After hours in the dark, this new sensation felt as comforting as a mother's heartbeat.

Sometime later, the blue star changed shape into a tiny square.

It grew until it dominated Ethan's field of vision, anticipation roiling in his gut.

Then it was ten feet ahead of him.

Then five.

Then he was stretching his arms out of the

opening of the duct, his shoulders crackling, the new freedom of movement as sweet as he imagined water might have been.

Hanging out of the end of the duct, he stared down into one twice as wide and intersected by other shafts.

A soft blue light filled the main airshaft—emanating from a bulb far below.

Down at the bottom, he glimpsed an air intake.

Must have been a hundred-foot drop down to those blades.

Like staring down a well.

At intervals of ten feet, more shafts fed into the main, some of them considerably larger.

Ethan glanced up. The ceiling was two feet above his head.

Shit.

He knew what his next move was, what it had to be, and he didn't like it.

Ethan climbed out into the airshaft with the same technique he'd used to ascend the chute—a pressure stance, each foot pushing into the opposite wall.

His bare feet achieved decent purchase on the metal, and despite the looming fall into spinning blades that awaited even the smallest mistake, he felt almost giddy to be free of that tiny shaft.

He descended in painstakingly slow increments, one step at a time, keeping pressure against the walls with his arms while he lowered his legs, then shifting the pressure back onto the balls of his feet.

Forty feet down, he rested at the opening to the first large horizontal shaft he'd encountered, sitting on the edge and staring down at the whirring blades as he ate the last of the carrots and bread.

He'd been so focused on surviving that it only now occurred to him to wonder what purpose all this infrastructure served.

Instead of continuing down, he glanced back into the shaft, noticing the darkness was interspersed with panels of light positioned at regular intervals. They extended on as far as he could see.

Ethan turned over onto his hands and knees and crawled across the metal for twenty feet until he reached the first one.

Stopped at the edge, a jolt of fear-tinged excitement coursing through him.

It wasn't a panel of light.

It was a vent.

He stared through it, down onto a flooring of checkered tile.

The air blowing through the ductwork had taken on a lovely warmth, like an ocean breeze in the dead of July.

For a long time, he waited.

Watching.

Nothing happened.

There was the sound of moving air, of his respirations, of the metal expanding and contracting, and nothing else.

Ethan took hold of the vent by its grating.

It lifted easily away, no screws, no nails, no welding holding it in place.

Setting the grate aside, he grabbed hold of the edge and tried to build the nerve to climb down.

Chapter 16

ETHAN LOWERED HIMSELF out of the duct until his bare feet touched the black-and-white checkered tile. He stood in the middle of a long, empty corridor. There was the hum of the fluorescent lights and the soft *whoosh* of air moving through the ductwork above him, but no other sound.

His feet made a quiet slap against the tile as he began to walk.

There were doors spaced out every twenty feet with numbers on them, and the one up ahead on his right was barely cracked and spilling a bit of light out onto the floor.

He reached it—number 37—and put his hand on the doorknob.

Listened.

No voices. No movement. Nothing to turn him away.

He pushed the door open another inch and looked inside.

There was a single bed on a metal frame against the far wall, perfectly made. A desk decorated with framed photographs and some tulips in a vase. His eyes passed over a floor-to-ceiling bookshelf, a Matisse print, an easel. Beside the door, a terrycloth robe hung from a hook in the wall, a pair of pink bunny slippers beneath it.

He went on down the silent corridor.

None of the doors were locked, and each one he took the risk of opening revealed a similar minimalist living space, brightened with a few flourishing touches of individuality.

After an impressive distance, the corridor terminated in a stairwell, Ethan standing at the top and staring down, counting four flights to the bottom.

A placard on the wall read *Level 4*.

He crept down to the next landing, which delivered him onto another corridor that looked identical to the one above.

Hard, sudden laughter resonated through the hall.

It drove Ethan back into the stairwell and primed him to flee. He was already figuring he could return to Level 4, use a chair from one of those apartments to climb back up into the airshaft. But the laughter died down, and after he'd waited a full minute, the corridor remained empty.

He padded thirty feet in, finally stopping in front of a pair of swinging doors, each inset with a small window.

A group of three men and two women occupied one of a dozen tables in a modest cafeteria, the smell of hot food making Ethan's stomach rumble.

One of the women said, "You know that's not true, Clay," pointing a fork at him that had speared a glob of what looked like mashed potatoes.

Ethan moved on down the corridor.

He passed a laundry.

A rec room.

A library.

An empty gymnasium.

Men's and women's locker rooms.

An exercise room where two women jogged side by side on treadmills and a man lifted free weights.

Ethan came to the stairwell at the far end and descended a flight of stairs that led out into the Level 2 corridor.

At the first door he came to, he stopped and peered inside through its circular window.

There was a gurney in the center, surrounded by lights, carts loaded with surgical instruments, heart monitors, IV stands, cautery and suction units, a fluoroscopy table, all immaculately clean and glimmering under the low light.

The next three doors were windowless and identified only by nameplates: *Lab A, Lab B, Lab C.*

Down toward the end of the corridor, one window glowed, and Ethan sidled up beside it.

On the other side of the glass—tapping and the murmur of soft, low voices.

He peered through the window.

The room was mostly dark, its glow coming from numerous monitors—twenty-five of them in five stacks of five mounted to the wall and perched above a large console that looked serious enough to launch a rocket.

Ten feet from where Ethan stood, a man sat staring up at them, his fingers moving at light speed across a keyboard as the images on the screens constantly changed. He wore a headset, and Ethan could just hear his voice coming through, though the words were lost.

On one of the screens, Ethan studied the slideshow of images . . .

The façade of a Victorian house.

The porch of a different house.

An alleyway.

A bedroom.

An empty bathtub.

A bathroom with a woman standing in front of a mirror, brushing her hair.

A man seated at a kitchen table eating a bowl of cereal.

A child sitting on a toilet reading a book.

A view of Main Street in Wayward Pines.

The playground at the park.

The cemetery.

The river.

The interior of the coffee shop.

The hospital lobby.

Sheriff Pope sitting behind his desk with his feet kicked up, talking on the telephone.

Ethan's line of sight was limited through the window, but he could just make out the left edge of another block of monitors and the sound of other people typing.

A pool of hot rage went supernova somewhere deep inside him.

He put his hand on the doorknob, started to turn it. Would have loved nothing more than to creep up behind that man as he watched people going about their private lives and snap his neck.

But he stopped himself.

Not yet.

Ethan backed away from the surveillance center and headed down the stairwell, emerging into the bottom corridor—Level 1.

Though difficult to tell from this distance, at the far end it appeared to extend beyond the stairwell into another section of the complex.

Ethan picked up his pace.

Every ten feet, he moved past a door with no

handle, no apparent method of entry beyond a keycard slot.

Third one down on his left, he stopped.

Glanced through the small window into darkness—just an empty room.

He did the same at the tenth door down, stopping and cupping his hands over his eyes so he could draw more detail out of the shadows.

The face of one of those creatures from the canyon crashed into the glass on the other side, its teeth bared and hissing.

Ethan stumbled back into the opposite wall, his system buzzing from the scare as the thing screeched behind the glass—thick enough to dampen most of the sound.

Footfalls echoed in the stairwell he'd just been in.

Ethan hurried down the corridor, moving as fast as he could, the fluorescent fixtures scrolling past in a stream of artificial light.

He glanced once over his shoulder as he reached the stairwell, saw two figures in black moving into the far end of the corridor a hundred yards back. One of them pointed and shouted something, and then they rushed toward him.

Ethan hustled through the stairwell.

A pair of automatic glass doors were sliding together straight ahead of him.

He turned sideways, barely managing to squeeze through as they closed after him.

It was the epic proportions of the next room

that took him aback, the mad scope of this place bringing him to a full stop.

He no longer stood on tile but on cold rock and at the edge of a cavern the size of ten warehouses—a million square feet at least if he had to guess, and the distance from floor to ceiling sixty feet in places. In all his life, he'd seen only one space more impressive—the Boeing Plant in Everett, Washington.

Giant globes of light hung down from the rocky ceiling, each one illuminating a thousand-square-foot section of floor space.

There were hundreds of them.

The glass doors had begun to spread open behind him, and he could hear the footsteps of those black-garbed men—they'd already covered half the distance of the corridor.

Ethan ran into the cavern and shot down a passageway between shelves laden with lumber of every dimension. The shelves were forty feet tall, three deep on either side, and extended the length of a football field, Ethan figuring they contained enough linear board feet to rebuild Wayward Pines five times over.

Numerous voices echoed through the cavern.

Ethan glanced over his shoulder, saw someone a couple of hundred feet back sprinting toward him.

He broke out of the narrow canyon between the shelves.

Straight ahead, the floor space was overrun by

hundreds of cylindrical reservoirs thirty feet tall and just as wide, each capable of holding tens of thousands of cubic feet, each labeled in huge, block letters as tall as Ethan.

Rice.

Flour.

Sugar.

Grain.

Iodized Salt.

Corn.

Vitamin C.

Soybeans.

Powdered Milk.

Malt.

Barley.

Yeast.

Ethan ran into the labyrinth of containers. He could hear footfalls—very close—but with all the spatial interference, it was impossible to pinpoint their location.

He stopped and leaned against a reservoir, breathing into his shirt in the crook of his arm, fighting to mask the noise of his panting.

A man in black fatigues bolted past, holding a walkie-talkie in one hand and something that resembled a cattle prod in the other.

Ethan waited ten seconds and then changed course, threading his way through the containers for another hundred yards until he emerged into a parking lot of cars.

The vehicles ranged in type from early eighties to present to models he'd never seen before—curvaceous, compact designs that looked more like radical concept cars than anything that belonged on a public street.

Every vehicle, without exception, sported gleaming chrome and unblemished paint jobs under the hanging globe lights, all looking as new and shiny as if they'd just rolled off the assembly line thirty seconds prior.

A group of men jogged into view on the far side of the parking lot.

Ethan ducked between a couple of red Jeep Cherokees, didn't know if he'd been seen, but he felt confident he'd spotted automatic weapons.

He crawled for several car lengths and then rose up slowly beside a driver's door until he was peering through the windshield of an early-eighties model Impala.

They were closer than he'd realized, just thirty feet away now and all armed with submachine guns. Two of them shined flashlights into the interior of every vehicle they passed while the third crawled behind on hands and knees, putting a light under each car.

Ethan headed in the opposite direction, not bothering to crawl, just running hunched over on the uneven rock and trying to make sure his head wasn't visible through any glass.

Near the edge of the parking lot, he stumbled

past a Crown Vic with tinted windows in the rear passenger doors. He stopped, and with absolute precision, pulled on the handle and tugged the door open without a sound.

The dome light blazed down, and Ethan scrambled inside, jerking the door shut after him with just a touch too much force.

Even from inside the car, he could hear the echo of the slammed door riding through the cavern.

Crouching down in the shadows behind the driver seat, Ethan glanced over the headrest and through the windshield.

The trio of men were all standing now, each slowly turning, trying to ascertain where the noise had originated.

They finally split up, two moving away from Ethan, but one heading straight toward his car.

As the man approached, Ethan got down behind the seat and curled up into as small and compact a ball as he could make himself.

The footsteps drew near.

He had his head tucked between his knees.

Couldn't see a thing.

Then the footsteps were right at his head, inches away on the other side of the door.

They didn't trail away.

They had stopped.

The urge to lift his head to see what was happening so strong it nearly overcame him.

He wondered if the man was spotlighting the interior of the Crown Vic.

Wondered how well the light would pass through the rear tinted windows.

If he couldn't get a decent glimpse inside, would he just open the door?

The footsteps went on, but Ethan didn't move—waited another five minutes until he could no longer hear them.

Finally, he sat up and stared through the windshield.

The men were gone.

He didn't see anyone.

Ethan eased the door open and crawled down onto the rock. If he strained to listen, he could hear voices, but they were much farther off, in some distant region of the cavern.

A hundred feet of crawling brought Ethan to the edge of the parking lot.

Straight ahead stood the cavern wall and the opening to a tunnel broad enough for two cars to travel abreast.

Ethan rose up onto his feet and crossed to the tunnel.

It was empty and well lighted and fell away from where he stood in a straight shot that descended at a ten or twelve percent grade over pristine pavement.

A sign had been affixed to the rock above the arched opening—white lettering on green background, just like the signage of the American interstate highway system.

But it listed only one destination . . .

WAYWARD PINES 3.5

Ethan glanced back at all the cars, thinking maybe he could borrow one of the older models, which were much easier to hotwire.

Something caught his eye—a chill blue light coming from a glass door in the rock fifty yards away.

The sound of footsteps and voices came back into range, still a good distance away, beyond the cars. Ethan thought he saw the beam of a flashlight strike one of the reservoirs, but he couldn't be sure.

He kept close to the wall of the cavern.

It curved gently as he jogged alongside it toward the glass door.

Five feet away, he stopped.

As the door slid open, he read a single word stenciled on the glass:

SUSPENSION

Ethan stepped inside.

The door zipped closed behind him.

It was much colder, just a few degrees above freezing, and his breath plumed in the chill. The light was frigid blue, like sunshine passing through sea ice, and the air was murky with a pale gas that hovered ten feet above, thick enough to completely mask the ceiling like a cloud. And yet this room had the clean, rinsed smell of a post-snowstorm night—odorless and pure.

The noise of hissing gas and soft beeps broke the silence.

Approximately the dimensions of a grocery store, the room housed row after row of charcoal-colored units—hundreds and hundreds of them—each the size of a drink machine, each spitting a white stream of gas from its roof like a smoking chimney.

Ethan walked down the first aisle and faced one of the machines.

A two-inch-wide panel of glass ran down the middle, nothing to see behind it.

To the left of the glass, a keypad was framed with several gauges and readouts, all of them zeroed out.

To the right of the glass, he studied a digital nameplate:

JANET CATHERINE PALMER
TOPEKA, KS
SUSPENSION DATE: 2.3.82
RESIDENT: 11 YEARS, 5 MONTHS, 9 DAYS

Ethan heard the door slide open, turned to see who'd entered, but the waves of gas blocked his view. He moved on down the aisle, deeper into the fog, glancing at the nameplate on each machine he passed, the suspension dates progressing steadily through the 1980s.

One stopped him altogether as voices mixed in with the sound of escaping gas and beeps.

Behind the center pane of glass, it looked as if the interior of the machine had been packed with black sand. Just barely poking through, he saw a white finger, motionless, its tip resting against the glass beneath a fingerprint smudge.

The gauges displayed what appeared to be a flat-lined heart monitor and a temperature reading of 21.1111°C.

The nameplate:

BRIAN LANEY ROGERS
MISSOULA, MT
SUSPENSION DATE: 5.5.84
INTEGRATION ATTEMPTS: 2

The next machine down stood empty, but Ethan recognized the first name, wondered if it was her:

BEVERLY LYNN SHORT
BOISE, ID
SUSPENSION DATE: 10.3.85
INTEGRATION ATTEMPTS: 3
TERMINATED

There was someone moving quickly toward him now. He tore himself away from Beverly's unit, mind reeling as he ran to the end of the aisle and started up the next.

What the hell did this mean?

There must have been a half dozen people in the room now, all chasing him, but he didn't care.

Just needed to see one more unit.

Had to see it.

And on the fourth row, midway down the aisle, with voices closing in, he stopped.

Stared at the empty machine.

His empty machine.

JOHN ETHAN BURKE
SEATTLE, WA
SUSPENSION DATE: 9.24.12
INTEGRATION ATTEMPTS: 3
TERMINATION IN PROGRESS

Reading his name didn't make it any more real.

He stood there not knowing what to do with the information in front of him.

Trying to piece together what it meant.

For the first time in what seemed like forever, he couldn't care less about running.

"Ethan!"

He knew this voice, although it took him a moment to link it back to the memory.

To the face it belonged to.

"We need to talk, Ethan!"

Yes, we do.

It was Jenkins. The psychiatrist.

Ethan started walking.

He felt like he'd been unraveling for days, but now he was getting down to the end of the string, wondering what exactly was going to happen when it all ran out.

"Ethan, please!"

He wasn't even looking at names anymore, or to see which machine was occupied, which one empty.

Only one thing mattered, one terrible suspicion gnawing his guts out.

"We don't want to hurt you! No one touches him!"

It was all he could do to make his legs work as he approached the last machine on the last row in the farthest corner of the room.

Men followed him now.

He could sense them close behind in the fog.

No chance at escaping now, but then, did it really matter anymore?

He arrived at the last machine and put his hand against the glass to brace himself.

Surrounded by black sand, a man's face pressed against that narrow window down the front.

Eyes open.

Unblinking.

No breath to fog the inside the glass.

Ethan read the nameplate and the year of suspension—2032. He turned around as Dr.

Jenkins emerged out of the fog, the small, unassuming man flanked by five of those black-clad men dressed in something approaching full riot gear.

Jenkins said, "Please don't make us hurt you."

Ethan shot a glance up the last aisle—two more figures loomed in the fog.

He was cornered.

Said, "What is this?"

"I understand you want to know."

"Do you."

The psychiatrist studied him for a moment. "You look terrible, Ethan."

"So I was what, frozen?"

"You were chemically suspended."

"What does that even mean?"

"To oversimplify, we use hydrogen sulfide to induce hypothermia. Once the core temperature is at ambient levels, we pack you in volcanic sand and crank up the sulfur gas to a concentration that kills all aerobic bacteria. Then we attack the anaerobic. Basically anything that supports cell senescence. This puts you in a highly efficient state of suspended animation."

"So you're telling me that, at least for a time, I was dead?"

"No. Dead . . . by definition . . . is something that can't be undone. We like to think of it as turning you off in such a way that allows us to turn you on again. To reboot you. Keep in mind,

335

I'm giving you the dummy's guide to a very delicate and complex process. One that took decades to perfect."

Jenkins moved forward with the caution he might have used to approach a rabid animal. His thugs kept close, inching forward themselves, but he waved them back, stopping two feet away from Ethan, and reaching out slowly until his hand touched Ethan's shoulder.

"I understand this is a lot to take in. That fact is not lost on me. You aren't crazy, Ethan."

"I know that. I've always known that. So what is this all about then? What does it mean?"

"You'd like for me to show you?"

"What do you think?"

"All right, Ethan. All right. But I have to warn you . . . I'm going to ask for something in return."

"What?"

Jenkins didn't answer. Instead, he just smiled and touched something to Ethan's side.

Ethan heard clicking, realized what was coming a half second before it hit him—like jumping into a freezing lake, every muscle flexing in unison, his knees locking, and a blast-furnace burn at the excruciating point of contact.

Then he was on the ground, his entire body vibrating and Jenkins's knee digging into the small of his back.

The pinch of a needle sliding into the side of his neck cut through the effects of the electromuscular disruption, and Jenkins must have hit a vein, because almost immediately, the pain of the Taser hit melted away.

The pain of everything melted away.

The euphoric rush coming fast and hard and Ethan struggling to see through it, to keep a finger on the fear of what was happening.

But the drug was too beautiful.

Too heavy.

It pulled him under into a painless bliss.

Chapter 17

BARELY TWO SECONDS have elapsed since he last grain of black sand emptied from the upper bulb of the hourglass when the door unlocks and swings open.

Aashif stands in the doorway smiling.

It is the first time Ethan has seen him without a hood, and it strikes him that this does not look like a man who is capable of doing the things to Ethan he has promised he will do.

His face is clean-shaven with only the faintest peppering of stubble.

Hair black and midlength and greased back.

"Which of your parents was white?" Ethan asks.

"My mother was British." Aashif steps into the room. At the desk, he stops and stares down at the sheet of paper. Points to it. "I trust it is not blank on the other side." He turns it over, studies it for a moment, and shakes his head as his eyes rise to Ethan's. "You were to write down something that made me happy. Did you not understand my instructions?"

"Your English is fine. I understood."

"Then maybe you do not believe I will do what I have said."

"No, I believe you."

"What then? Why did you not write something?"

"But I did."

"In invisible ink?"

Now Ethan smiles. It takes everything within his power to stifle the tremor that keeps threatening to move through his hands.

He holds up his left.

"I wrote this," he says, showing the tattoo he carved into his palm with the tip of the ball-point pen—dark blue and sloppy, his hand still bleeding in places. But given the time constraints and the circumstance, it was the best he could do. He says, "I know that soon I will be screaming. In terrible pain. Every time you wonder what I'm thinking, even though I may not be able to speak, you can just look at my hand and take those two words to heart. It's an American saying. I trust you understand its full meaning?"

"You have no idea," Aashif whispers, and for the first time, Ethan registers unchecked emotion in the man's eyes. Through the fear, he makes himself catalog the satisfaction of having broken this monster's cool, knowing it may be his only moment of victory in this brutal transaction.

"Actually, I do," Ethan says. "You will torture me, break me, and eventually murder me. I know exactly what's coming. I just have one request." ·

This elicits a subtle smile.

"What?"

"Quit telling me how much of a stud you are, you piece of shit. Whip it out and show me."

All day, Aashif shows him.

Some hours later, Ethan snaps back to consciousness.

Aashif sets the bottle of smelling salts on the table beside the knives.

"Welcome back. Have you seen yourself?" the man asks him.

Ethan has lost all concept of how long he's been down here in the brown-walled room without windows that smells of death and rancid blood.

"Look at your leg." Aashif's face is beaded with sweat. "I said look at your leg."

When Ethan refuses, Aashif reaches his bloody fingers into an earthenware vessel, comes out with a handful of salt.

He flings it at Ethan's leg.

Screams through the ball gag.

Agony.

Unconsciousness.

"Do you understand how completely I own you now, Ethan? How I will always own you? Do you hear me?"

Truer words.

Ethan has placed himself in another world, trying to follow a line of thought that leads to his wife, to her giving birth to their firstborn, and him in the hospital with her, but the pain keeps dragging him back into now.

"I can make it end," Aashif purrs into his ear. "I can also keep you alive for days. Whatever I want. I know it hurts. I know you're in more pain than you even knew a person was capable of experiencing. But consider that I've only been working on one leg. And I'm very good at this. I will not allow you to bleed to death. You will only die when it pleases me."

There is undeniable intimacy between them.

Aashif cutting.

Ethan screaming.

At first, Ethan hadn't watched, but now he can't tear his eyes away.

Aashif forces him to drink water and shovels lukewarm beans into his mouth, all the while talking to him in the most casual tone, as if he were merely a barber and Ethan had popped in for a trim.

Later, Aashif sits in the corner drinking water and watching Ethan, studying his handiwork with a mix of amusement and pride.

He wipes his brow and rises to his feet, the hem of his dishdasha dripping Ethan's blood.

"Tomorrow morning first thing, I will castrate you, cauterize the wound with a blow torch, and then go to work on your upper body. Think about what you want for breakfast."

He turns off the light on his way out of the room.

All night, Ethan hangs in darkness.

Waiting.

Sometimes he hears footsteps stop outside the door, but it never opens.

The pain is titanic but he manages to think clearly about his wife and the child he will never know.

He whispers to Theresa from this dungeon and wonders if she can hear him.

He moans and he cries.

Trying to come to grips with the idea that he is meeting *this* end.

Even years later, it will be this moment—hanging alone in the dark with nothing but the pain and his thoughts and the waiting for tomorrow—that will haunt him.

Always waiting for Aashif's return.

Always wondering what his son or daughter will look like.

What their name will be.

Always wondering how Theresa will get on without him.

She will even say to him four months later, sitting at the breakfast table in their kitchen in Seattle as the rain falls, "It's like you never came back to me, Ethan."

And he will say, "I know," as the cries of his son come through the baby monitor, thinking, *Aashif didn't just take physical pieces out of me.*

And then the door finally opens, razor blades of light streaming in, bringing Ethan back to consciousness, back to the pain.

When his eyes adjust to the onslaught of daylight, it isn't the silhouette of Aashif he sees but the bulky profile of a SEAL in full gear holding an M-4 with an ACOG whose barrel gives off wisps of smoke.

He shines a light on Ethan and says with a thick, west-Texas drawl, "Jesus."

Theresa thinks the leg wounds are from the crash.

The SEAL is a Chief Petty Officer, last name Brooks, and he carries Ethan on his back up a narrow flight of stairs, out of the basement dungeon into a kitchen where pieces of meat are burning on a skillet.

Breakfast interruptus.

Three Arab men lie dead in the hall, and five members of the SEAL team occupy the cramped kitchen, one of them kneeling down beside Aashif, tying a strip of cloth around his left leg above the knee, which bleeds from a gunshot wound.

Brooks lowers Ethan into a chair and growls at his medic, "Get away from him." He stares down at Aashif. "Who cut up this soldier?"

Aashif responds to the question with something in Arabic.

"Me no hablo whatever the fuck you just said."

"It's him," Ethan says. "He did this to me."

For a moment, there is nothing in the kitchen but the stench of burning meat and the gunpowder from the firefight.

"We'll have air in two minutes," Brooks says

to Ethan. "This is the only cocksucker left and there's no one in this room gonna say shit about what you do."

A soldier standing by the stove and holding a sniper rifle says, "Fuckin-a."

"Can you stand me up?" Ethan asks.

Brooks hauls Ethan out of his seat, Ethan groaning as he inches his way across the kitchen toward Aashif.

When they're standing over him, the SEAL unholsters a SIG.

Ethan takes it out of his hand, checks the load.

It will occur to him months from now that if this had been a movie, he wouldn't have done it. Wouldn't have sunk to the level of this monster. But the ugly truth is it never even crosses Ethan's mind *not* to do it. And though he will continually dream about the crash, about all the things Aashif did to him, this moment will never haunt him. He will only wish it could have lasted longer.

Ethan is naked, on his feet only with the support of Brooks, his legs like something that belongs in a butcher shop.

He tells Aashif to look at him.

In the distance, he can hear the distinctive *whop-whop* of the approaching Black Hawk.

Beyond that, it is as quiet as mass out on the street.

The torturer and the tortured hold eye contact for a long second.

Aashif says, "You're still mine, you know."

As he smiles, Ethan shoots him through the face.

The next time he comes to consciousness, he's leaning against the window of the Black Hawk, staring three hundred feet down at the streets of Fallujah, morphine gliding through his system and Brooks's voice screaming in his ear that he's safe, that he's going home, and that two days ago, his wife gave birth to a healthy baby boy.

Chapter 18

ETHAN OPENED HIS eyes.

His head leaned against a window and he was staring down at mountainous terrain scrolling past at a hundred and fifty miles per hour. Cruising, if he had to guess, at twenty-five hundred feet AGL. He'd flown an air ambulance for six months after returning from Iraq and before applying to the Secret Service, and he recognized not only the voice of the Lycoming turbines roaring above his head but the dimensions of the BK117 airframe. He'd flown this model with Flight for Life.

Raising his head off the glass, he moved to scratch an itch on the side of his nose, but found his hands cuffed behind his back.

The passenger cabin had been arranged in a standard configuration—four seats divided between two facing rows, and a cargo space in the rear of the fuselage, hidden behind a curtain.

Jenkins and Sheriff Pope sat across, and Ethan felt pleased to see the lawman's nose still bandaged.

Nurse Pam—having traded her classic nurse's uniform for black cargo pants, a long-sleeved black T, BDUs, and an H&K tactical shotgun—sat beside him, a half-moon trail of sutures curving from a shaved portion of her skull, across her temple, and midway down her cheek. Beverly had been responsible for that, and Ethan noted a flicker of rage at the memory of what had been done to that poor woman.

Jenkins' voice crackled through the headset. "How you feeling, Ethan?"

Though he felt groggy from the meds, his head had already begun to clear.

But he didn't answer.

Just stared.

"Apologies for the shock yesterday, but we couldn't take any chances. You've proven you're more than capable at handling yourself, and I didn't want to risk any further loss of life. Yours or my men."

"Loss of life, huh? That's what you're so worried about now?"

"We also took the liberty of rehydrating you, giving you some nourishment, new clothes. Seeing to your injuries. I have to say . . . you look much better."

Ethan glanced out the window—endless pine forests streaming through valleys and over hills that occasionally climbed above the timberline into sheer rock escarpments.

"Where are you taking me?" Ethan asked.

"I'm keeping my word."

"To whom?"

"You. I'm showing you what this is all about."

"I don't under—"

"You will. How much longer, Roger?"

The pilot broke in over the headset. "Have you on the ground in fifteen."

It was a jaw-dropping sweep of backcountry.

No roads, no houses as far as Ethan could see.

Just forested hills and the occasional squiggle of water through the trees—glimpses of stream and river.

Soon, the pine forest fell away behind them and Ethan could tell by the pitch change of the twin-turbine that the pilot had initiated their descent.

They flew over brown, arid-looking foothills, which over the course of ten miles flowed down into a vast hardwood-conifer forest.

At two hundred feet AGL, the helicopter banked and circled the same square mile of real estate for several minutes while Pope studied the terrain through a pair of binoculars.

He finally spoke into his mike. "We're looking good."

They set down in a large clearing surrounded by towering oaks in full autumn color, the rotors stirring the grass in long wavelengths that expanded out from the helicopter in concentric circles.

Ethan gazed across the field while the engines powered down.

Jenkins said, "Would you join me for a little hike, Ethan?"

Pam reached over, unbuckled his lap belt and shoulder harness.

"Cuffs too?" she asked.

Jenkins looked at Ethan. "You'll behave?"

"Sure."

Ethan leaned forward so Pam could access the keyhole.

The bracelets popped open.

He stretched his arms out and massaged his wrists.

Jenkins looked at Pope, opened his hand, said, "You bring something for me like I asked?"

The sheriff filled it with a stainless-steel revolver that looked beefy enough to have been bored out for .357 Magnum cartridges.

Jenkins looked dubious.

"I've seen you shoot," Pope said. "You'll be fine. Anywhere near the heart, or better yet a head shot, and you're golden."

Pope reached back behind his seat and came up with an AK-47 outfitted with a hundred-round drum. Ethan watched him switch the mode from safety to three-round burst.

Jenkins pulled off his headset. Then he swept aside the curtain between the passenger cabin and the cockpit, said to the pilot, "We'll be on channel four, and you'll hear from us if we need to leave in a hurry."

"I'll keep my finger on the engine start."

"You radio at the first sign of trouble."

"Yes, sir."

"Arnie left you a gun?"

"Two, in fact."

"We won't be long."

Jenkins opened the cabin door and climbed out.

After Pope and Pam, Ethan followed, stepping down onto the skid and then into the soft, waist-high grass. He caught up with Jenkins, and the four of them moved quickly across the field, Pope out in front with the assault rifle, Pam bringing up the rear.

It was late in the day—a crisp, golden afternoon.

Everyone seemed twitchy and nervous, like they were out on a patrol.

Ethan said, "Ever since I came to Wayward Pines, you've done nothing but fuck with me. What are we doing out here in the goddamned wilderness? I want to know right now."

They entered the woods, slogging their way through a riot of underbrush.

The noise of birds getting louder.

"But Ethan, this isn't the wilderness."

Ethan glimpsed something barely visible through the trees, realized he'd initially missed it because of all the vegetation. He quickened his pace, now clawing his way through the bushes and saplings that comprised the forest understory, Jenkins following closely behind.

When Ethan arrived at the base of it, he stopped and looked up.

For a moment, he didn't understand exactly what he was staring at. Down low, the beams were wrapped in several feet of dead and living vines, the brown and the green camouflaging the shape of the structure, blending it so seamlessly into the color of the forest that if you looked at it askance, it disappeared.

Higher up, the color of the steel beams showed through—rust so deep it verged on red. Centuries of oxidation. Three oak trees had grown up right through the heart of it, twisting and turning as they climbed, some of the branches even providing support for the girders. Only the framework of the lower six floors still stood—the corroded skeleton of a building. A handful of beams near the top had bent over and curled like ringlets of auburn-colored hair, but most of the steelwork had long ago collapsed into the center to be subsumed by the forest floor.

The sound of birds coming from the ruin was tremendous. Like an avian high-rise. Nests everywhere Ethan looked.

"Remember when you told me you wanted to be transferred to a hospital in Boise?" Jenkins asked.

"Yeah."

"Well, I've brought you to Boise. Right into the center of town."

"What are you talking about?"

"You're looking at the U.S. Bank building. Tallest skyscraper in Idaho. That's where the Secret Service's Boise field office is located, right? Up on seventeen?"

"You're out of your mind."

"I know this looks like a forest floor, but we're actually standing in the middle of Capitol Boulevard. The state capitol is just a third of a mile through those trees, although to find any trace of it, you'd have to dig."

"What is this? Some kind of trick?"

"I told you."

Ethan grabbed the man by his collar and pulled Jenkins in close. "Start making sense."

"You were put into suspended animation. You saw the units—"

"For how long?"

"Ethan—"

"How. Long."

Jenkins gave a slight pause, Ethan realizing there was something in him that almost didn't want to hear the answer.

"One thousand eight hundred fourteen years . . ."

Ethan let go of Jenkins's shirt.

". . . five months . . ."

He staggered back.

". . . and eleven days."

Looked at the ruin.

Looked at the sky.

"You should get off your feet," Jenkins said. "Let's sit." As Ethan eased down into a bed of ferns, Jenkins glanced up at Pope and Pam. "You guys give us a minute, all right? But don't go far."

They walked off.

Jenkins sat down across from Ethan.

"Your mind is racing," he said. "Will you try not to think for a minute and just listen to me?"

It had rained here recently—Ethan could feel the dampness of the ground through the pair of brown fatigues they'd dressed him in.

"Let me ask you something," Jenkins said. "When you think of the greatest breakthrough discovery in history, what comes to mind?"

Ethan shrugged.

"Come on, humor me."

"Space travel, theory of relativity, I don't—"

"No. The greatest discovery in the history of mankind was learning how man would become extinct."

"As a species?"

"Precisely. In 1971, a young geneticist named David Pilcher made a startling discovery. Keep in mind this was before RNA splicing, before DNA polymorphism. He realized the human genome, which is essentially the entirety of our heredity information, which programs cell growth, was changing, becoming corrupted."

"By what?"

"By what?" Jenkins laughed. "By everything. By what we'd already done to the earth, and by all that we would do in the coming centuries. Mammal extinction. Deforestation. Loss of polar sea ice. Ozone. Increased carbon dioxide levels in the atmosphere. Acid rain. Ocean dead zones. Overfishing. Offshore oil drilling. Wars. The creation of a billion gasoline-burning automobiles. The nuclear disasters—Fukushima, Three Mile Island, Chernobyl. The two-thousand-plus intentional nuclear bomb detonations in the name of weapons testing. Toxic waste dumping. Exxon-Valdez. BP's Gulf oil spill. All the poisons we put into our food and water every day.

"Since the Industrial Revolution, we've treated our world like it was a hotel room and we were rock stars. But we aren't rock stars. In the scheme of evolutionary forces, we are a weak, fragile species. Our genome is corruptible, and we so abused this planet that we ultimately corrupted that precious DNA blueprint that makes us human.

"But this man, Pilcher—he saw what was coming. Maybe not specifically, but in broad strokes. Saw that, over successive generations, because of the substantial environmental changes we were bringing to bear, there was the potential for tachytelic anagenesis. To put it in terms you might understand—rapid, macroevolutionary change. What am I saying? From human to something *other* in thirty generations. To put it in Biblical terms, Pilcher believed a flood was coming, so he decided to build an ark. Are you following me?"

"Not at all."

"Pilcher thought if he could preserve a number of pure humans before the corruption reached critical mass, they could, in effect, sit out the evolutionary changes that would lead to the destruction of human civilization and our species. But to achieve this, it would require a robust suspended animation technology.

"He set up a lab and dropped his billions into R&D. Nailed it by 1979 and started work fabricating a thousand suspension units. Meanwhile, Pilcher had been looking for a small town to house his cargo, and when he stumbled across Wayward Pines, he knew it was perfect. Secluded. Defendable ground. Closed in by those high mountain walls. Tough to access. Tough to leave. He bought up all the residential and commercial property and started construction on a bunker complex deep in the surrounding mountains. It was a massive project. Took twenty-two years to finish."

"How did the supplies keep all of this time?" Ethan asked. "Wood and food couldn't have lasted nearly two thousand years."

"Until the crew reanimated, the warehouse cavern, the dormitories and surveillance center—literally every square inch of that complex—existed in a vacuum. It wasn't perfect, and we did lose some material, but enough survived to rebuild the Wayward Pines infrastructure, which time and the elements had completely erased. But the cave system we utilized contained minimal moisture content in the air, and since we were able to kill off ninety-nine-point-nine percent of all bacteria, it turned out to be almost as efficient as suspension itself."

"So the town is completely self-sufficient?"

"Yes, it functions like an Amish village or a preindustrial society. And as you saw, we have vast stores of staples that we do package and truck into town."

"I saw cows. Did you create suspension chambers for livestock as well?"

"No, we just put some embryos in stasis. Then used artificial wombs."

"There was no such thing in 2012."

"But there was in 2030."

"Where's Pilcher now?"

Jenkins grinned.

Ethan said, "You?"

"Your colleagues, Kate Hewson and Bill Evans—when they disappeared in Wayward Pines, they were trying to find me. Some of my business dealings had fallen onto the Secret

Service radar. That's why you're sitting here right now."

"You kidnapped federal agents? Locked them away?"

"Yes."

"And many others . . ."

"Aside from my handpicked and extravagantly compensated crew, I didn't think I'd get much in the way of volunteers for an endeavor of this nature."

"So you abducted people who came to Wayward Pines."

"Some came to town and I took them there. Others, I sought out."

"How many?"

"Six hundred and fifty were conscripted over the course of fifty years."

"You're a psychopath."

Pilcher seemed to consider the accusation, his cool, dark eyes intense and thoughtful. It was the first time Ethan had really looked into the man's face, and he realized the shaved head and good skin belied Pilcher's age. The man must have been in his early sixties. Possibly older. Ethan had up until this moment written off his utterly precise, controlled manner of speaking as a gimmick, a shrink's ruse, but now he saw it for what it was—clear evidence of an immense intellect. It struck him that he was sitting out here under a canopy of oak trees with the sharpest mind he'd ever encountered. Something both thrilling and terrifying in that.

Pilcher finally said, "I don't see it quite that way."

"No? How then?"

"More like . . . the savior of our species."

"You stole people from their families."

"You still don't get it, do you?"

"Get what?"

"What Wayward Pines is. Ethan . . . it's the last town on earth. A living time capsule for our way of life. For the American Dream. The residents, the crew, me, you . . . we're all that's left of the species *Homo sapiens*."

"And you know this how?"

"I've sent out a handful of reconnaissance teams over the years. Those who made it back reported the most hostile conditions imaginable. Without the protection and infrastructure of a place like Wayward Pines, no one could survive. Since my crew came out of suspension fourteen years ago, we've had a radio beacon continuously transmitting a distress call on every known emergency frequency. I even made the decision to broadcast the coordinates of Pines on the remote chance there were other humans out there. No one's shown up on our doorstep. No one's ever made contact. I said this is Boise, but it's not. There is no Boise, no Idaho, no America. Names no longer mean a thing."

"How did it all end?"

"We'll never know, will we? I went to sleep shortly after you so I could still have twenty-five years in Wayward Pines postsuspension. And after 2032, we were all sleeping in the mountain. But if I had to guess? By 2300, I estimated we'd see major abnormalities cropping up. And with diversity being the raw material of evolution, by 2500, we could've been classified as a completely different species. Each generation getting closer and closer to something that could thrive in this toxic world. Something less and less human.

"You can imagine the social and economic ramifications. An entire civilization built for humanity crumbling. I'm guessing there were genocides. Maybe the end came over forty terrible years. Maybe it took a thousand. Maybe a full-scale nuclear war wiped out billions in the span of a month. I'm sure many thought it was end times. But we'll never have that piece of knowledge. All we know is what's out there now."

"And what is that?"

"Aberrations. We call them abbies. Those translucent-skinned creatures that nearly killed you in the canyon. Since coming out of suspension, I've traveled only three times by helicopter, including today. It's quite risky. Farthest we got was Seattle. Or where Seattle used to be. We had to haul fuel. Barely made it back. Extrapolating from what I saw, there must be hundreds of millions of those creatures just on this continent alone. They're predators, of course, and if their population is as healthy as I'm projecting, this would point to a burgeoning deer or other ruminant population. It's even possible that some descendant of the bison is once again roaming the plains in large numbers.

"Because we can't leave the valley to conduct research, we have only a small sample from which to gauge which species survived the last two thousand years unscathed. Birds seem to have come through unaffected. Some insects. But then you'll realize something's missing. For instance, there are no crickets. No lightning bugs. And in fourteen years, I haven't seen a single bee."

"What are these abbies?"

"It's easy to think of them as mutants or aberrations, but our name for them truly is a misnomer. Nature doesn't see things through the prism of good or bad. It rewards efficiency. That's the beautiful simplicity of evolution. It matches design to environment. In trashing our world, we forced our own transformation into a descendant species from *Homo sapiens* that adapted, through natural selection, to survive the destruction of human civilization. Line our DNA sequences up side by side, and only seven million letters are different—that's about half of a percent."

"Jesus."

"From a logistical standpoint, abbies are hugely problematic. They're far more intelligent than the great apes and exponentially more aggressive. We've captured a handful over the years. Studied them. Tried to establish communication, but it's all failed. Their speed and strength is more in line with your average Neanderthal man. At sixty pounds, they're lethal, and some of them grow to two hundred. You were lucky to survive."

"That's why you've built fences around Wayward Pines."

"It's sobering when you realize we aren't at the top of the food chain anymore. Occasionally, an abby will get through, but we keep the outskirts of town on motion sensors and the entire valley under sniper surveillance, day and night."

"Then why didn't you just—"

"Take *you* out?" Jenkins smiled. "At first, I wanted the people to do it. Once you reached the canyon, we knew a pack of abbies was in the area. You were unarmed. Why waste ammo?"

"But the residents . . . they don't know about any of this?"

"No."

"What do they think?"

"They woke up here after an accident just like you did—reinjured, of course, in the appropriate places. Through our integration program, they come to understand there's no leaving. And we have rules and consequences to minimize the complications that arise when someone from 1984 lives next door to someone from 2015. For the residents to thrive, to reproduce, they can't know they're all that's left. They have to live like the world is still out there."

"But it's not. So what's the point of the lie? When you bring them out of suspension, why not just tell them, 'Congratulations! You're the sole survivors!'"

"We did that very thing with the first group. We'd just finished rebuilding the town, and we brought everyone down to the church and said, 'Look, here's the deal.' Told them everything."

"And?"

"Within two years, thirty-five percent had committed suicide. Another twenty percent left town and were slaughtered. Nobody married. No one got pregnant. I lost ninety-three people, Ethan. I cannot—no—*humanity* cannot afford losses on that scale. Not when our species is this endangered, down to our last eight hundred and eleven souls. I'm not saying our method is perfect, but in all these years, and after trying almost everything, it's proven the most effective system for growing our population that we've landed on."

"But they always wonder, right? About what's out there? About where they really are?"

"Some do, but we're an adaptable species.

Through conditioning, like good humans, most come to accept their environment, as long as it isn't completely devoid of hope."

"I don't believe they accept that the world is still out there, when you won't let them see it."

"You believe in God, Ethan?"

"No."

"Many did. Adopted moral codes. Created religions. Murdered in the names of gods they'd never seen or heard. You believe in the universe?"

"Sure."

"Oh, so you've been to space. Seen those distant galaxies firsthand?"

"Point taken."

"Wayward Pines is just a shrunken world. A small town never left. Fear and faith in the unknown still apply, just on a smaller scale. The boundaries of the world you came from were space and God. In Pines, the boundaries are the cliff walls that protect the town, and the mysterious presence in the mountains, aka me."

"You're not a real psychiatrist."

"No formal training, but I play one back in town. I find it helpful to gain the trust of the residents. Stay in touch with the mood of the town. Encourage people in their struggles, their doubts."

"You had the people murder Beverly."

"Yes."

"And Agent Evans."

"He forced my hand."

"You'd have had them murder me."

"But you escaped. Proved yourself even more adept than I first thought."

"You've created a culture of violence."

"That's nothing new. Look, when violence becomes the norm, people adapt to the norm. No different than the gladiator games or throwing Christians to the lions or public hangings in the old West. An atmosphere of self-policing isn't a bad thing."

"But these people aren't really free."

"Freedom is such a twenty-first-century construct. You're going to sit here and tell me that individual freedom is more vital than the survival of our species?"

"They could decide that for themselves. There'd be dignity in it at least. Isn't that what makes us human?"

"It's not their decision to make."

"Oh, it's yours?"

"Dignity is a beautiful concept, but what if they made the wrong choice? Like that first group. If there's no species left to even perpetuate such an ideal, what's the point?"

"Why haven't you killed me?"

Pilcher smiled, as if glad that Ethan had finally broached the subject. He cocked his head. "You hear that?"

"What?"

"Silence."

The birds had gone quiet.

Pilcher pushed against his legs and struggled onto his feet.

Ethan stood too.

The woods had become suddenly still.

Pilcher pulled the gun out of his waistband.

He unclipped his walkie-talkie, brought it to his mouth.

"Pope, come back, over."

"Yep, over."

"Where are you, over?"

"Two hundred meters north. Everything all right, over?"

"I'm getting the feeling it's time we ran for the hills, over."

"Copy that. On our way. Over and out."

Pilcher started toward the clearing.

In the distance behind them, Ethan could hear the ruckus of branches snapping and dead leaves crunching as Pope and Pam headed back their way.

"It was a big deal, Ethan, for me to fly you a hundred and thirty miles down here to the Boise ruins. I hope you appreciate the gesture. We've had our handful of problem residents over the years, but no one like you. What do you think I value most?"

"No idea."

Ethan glimpsed the meadow through the oaks.

Red leaves drifted lazily down from the branches above.

"Control. There's an underground contingent in Pines who presents a façade of compliance. But secretly, they want to take over. Call it . . . an insurgency. A rebellion. They want to break free, to pull back the curtain, to change how things are done. You understand that would mean the end of Pines. The end of us."

They came out of the trees, the helicopter a hundred yards away, its bronze paint job gleaming in the late-afternoon sun.

A part of Ethan thinking, *What a perfect autumn day.*

"What do you want from me?" Ethan asked.

"I want you to help me. You have a rare skill set."

"Why do I get the feeling you're implying I have no choice in the matter?"

"Of course you do."

A breeze lapped at Ethan's face, the meadow grasses bending toward the ground.

They reached the helicopter and Pilcher pulled open the door, let Ethan climb in first.

When they were seated and facing each other, Pilcher said, "All you've wanted to do since you woke up in Pines is leave. I'm giving you that opportunity, plus a bonus. Right now. Look behind you."

Ethan glanced over his seat into the cargo hold, pushed back the curtain.

His eyes became wet.

It had been right there the whole time—a brutal fragment of knowledge he hadn't allowed himself to even acknowledge. If what Pilcher said was true, then he would never see his family again. They'd be nothing more than ancient bones.

And now, here they were—Theresa and Ben unconscious and strapped to a pair of stretchers with a black duffel bag between them.

His boy did not look like a boy.

"After I put you into suspension, I looked you up, Ethan. I thought you had real potential. So I went to your family."

Ethan wiped his eyes. "How long have they been in Pines?"

"Five years."

"My son . . . he's—"

"He's twelve now. They both integrated well. I thought it would be better to have them stable and settled before attempting to bring you in."

Ethan didn't bother to mask the rage behind his voice, his words coming like a growl. "Why did you wait so long?"

"I didn't. Ethan, this is our third attempt with you."

"How is that possible?"

"One of the effects of suspension is retrograde amnesia. Each time you reanimate, your mind resets to just before your first suspension. In your case—the car wreck. Although, I suspect some memories linger. Maybe they emerge in dreams."

"I've tried to escape before?"

"First time, you made it across the river, nearly got yourself killed by the abbies. We intervened, saved you. Second time, we made sure you discovered your family, thinking that might help. But you tried to escape with them. Nearly got all of you killed."

"So this time you went after my mind?"

"We thought if we could induce psychosis, maybe we'd have a chance. Shot you full of some powerful antipsychotics."

"My headaches."

"We even tried to use your history of torture against you."

"What are you talking about?"

"I have your military file. Your report from what happened to you in Fallujah. We tried to tap into that during Pope's interrogation."

"You're . . . sick."

"I never expected you to actually break into the bunker. We were going to just let the abbies have you. But when I saw you standing in suspension, something occurred to me. You're stubborn. A fighter to the end. You were never going to accept the reality of Wayward Pines. I realized I needed to quit fighting you. That instead of a liability, you might actually be an asset."

"Why didn't you just tell me about all of this?"

"Because I didn't know what you would do

with the knowledge, Ethan. Suicide? Escape? Try to make it on your own? But I realize now that you're one of the rarities."

"What do you mean?"

"The people in town, for the most part, can't handle the truth of what's out there. But you . . . you can't handle the lie. The not knowing. You're the first resident I've ever shared any of this with. Of course, it's crushed your family to see the difficulty you've had."

Ethan turned back around and glared at Pilcher. "Why did you bring them here?"

"I'm giving you a choice, Ethan. They know nothing about the world outside of Pines. But you do. Say the word, and I'll leave you here in this field with your family. There's a duffel bag packed with food and supplies, even a few weapons. You're a man who wants things on his terms, and I respect that. If that's what's most important to you, have at it. You can reign in hell here on the outside, or serve in heaven, back in Pines. Your choice. But if you come back to Pines, if you want that safety and support for your family, for yourself, it's on my terms. And my terms, Ethan, come with severe penalties. If you fail me, if you betray me, I will make you watch while I take your son and—"

The sudden noise cut Pilcher off. At first, Ethan thought someone had fired up a jackhammer out in the forest, but then the fear hit him right between the eyes.

It was the *tat-tat-tat* of the AK.

Pam's voice exploded over the radio. "Start the chopper! They're coming!"

Pilcher glanced into the cockpit. "Get us out of here," he said.

"Working on it, boss."

Ethan heard the turbines of the BK117 starting up, the thunderous boom of Pam's shotgun. He moved over to the window, staring back toward the woods as the gunfire grew louder.

Already, it was too noisy inside the helicopter to talk, so he tugged on his headset and motioned for Pilcher to do the same.

"What do you want me to do?" Ethan asked.

"Help me run Pines. From the inside. It'll be a helluva job, but you were made for it."

"Isn't that what Pope's doing?"

Ethan saw movement in the trees as the turbines began to whine, the cabin vibrating as the RPMs increased.

Pope and Pam broke out of the forest, back-pedaling into the clearing.

Three abbies leaped out of the trees and Pope cut two of them down with a long burst of full auto while Pam put a pair of slugs through the third one's chest.

Ethan lunged to the other side of the cabin and looked out the window.

"Pilcher."

"What?"

"Give me your gun."

"Why?"

Ethan tapped the glass, motioning to a pack of abbies emerging on the far side of the field—at least four of them, all barreling toward Pam and Pope at a fast, low sprint that utilized all four appendages.

"You with me, Ethan?"

"They're going to be killed."

"Are you with me?"

Ethan nodded.

Pilcher slapped the .357 into his hand.

Ethan ripped off his headset and shouted into the cockpit, "How long?"

"Thirty seconds!"

Ethan cranked open the door and jumped down into the grass.

The noise and the wind from the rotors screaming in his ear.

Pope and Pam were fifty yards away and still backing toward the chopper while laying down a torrent of suppressing fire.

They'd killed a dozen of them already—pale bodies strewn across the grass—and still more were coming.

More than Ethan could count.

He ran in the opposite direction.

Twenty yards past the copter, he stopped and planted his feet shoulder-width apart.

Stared at the revolver in his hand—a double-action Ruger with a six-shot cylinder.

He raised it.

Sighted down the barrel.

Five of them charging at full speed.

He thumbed back the hammer as frantic machine-gun and twelve-gauge fire roared over the turbines.

The abbies were thirty feet away, Ethan thinking, *Anytime you want to start shooting, that might be a good idea. And no double taps. You need single-fire kill shots.*

He drew a bead on the one in the center, and as it came up into the crest of its stride, squeezed off a round that sheered away the top of its head in a fountain of gore.

At least he was shooting hollow points.

The other four kept coming, unfazed.

Twenty feet away.

He dropped the two on the left—one shot apiece through the face.

Hit the fourth one in the throat.

The last abby inside of ten feet now.

Close enough to smell it.

Ethan fired as it jumped, the bullet only grazing its leg, Ethan adjusting his aim as the abby rocketed toward him.

Pulled back the hammer, pulled the trigger as the monster hit, teeth bared, its scream at this proximity louder than the turbines.

The bullet went through its teeth and tore out of the back of its skull in a spray of bone and brain as it crashed into Ethan.

He didn't move.

Stunned.

His head jogged so hard that flashes of light were detonating everywhere he looked, and his hearing was jumbled—muffled and slowed down so that he could pick out all the individual pieces of sound that built the symphony of chaos around him.

Shotgun blasts.

The AK.

The spinning rotors.

The screams of the abbies.

Telling himself, *Get up, get up, get up.*

Ethan heaved the dead weight of the abby off his chest and sat up. Tried to look across the field, but his vision was stuck on blurry. He blinked hard several times and shook his head, the world slowly crystallizing like someone turning the focus knobs on a pair of binoculars.

Dear God.

There must have been fifty of them already in the clearing.

Dozens more breaking out of the trees with every passing second.

All moving toward the helicopter in the center of the field.

Ethan struggled up onto his feet, listing left in the wake of the hit, his center of balance annihilated.

He stumbled toward the helicopter.

Pam was already inside.

Pope standing several feet out from the skid, trying to hold the abbies off. He had shouldered the rifle and was taking precision shots now, Ethan figuring he must be down to the final rounds of his magazine.

Ethan patted him on the shoulder as he stepped onto the skid, screamed in his ear, "Let's go!"

Pilcher opened the door and Ethan scrambled up into the cabin.

He buckled himself in, glanced out the window.

An army of abbies flooded across the field.

Hundreds of them.

Ten seconds from the chopper and closing in like a mongrel horde.

As he put on his headset, Pilcher pulled the cabin door closed, locked it, said, "Let's go, Roger."

"What about the sheriff?"

"Pope's staying."

Through his window, Ethan saw Arnold throw down his AK and try to open the door, struggling with the handle but it wouldn't turn.

Pope stared through the glass at Pilcher, a beat of confusion flashing through the lawman's eyes, followed quickly by recognition.

Then fear.

Pope screamed something that never had a chance of being heard.

"Why?" Ethan said.

Pilcher didn't avert his eyes from Pope. "He wants to rule."

Pope beat his fists against the window, blood smearing across the glass.

"Not to rush you or anything, Roger, but we're all going to die if you don't get us out of here."

Ethan felt the skids pivot and go airborne.

He said, "You can't just leave him."

Ethan watched as the chopper lifted off the ground, the sheriff hooking his left arm around the skid, fighting to hang on.

"It's done," Pilcher said, "and you're my new sheriff. Welcome aboard."

A mob of abbies swarmed under Pope, jumping, clawing, but he'd established a decent grip on the skid and his feet dangled just out of reach.

Pilcher said, "Roger, take us down a foot or two if you wouldn't mind."

The chopper descended awkwardly—Ethan could tell the pilot hadn't flown in years—lowering Pope back down into the madness on the ground.

When the first abby grabbed hold of Pope's leg, the tail of the chopper ducked earthward under the weight.

Another one latched onto his other leg, and for a horrifying second, Ethan thought they would drag the chopper to the ground.

Roger overcorrected, climbing fast to a twenty-foot hover above the field.

Ethan stared down into Pope's wild eyes.

The man's grip on the skid had deteriorated to a single handhold, his knuckles blanching under the strain, three abbies clinging to his legs.

He met Ethan's eyes.

Screamed something that was drowned out by the roar of the turbines.

Pope let go, fell for half a second, and then vanished under a feeding frenzy.

Ethan looked away.

Pilcher was staring at him.

Staring through him.

The helicopter banked sharply and screamed north toward the mountains.

It was a quiet flight, Ethan's attention divided between staring out his window and glancing back through the curtain at his sleeping family.

The third time he looked in on them, Pilcher said, "They'll be fine, Ethan. They'll wake up tonight, safe and warm in bed. That's what matters, right? Out here, you would all surely die."

It was getting on toward dusk.

Ethan dead tired, but every time he shut his eyes, his thoughts ran in a hundred different directions and at blinding speeds.

So he tried to just watch the world move by.

His view was west.

The sun was gone, and in the wake of its passing, mountain ranges stood profiled against the evening sky like a misshapen saw blade.

There was nothing to see of the pine forest a thousand feet below.

Not a single speck of light anywhere that existed because of man.

They flew through gaping darkness.

With the cabin lights dimmed and the glow of the instrument panel in the cockpit hidden behind the curtain, Ethan could just as well have been adrift in a black sea.

Or space.

He had his family behind him, and there was comfort in that fact, but as he leaned against the freezing glass, he couldn't help but feel a plunging stab of fear.

And despair.

They were alone.

So very much alone.

It hit him center mass.

These last few days, he'd been fighting to get back to his life outside of Wayward Pines, but it was gone.

Gone for nearly two thousand years.

His friends.

His home.

His job.

Almost everything that defined him.

How was a man supposed to come to terms with a thing like that?

How did one carry on in the face of such knowledge?

What got you out of bed and made you want to breathe in and out?

Your family. The two people sleeping behind you.

Ethan opened his eyes.

At first, he didn't quite believe what he saw.

In the distance below, a wellspring of light shone in the midst of all that darkness.

It was Pines.

The house lights and porch lights.

The streetlights and car lights.

All merging into the soft nighttime glow of a town.

Of civilization.

They were descending now, and he knew that down in that valley, there stood a Victorian house where his wife and his son lived.

Where he could live too.

There was a warm bed to crawl into.

And a kitchen that would smell of the food they cooked.

A porch to sit out on during the long, summer evenings.

A yard where he might play catch with his son.

Maybe it even had a tin roof, and there was nothing he loved more than the sound of rain drumming on tin. Especially late at night in bed, with your wife in your arms and your son sleeping just down the hall.

The lights of Wayward Pines glowed against the cliffs that boxed it in, and for the first time, those steep mountain walls seemed inviting.

Fortifications against all the horror that lay beyond.

Shelter for the last town on earth.

Would it ever *feel* like home?

Would it be all right if it did?

You think man can destroy the planet? What intoxicating vanity. Earth has survived everything in its time. It will certainly survive us. To the earth . . . a million years is nothing. This planet lives and breathes on a much vaster scale. We can't imagine its slow and powerful rhythms, and we haven't got the humility to try. We've been residents here for the blink of an eye. If we're gone tomorrow, the earth will not miss us.

Michael Crichton

From *Jurrassic Park* by Michael Crichton, copyright © 1990 by Michael Crichton. Used by permission of Alfred A. Knopf, a division of Random House, Inc.

Epilogue

HE SITS IN the quiet of his office, his boots up on the desk, studying the brass star in his hand and running his fingers over the WP inset in the center, the lettering in some black stone—obsidian perhaps. He wears dark brown canvas pants and a hunter-green long-sleeved button-down, just like his predecessor. The fabric feels new and over starched.

There is an extensive briefing scheduled with Pilcher and his team tomorrow, but today has been uneventful.

And strange.

For eight hours, he sat in the stillness of his office, lost in thought, and the phone interrupted him only once—Belinda, the receptionist, at the noon hour asking if he'd like her to pick up anything for lunch.

He watches the second hand and the minute hand click over to the twelve.

It is five o'clock.

Sliding his boots off the desktop, he rises and puts on his Stetson, slips his brass star into his pocket. Maybe tomorrow he'll bring himself to finally pin it on.

Or maybe not.

Like the first day of any new thing, it has

been a long one, and he's glad to see it end.

He looks at the three antique gun cabinets—a lustful, fleeting glance—and exits his office, heading down the hallway toward reception.

Belinda's desk is covered in playing cards.

"I'm taking off," Ethan says.

The white-haired woman lays down an ace of spades and looks up with a warm smile that does absolutely nothing to divulge a single telling aspect of who she really is. "How was your first day?"

"It was fine."

"You have a good night, Sheriff. We'll see you in the morning."

It is a cool, clear evening.

Already the sun has slipped behind the mountain walls, and there is a crisp chill settling in that may herald the first frost of the season.

Ethan heads down the sidewalk of a quiet neighborhood.

An old man sitting in a rocking chair on a covered porch calls out, "Evening, Sheriff!"

Ethan tips his hat.

The man raises a steaming mug.

Raises it like a toast.

Somewhere in the near distance, a woman calls out, "Matthew! Time for dinner!"

"Come on, Mom! Just five more minutes!"

"No, right now!"

Their voices echo and fade across the valley.

On the next street down, he walks alongside an entire block devoted to a community garden, several dozen people hard at work, filling large baskets with fruit and vegetables.

The scent of overripe apples skirts along on the breeze.

Everywhere Ethan looks, lights are coming on inside houses, the air becoming fragrant with the smell of suppers cooking.

Through cracked windows, he hears clanging dishes, indistinct conversations, ovens opening, closing.

Everyone he passes smiles and says hello.

Like a Norman Rockwell painting come to life.

He crosses Main and follows Sixth Street for several blocks until he arrives at the address Pilcher gave him.

It is a three-story Victorian, canary yellow with white trim, its most prominent feature a window shaped like a teardrop centered just below the pitch of the tin roof.

Through a large window on the first floor, he sees a woman standing at a kitchen sink, dumping a pot of boiling pasta into a colander, bellows of steam rising into her face.

As he watches her, he feels an anxious thumping in his chest.

It is his wife.

Up the stone path through the front yard, up three brick steps, and then he is standing on the porch.

He knocks on the screen door.

After a moment, the light winks on.

She opens the door crying and staring at him through the screen while footsteps clomp down a staircase.

Ethan's son walks up behind her, puts his hands on his mother's shoulders.

"Hi, Dad."

Not the voice of a little boy.

"Jesus, you're taller than your mother."

There is still the screen between them and through the wire mesh, Theresa looks much the same, although her blonde hair is as long as she's ever worn it.

"I heard they made you sheriff," Ben says.

"That's right." A long, emotion-packed moment crawls by. "Theresa."

She wipes her eyes with both hands.

"It smells wonderful," Ethan says.

"I'm cooking spaghetti."

"I love your spaghetti."

"I know." Her voice breaking.

"They told you I was coming?"

She nods. "You're really here, Ethan?"

"Yes."

"To stay this time?"

"I will never leave you again."

"We've waited so long." She has to keep wiping her face. "Ben, go stir the sauce, please."

The boy hurries off to the kitchen.

"Would it be all right if I came inside?" Ethan asks.

"We lost you in Seattle. Then we lost you here. I can't take it. He can't take it."

"Theresa, look at me." She looks at him. "I will never leave you again."

He worries she's going to ask what happened. Why he isn't dead. It's a question he's been dreading and preparing for all day.

But it doesn't come.

Instead, she pushes open the door.

He has feared seeing a hardness in her face, feared it more than anything, but under the glow of the porch light, there is no bitterness here. Some brokenness. The beginnings of wrinkles around her mouth that weren't there before. Around those bright green eyes that slayed him all those years ago. A lot of tears. But also love.

Mainly love.

She pulls him across the threshold into their home.

The screen door slams shut.

Inside the house, a boy is crying.

A man failing to hold back tears of his own.

Three people entangled in a fierce embrace with no letting go in sight.

And outside, at the exact moment the streetlamps cut on, a noise begins somewhere in the hedges that grow along the porch, repeating at perfect intervals, as steady as a metronome.

It is the sound of a cricket chirping.

Afterword
by Blake Crouch

ON APRIL 8, 1990, the pilot episode of Mark Frost and David Lynch's iconic television series *Twin Peaks* aired on ABC, and for a moment, the mystery of *Who Killed Laura Palmer?* held America transfixed. I was twelve at the time, and I will never forget the feeling that took hold of me as I watched this quirky show about a creepy town with damn fine coffee and brilliant cherry pie, where nothing was as it seemed.

Twin Peaks was ultimately canceled, the brilliant director and actors went on to do other things, but the undeniable magic present in those early episodes still haunts me two decades later. Shows like *Northern Exposure*, *Picket Fences*, *The X-Files*, and *Lost* occasionally veered into that eerily beautiful creepiness that defined *Twin Peaks*, but for the most part, for this fan at least, nothing else has ever come close.

They say all art—whether books, music, or visual—is a reaction to other art, and I believe that to be true. As good as *Twin Peaks* was, the nature of the show, in particular how abruptly and prematurely it ended, left me massively unsatisfied. Shortly after the show was cancelled, I was so heartbroken I even tried to write its mythical third season, not for anyone but myself, just so I could continue the experience.

That effort failed, as did numerous other attempts as I matured, both as a person and a writer, to recapture the feeling my twelve-year-old self had experienced back in 1990.

Pines is the culmination of my efforts, now spanning twenty years, to create something that makes me feel the way *Twin Peaks* did. In no way am I suggesting that *Pines* is as good as Lynch's masterpiece, or even something that is likely to take *you* back to the feeling of that series. The show was so utterly its own thing that any attempt to recreate its aura would be inherently doomed to fail. But I feel the need to express how much *Pines* is inspired by Lynch's creation of a small town in the middle of nowhere—beautiful on the outside, but with a pitch-black underbelly.

Pines would never have come about, and I may never have become a writer, if my parents hadn't let me stay up late on Thursday nights, that spring of 1990, to watch a show the likes of which we will never see again.

So thanks, Mom and Dad. Thanks, Mr. Lynch and Mr. Frost. And, of course, the inimitable Agent Dale Cooper.

Pines is not *Twin Peaks*, not by a long shot, but it wouldn't be here without it.

I hope you enjoyed my show.

Blake Crouch,
Durango, Colorado
August 2012

Acknowledgments

MY AGENT, David Hale Smith, and everyone at Thomas & Mercer has given 110 percent to help get this book off the ground. It is a privilege to know and work with such a tremendously talented group of people who are changing the way we read for the better.

A heartfelt thanks to Andy Bartlett, Jacque Ben-Zekry, Rory Connell, Vicky Griffith, Mia Lipman, Paul Diamond, Amy Bates, Jeff Belle, Daphne Durham, Jon Fine, Alex Carr, Philip Patrick, Alan Turkus, Sarah Gelman, Jodi Warshaw, and Leslie LaRue, and finally a shout-out to my KDPeeps—Brian Mitchell, Brian Carver, and Nader Kabbani.

I am incredibly fortunate to count as friends some fantastic writers and wildly astute readers. These folks gave amazing feedback on early drafts of *Pines* and made the book better in every conceivable way. So many thanks to my writing partner, Joe Konrath, Maria Konrath, my brother, Jordan Crouch, my terrific cover artist, Jeroen ten Berge, Ann Voss Peterson, Suzanne Tyrpak, Selena Kitt, and Marcus Sakey. A special thanks to Barry Eisler for a particularly adroit read.

Finally, hugs and kisses to my dear family—Rebecca, Aidan, and Annslee. Thanks for sharing me with this book I've been dying to write. I love you.

About the Author

BLAKE CROUCH WAS born in the North Carolina piedmont in 1978. He earned his undergraduate degrees in English and creative writing from the University of North Carolina–Chapel Hill, publishing his first two novels within five years of graduation. Since then he has published eight additional novels as well as multiple novellas, short stories, and articles. His novels *Fully Loaded*, *Run*, and *Stirred*, which was cowritten with J. A. Konrath, have each earned spots in the top ten of the Kindle bestseller list. Three novels, one novella, and one short story have all been optioned for film. He lives today in Durango, Colorado.

Center Point Large Print
600 Brooks Road / PO Box 1
Thorndike, ME 04986-0001 USA

(207) 568-3717

US & Canada:
1 800 929-9108
www.centerpointlargeprint.com